Decentralization in the Global Era

Decentralization in the Global Era

Television in the regions, nationalities and small countries of
the European Union

**Edited by
Miquel de Moragas Spà
and
Carmelo Garitaonandía**

John Libbey

JL

LONDON · PARIS · ROME

British Library Cataloguing in Publication Data
Decentralization in the Global Era:
Television in the Regions, Nationalities and Small Countries of the European Union
  I. Moragas Spà, Miquel de   II. Garitaonandía, Carmelo
  384.55094

ISBN 0 86196 475 6

Published by

John Libbey & Company Ltd, 13 Smiths Yard, Summerley Street,
London SW18 4HR, England
Telephone: +44 (0)181-947 2777: Fax +44 (0)181-947 2664
John Libbey Eurotext Ltd, 127 avenue de la République, 92120 Montrouge, France.
John Libbey - C.I.C. s.r.l., via Lazzaro Spallanzani 11, 00161 Rome, Italy

CONTENTS

Editors
Miquel de Moragas Spà, Carmelo Garitaonandía

Authors
Gaëlle Canova-Lamarque, Mike Cormack, Maria Corominas, Panayote E. Dimitras, Carmelo Garitaonandía, Ellen Hazelkorn, Nicholas W. Jankowski, Hans J. Kleinsteuber, Bernat López, Miquel de Moragas Spà, J. -M. Nobre-Correia, Michel Perrot, Jørgen Poulsen, Giuseppe Richeri,Francisco Rui Cádima,Barbara Thomaß

General Co-ordination
Bernat López

Documentation
Rosabel Argote and Marta Civil

EURORETV
Network for the Study of Television in the Regions, Nationalities and Small Countries of Europe

This book was published jointly by EURORETV and CEDIC (Communication Research Centre, Generalitat de Catalunya, with the support of the Generalitat de Catalunya's Department for Foreign Initiatives.

The basic research on which this book is based is the result of a co-operative research project involving the Autonomous University of Barcelona and the University of the Basque Country, with the support of the Spanish Ministry of Education's Scientific and Technical Research Council (DGICYT).

Foreword

The audio-visual sector occupies an increasingly important place in the debate on modern-day Europe, not only because of its impact on European political and cultural life, but also because of its social and economic implications, and its influence on the overall development of Europe. The report *Europe and the Global Information Society*, which gathers together a number of recommendations to the European Council, opens with the telling statement that information and communication technologies are giving rise to a new industrial revolution, as important and profound as its predecessors.[1]

The importance of the audio-visual sector was stated in Community documents concerning cultural and communications policies in the 1980s, as early as 1984, with the publication of the Green Paper *Television Without Frontiers* (COM (84) 300 fin, 24 June, 1984). More recently, the documents on development and competitiveness and, more particularly, the Commission's White Paper *Growth, Competitiveness, Employment. The Challenges and Ways Forward into the 21st Century* (COM (93) 700 fin, 5 December, 1993), have noted the expansion of the audio-visual sector's areas of influence, going so far as to refer to it as a strategic sector with regard to competitiveness and employment.

Be that as it may, this consideration of the audio-visual sector has, almost systematically, ignored one of the potentially most important communication levels or spaces of the future: the regions, small cultural, political and linguistic communities.

These communication spaces, which fall between local and State/national communication, although they play a very uneven part in the European audio-visual scene at present, will in

---

1. *Europe and the Global Information Society. Recommendations to the European Council.* Brussels, 1994, CD-84-290-ES-C.

future have a much higher profile within the synergies and strategies of the audio-visual sector as a whole.

Moreover, and leaving aside the still manifestly centralist strategies of the various member States, the need to create or stimulate a 'common or unified market' for the communication sector in Europe has caused priority to be given to programmes supporting the new trans-European communication spaces, especially in the case of television, while ignoring or underestimating the importance of these new regional ventures.

Without denying the importance and the potential of this great new European space, the various chapters of the present book also show the need to bear in mind the importance of the 'diversity' factor, beyond the one constituted by the different States, not only as regards cultural, political and linguistic aspects, but also as regards the potential of this diversity to create new markets, and to contribute to the much sought after competitiveness in the European cultural industries. In modern communication conditions, with the possibility of using transnational (satellite), but also local (over-the-air and cable broadcasting) communication networks, it should be remembered that diversity, besides being an intrinsic cultural value, can also be an asset as regards competitiveness. Diversity should not necessarily be considered only as a threat to or a fragmentation of the European audio-visual market, but rather as another opportunity for this market.

The aim of this book is to initiate a comparative study of the communication spaces in the regions of Europe and to provide an introduction to the present situation. The reader will find a detailed account of television in the regions of the 'twelve' (that is, of the European Union prior to the entry of Austria, Sweden and Finland), as well as an evaluation of the measures and actions taken under European policy within the sector, and a discussion of the functions (cultural, political, economic, technological) which may be ascribed to television companies in the future regional communication spaces.

The publication of twelve reports – one for each State – instead of individual reports for every region, is justified not only by practical considerations, but also by the fact that within the context of regional television, nation-states continue to have enormous importance and influence in legal and political matters. Moreover, regional and local television stations have been largely shaped by the existence of national television companies which until recently were controlled by State monopolies or highly centralized legislation.

The reader of this book will find regional television models which differ widely from one State to another. This is due not only to the geographical, social and economic differences between the countries involved, and the different configuration of the respective States (centralized, regional, autonomous, federal), but also to the diversity reigning in the various television systems. We are dealing with a non-standard phenomenon, with numerous ventures which are still in their infancy, but which are generally on the increase.

The present study is the work of a research group which brings together communication experts from several European universities, known as EURORETV (Network for the Study of Television in the Regions, Nationalities and Small Countries of Europe). This group, which originated from work carried out by the Departments of Journalism of the Autonomous

University of Barcelona and the University of the Basque Country, was created in order to promote research and documentation on television in the regions, nationalities and small countries of Europe.

The twelve reports in this book, which correspond to Belgium, Denmark, France, Germany, the United Kingdom, Greece, Holland, Ireland, Italy, Luxembourg, Portugal and Spain, conform to a single, pre-established blueprint, although the authors have been free to adapt their analyses to the particular and diverse situations prevailing in their respective countries: from the most highly centralized systems, to others, including the case of Spain, where some regions and nationalities act in the field of television more like small States than regions.

In addition to all the contributors, we should like to thank the following for their help in preparing this book: Professors José Antonio Mingolarra, José Vicente Idoyaga, Marcial Murciano, Manuel Parés and Maria Corominas. Our sincere thanks also go to Marta Civil and Rosabel Argote for their excellent work in co-ordinating documentation, and, especially, to Bernat López as general co-ordinator of this edition.

Finally, we should like to express our thanks for the encouragement given by Antoni Gutiérrez Díaz, former Chairman of the Committee on Regional Policy of the European Parliament, and for having entrusted us with the organization of a public hearing at the European Parliament (Brussels, March 1994) entitled 'The role of regional television', during which we submitted a report on this topic.[2] Similarly, we should like to express our thanks for the support and trust received at all times from the autonomous Catalan government, the Generalitat, through the 'Centre d'Investigació de la Comunicació' (Communication Research Centre) and its director, Wifredo Espina, as well as from Joan Maria Vallvé and Joaquim Llimona, of the 'Comissionat per a Actuacions Exteriors' (Department for Foreign Initiatives).

This research might never have been carried out if it had not been for the initial financing granted by the DGICYT (Scientific and Technical Research Council) of the Spanish Ministry of Education which, under its programme 'Promoción General del Conocimiento', approved the joint research project proposed by the Autonomous University of Barcelona and the University of the Basque Country, thereby giving considerable assistance in the preparation of this work.

It is hoped that this book, the result of the combined efforts of those already mentioned, will lead the way in the development of a line of research which will facilitate the adoption of measures to create new audio-visual spaces in Europe; measures which will allow the development of a European cultural identity which is built on the will to share a common tradition and ethos, but also on the diversity of Europe's values and constituent parts.

Miquel de Moragas Spà and Carmelo Garitaonandía
Barcelona–Bilbao, January 1995

---

2. *The role of regional television*, Working documents 1, 2, 3 and 4. EP 208.155. Brussels, 1994. Edition in the nine official Community languages.

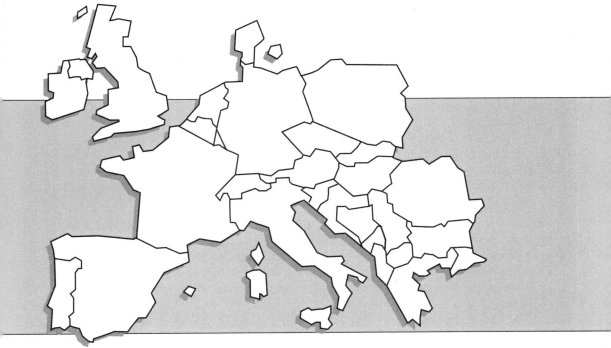

1 Television in the regions and the European audio-visual space

Miquel de Moragas Spà and Carmelo Garitaonandía

This book deals with television in the regions, with the various models of television existing within the huge variety of European regions. We believe that it would have been mistaken and misleading to use the more usual concept of regional television applied to models as widely different as a Dutch local television station, a regional centre of France 3, and the private television companies of ITV in the United Kingdom (currently Channel 3). The concept of regional television has often been used to describe a form of television specializing in local news and folklore; moreover, the very idea of 'regional' has usually been linked with narrow local interest and decentralization of a purely administrative nature.

The regions of Europe are not the result of mere geographical or administrative divisions, but in many cases are the result of long historical processes, the legacy of the feudal structure, of Romanization, or of even earlier times, which have created a profound and important diversity of culture and language in the continent.

These and other underlying factors are those which determine the reasons behind the setting up of broadcasting stations in the regions, as well as their organizational and structural differences: area of coverage, legal status of the company, budget, programming and production conditions, financing, language, etc.

Thus, for example, it was mainly political and commercial reasons which led to the creation of the private ITV companies in the United Kingdom; institutional reasons which determined the important role of the *Länder* in the organization of television in Germany; reasons concerning the decentralization of national television companies (BBC, TVE, FR3, RAI 3, etc.) which explain the emergence of regional centres of public television companies in the United Kingdom, Spain, France and Italy. Political demands of some regions with a specific historical and cultural tradition and language to consolidate their own media explain the case of TV3 in Catalonia, Euskal Telebista in the Basque Country, S4C in Wales, Omrop Fryslân in Holland and Teilifís na Gaelige, the future Gaelic language television channel in the Republic of Ireland.

Although television in Europe was born as a reflection of the nation-state, the 1980s witnessed a general breakdown in television monopolies. The chief reasons for this process were privatization initiatives, followed by decentralization initiatives. Although economic factors are increasingly influential in the development of television in Europe, the creation, existence and disappearance of television ventures in the regions has depended above all on political and cultural factors.

The states retain and lose authority in the communication sector

The European States have not lost their influence and leading role in communication policies, although they are no longer the only players involved in those policies, and they now have to share the lead with other, new agents. This loss of influence by the nation-states is occurring on three fronts: privatization, transfer of authority to supra-national European levels and, as we shall see in greater detail, decentralization, with the gradual shift of authority in matters of communication to the regional, autonomous and local levels.

Nowadays, names such as Springer, Bertelsmann, CLT, Fininvest, Hachette, Hersant and Canal Plus are as important in the European communication sector as in the past has been the case with the BBC, RAI, RTVE, ORTF, etc. The presence of the private sector establishes new criteria in the control of information and culture. The presence in the financial sector, of the major banks and service companies (gas, water, electricity), and of the great construction companies in the new communication business, means a shift from political to commercial and financial factors.

The concentration of companies in this private sector certainly poses major problems for the plurality of information, which have been the subject of numerous political and economic analyses (Charon, 1991; de Miguel, 1993; Sánchez Tabernero, 1993; Commission of the European Communities, 1992 and 1994). In this context, the defenders of free initiative in the communication sector argue that the proliferation of small companies seriously weakens European competitiveness, compared with the large US companies. Restrictions on concentration are seen as real obstacles to the activities of the economic operators within the sector.

The importance of private groups in the audio-visual sector is so great that it is impossible to imagine the future of television in the regions without their involvement. However, the concentration of companies is not necessarily incompatible with territorial decentralization, even though it appears to be so in many cases. Although at the moment, most television initiatives in the regions correspond to the public sector, the participation of multimedia groups in regional and especially local broadcasting projects is becoming increasingly important, albeit on an experimental basis.

We should also bear in mind that, until now, the legal ruling of most European States has raised numerous obstacles to the presence of the private sector in the regional audio-visual field, establishing various forms of centralist regulation which have prevented the access of private initiatives to television in the regions and the municipalities.

Another major 'drain' of power away from the States in the audio-visual sector is toward the supra-national levels, which in the case of the European Union has been toward the European authorities.

The European Union's communication policy, as in other sectors, consists of an on-going debate between the member States and the Union itself concerning the transfer or the retaining of powers, and which brings the various countries together in a new and wider framework, changing their participation in the forms of production, consumption and financing of culture and communication.

Within this context, the emerging idea has been the need to create a common cultural market capable of guaranteeing both the survival of European cultural identity and its industrial competitiveness (Vasconcelos et al., 1994). European communication policies are therefore defined as a form of resistance against the great powers (United States, Japan) whose industry, apart from casting a shadow over the cultural identity and supremacy of Europe, impoverishes its economy and curbs the creation of jobs.

However, this debate on the European 'common' space has opened up a new front on which the member States are losing their powers in the field of communication: regionalization (Robins and Morley, 1992). Strangely enough, to the question 'what is European?' comes the answer 'diversity', and together with the creation of a common audio-visual space, all the various audio-visual landscapes making up that whole have been mapped out: city, region, State and Europe. A European audio-visual policy will only be complete if it covers each and every one of these four spheres. An audio-visual void on the regional and local level would not only be detrimental to the regions and cities themselves, but would also deprive Europe of a vital link in its global communication policy, which should supposedly generate multiple synergies: in company organization, professional training, production and distribution, segmentation of audiences and advertising strategies, in the distribution of information and cultural functions, in technological development, etc.

Various implications of communication policies: mass media, telecommunications and development

An analysis of the functions and viability of television in the regions cannot be undertaken without reference to the major changes taking place in communications systems in Europe, and, in general, in the most developed countries of the world.

One such outstanding change is the fact that communication, particularly television, influences not only politics, culture and education, as we all know, but also other new sectors such as finance, industrial production, science, social welfare, health, etc.

7

This new influence of communication is a consequence of its own rapid changes, especially the convergence of mass media, telecommunications and information technology, which has had important (direct) effects on the communications system and no less important (secondary) effects on the economic, social and cultural system as a whole.

Modern communication policies must involve, therefore, the co- ordination of three major areas: the media, cultural management and telecommunications, on the basis of the important repercussions these areas have had in sectors such as social welfare, the economy and technological development.

The regions are also affected by these transformations. On the one hand, because their own economic development depends on the above-mentioned inter-relationship (media, culture, telecommunications); on the other hand, because the new communication technologies have their own territorial logic, which is characterized less by suppressing spaces than by increasing their differentiation. The new information-based society is not a 'transnational society', but rather a society which is at one and the same time both 'local and global', and which can be described as simultaneously transnational, national, regional and local.

Research on an emerging phenomenon

The presence of television in the regions is a relatively recent phenomenon. With the exceptions of ITV in the United Kingdom and ARD in Germany, the first ventures in regional television within Europe did not occur until the late 1960s and 1970s, when the State radio and television companies (RAI, BBC, RTVE, etc.) had achieved full coverage of their territories, and began to widen their range with second and even third channels (TVE2, RAI3, FR3). This was the first stage, in which the only form of television in the regions corresponded to off-the-network trials by State broadcasting bodies involving the transmission of a few minutes specific programming in some particular regions.

During those years, the driving force behind the interest and the demands of social movements, more than territorial decentralization, was the need to regulate citizens' 'access' or to broaden their 'participation' in the media, in a search for more democratic ways of organizing television. The recognition of the importance of territorial decentralization and autonomy, on the regional and local level, for the democratization of communication was not explicitly formulated until the 1980s, which saw the beginnings of a certain disenchantment with the processes of 'central decentralization', and witnessed the birth of new, fully independent models of regional television, independent of the State television companies. The new autonomous television companies were able to be more agile in adapting their programming to the demands of their audience, free from the control and strategies of the central television companies. The first television companies to broadcast special programmes independently in the regions were in countries in which there existed strong claims to distinctive identities (political, cultural and linguistic). Television would come to be seen as a vital means of propagating a distinctive identity and ensuring its survival. One of the first TV stations of this type was Sianel Pedwar Cymru (S4C), the Welsh channel in the United Kingdom, which was founded in 1980 after a long political struggle and began broadcasting in 1982. Other channels such as Euskal Telebista in the Basque Country or TV3 in Catalonia, began broadcasting in 1982 and 1983, respectively.

Although the late 1980s and the 1990s are characterized by the emergence of private national (hertzian) and transnational (satellite) companies, we also see during this period a proliferation of ventures in regional and local television. In Belgium and Denmark, for example, there is an interesting phenomenon of transfer of former experience in local and regional radio to the world of television. In Holland, the regional television channel Omrop-Fryslân sought independence from the Dutch television company NOS. In Luxembourg, the RTL station Hei Elei, founded in 1969 by CLT to broadcast short transmissions in the Luxembourgish language, in 1991 extended its specifically local programming to 20 hours per week, achieving a large audience. The State television companies (BBC, RAI–3, FR3/France 3, TVE–2, etc.) for their part, and not without some difficulty, extended their off-the-network programmes to match these new ventures in independent television and also to meet the new political, cultural and economic demands of regionalization.

The emergence of regional television projects, admittedly still of secondary importance within the context of the full range of European television, can also be seen in some 'small States' which, in terms of their market and audience, can be compared with some large regions. Such is the case of the Republic of Ireland, where the first channel committed to broadcasting exclusively in Gaelic (Teilifís na Gaelige) was created in 1993, with a view to commencing transmission in 1996.

It is now up to researchers in television to interpret these emerging phenomena and to carry out a prospective study. At present, our knowledge of the situation allows us to formulate the hypothesis that, following a stage characterized by privatization, it is possible that television in Europe will enter a phase in which decentralization processes will gain ground in local and regional television, within the wider context of an increased television supply in a new era of segmented audiences.

Studies and documentation on television in the regions

So far, there have been few comparative studies on television in the European regions. The first initiatives came from the Council of Europe, which in 1987 organized an introductory seminar on the subject, within the framework of the so-called 'Project 10: Culture and Regions. Cultural Trends in Regional Development' (Council of Europe, 1987). In 1989, the Committee for Cultural Co-operation, also of the Council of Europe, commissioned a study from the researcher Pierre Musso on television in 12 European regions; this study was presented at the symposium 'Régions d'Europe et Télévision' (Musso et al., 1991), which was held in Lille in conjunction with the Regional Council of Nord/Pas de Calais. Subsequently, the same author carried out a second comparative study on television and the press, 'Presse écrite et télévision dans les régions d'Europe', which was presented at the symposium on 'Press, television and the regions of Europe', organized in 1993 by the Council of Europe in Krakow (Council of Europe, 1993).

Other initiatives have centred on CIRCOM Regional (Co-operative Internationale de Recherche et d'Action en Matière de Communication), the first European association of regional television companies, which was created in 1983, with the aim of encouraging the co-production and exchange of programmes. CIRCOM Regional, which brings together some 300 stations, holds an annual conference and has a directory on television in the regions in Europe.

The close relationship between television and linguistic identity has led the subject of television in the regions and small countries to be taken up by studies and recommendations concerning the less widely spoken or minority languages in Europe. Various initiatives of this kind have emerged from the European Bureau for Lesser Used Languages (EBLUL), an organization which has received support from the European Commission. In 1986, the Bureau asked Miquel de Moragas Spà to give the introductory paper in the symposium 'Lesser used languages and the media in the EEC' (Moragas Spà, 1986). In 1991, the same institution published an important document (EBLUL, 1991) on the rights of less used languages to gain access to the modern audio-visual media. EBLUL has also fostered and financed the MERCATOR network of information centres, whose purpose it is to gather, systematize and distribute information and documentation on various aspects of lesser used languages. MERCATOR has four specialist centres, each of them in a different European city. The centre which specializes in the media is at the University of Wales (Aberystwyth). The most recent work carried out by this centre under the supervision of Ned Thomas is the publication of a guide to the European media which use those minority languages (Davies, 1993).

Among the few research studies and monographs on television in the regions of Europe are those contained in the special issues of the magazine *Dossiers de l'Audiovisuel* – published by the French Institut National de l'Audiovisuel (INA) – devoted to television in the regions,[1] and the studies by Carmelo Garitaonandía (1990, 1993).

Generally speaking, reports on television in the various European countries, even the yearly reports of the television companies themselves, have paid little attention to what has been going on in the regions. This situation makes it necessary to devote greater energy on direct research and has led to the setting up of a team to anneal the changes taking place in the audio-visual field at the local and regional levels, and to perform a periodic update on the results and conclusions. To this end, EURORETV (Network for the Study of Television in the Regions, Nationalities and Small Countries of Europe) was set up in 1992. The activities of this group have given rise to the publication of this book. In March, 1994, EURORETV held a public hearing with the Committee on Regional Policy, Regional Planning and Relations with Regional and Local Authorities of the European Parliament to discuss the relationship between television and the regions. Among the conclusions arising from this meeting was the importance of comparative research on television in the regions as a foundation for the establishment of new media policies which will take into account this important sector of the European audio-visual space (Moragas Spà and Garitaonandía, 1994).

1. *L'Audiovisuel en Région, Dossiers de l'Audiovisuel*, no. 4, November-December 1985; *La télévision régionale en Europe, Dossiers de l'Audiovisuel*, no. 33, September-October 1990.

The differences between the European regions as translated in the complex typology of regional television companies

A study of television in the European regions, if it wishes to address the diversity of existing models, requires a varied and complex typology. In spite of their variety, the public and private television companies of European countries are much more homogeneous than those of the regions. This varied typology of regional television is in part due to the great political, economic, geographical, demographic, cultural and linguistic differences which exist between the European regions, and also partly due to the different historical processes undergone by the various national television systems. Consider, for example, the different television regulation and deregulation processes experienced by the large European States: France, Germany, Italy, the United Kingdom and Spain.

This heterogeneous state of affairs that we refer to as a region has as its upper boundary the nation-state and as its lower boundary the urban centre. The 'region' can be defined as an area of territory associated with a specific identity which in terms of size is smaller than the nation-state, but considerably larger than an urban centre. However, between the nation-state and the urban centre there are a multitude of types of region. From the 'regions' with a strong sense of their own identity, language and an autonomous political structure in relation to the central state, to the administrative regions, with very little authority of their own, and even those regions with a distinctive cultural and linguistic identity, but which lack any corresponding political autonomy.

Moreover, the definition of a region as a space somewhere between nation and urban centre is inappropriate in the case of some regions and linguistic areas whose territory in fact lies in more than one State. The traditional notion of a region as part of a single country or nation becomes more problematic when we consider cross-border co-operation. In fact, as a consequence of common cross-border interests of an economic, social and cultural nature, we have witnessed the emergence of a number of programmes produced by regional television companies from different countries: *Vis à Vis* (by the French television channels F3 Alsace and F3 Lorraine-Champagne-Ardennes in conjunction with the German channel SWF), *Euro3* (by the French channel F3 Nord-Pas de Calais, the British channel TVS, the Belgian channel RTBF and the German channel WDR), *Euro-Sud* (by F3 Aquitaine, TVE-País Vasco and the Portuguese RTP-Oporto), etc.

Local television – which is also enormously varied – has a regional dimension, too. Many local television companies in fact act as the television station of the regions to which they belong; similarly, some regional stations operate as local television.

In view of the preceding considerations, and in order to reduce all this diversity to its lowest common denominator, we propose the following television typology classification, based on the work of various specialists in the field (CIRCOM, 1983; Musso, 1991; Zimmerman, 1990; Garitaonandía, 1993):

(a) Television production delegated to the region

This refers basically to regional production centres which work for a national television

11

company to which they are responsible. They do not generally transmit to their own locality or region, their production is small and subject to orders from central management. This is the case, for example, of the regional centres ERT-Thessaloniki (Greece) and RTP-Porto (Portugal).

(b)   Decentralized television

It consists of regional centres depending on a central television company which have the responsibility of producing a news bulletin, lasting between 15 and 30 minutes, for their own region. They also take part in the production of news items and reports for the central news service. This is the case of the regional centres of Danish television's DR, of RAI–3, etc.

(c)   Regional off-the-network television

These are regional centres of a State television company which broadcast one or two hours daily off-the-network. In addition to regional news, they offer reports, cultural programmes, entertainment, sport and, in some cases, regional advertising. They often enjoy a certain degree of independent production capacity, which they use for their own programming requirements, or to make programmes intended for State-wide transmission.

This is the case of the regional centres of some large public channels which have become established in those European regions with a distinctive identity, such as the BBC in Scotland, France–3 in Alsace and TVE in Catalonia.

(d)   Federated television

A number of legally independent television bodies contribute to the national channel under their authority and specific programming for their respective regions, as well as participating in the co-ordination of that national channel.

This is the typology we find in the radio and television organizations in the German *Länder* and in the private companies of ITV in the United Kingdom.

(e)   Independently managed television

In this category we consider the independent regional broadcasting stations which produce and transmit to their own regions a complete and competitive programming schedule either throughout or for a major part of the available broadcasting time.

To this type belong the autonomous television channels in Spain (Catalonia, Basque Country, Galicia, Andalusia, Madrid and Valencia), Omrop Fryslân (Holland), S4C (Wales), etc.

(f)   Regional television with supra-regional, national and/or international coverage

This is the case of those independent regional television stations, generally similar to those of the two previous categories, which transmit not only to their own regions, but also to larger territorial areas (several regions, the whole State to which they belong, or even beyond the borders of the State).

This is the case, for example, of RTBF and BRTN in Belgium, the German third channels of WDR (West 3), NDR (N3) and BR (Bayern 3), which broadcast via satellite and can be received by cable or satellite dishes in other parts of Germany and Europe, and Catalan Television (TV3), which in fact is received in almost all Catalan speaking areas: Catalonia, Valencia, the Balearic Islands, Andorra and Roussillon (France).

(g) Local television with a regional outreach

Although they cannot properly be called 'regional television stations', we must take into account in a final category those local television stations, especially those which broadcast over the air, whose area of broadcasting and influence encompasses a major part of the region in which they are located.

To this type belong stations such as Télé Lyon Métropole in France (Lyon), Tele Lombardia in Italy (Milan), IA Brandenburg in Germany (Berlin), etc.

(h) News programmes: a sign of viability

Until now, the complexity and high production costs in television have curbed the expansion of local and regional television companies, which have been unable to compete with the spectacular quality and abundant programming resources of the large television channels. However, this situation has begun to change. New light production technologies have brought quality programming and a high technical standard of broadcasting within the reach of local and regional television.

Although, at present, local and regional television clearly takes second place to the older public channels and the new private national and international channels, it is alive in all the countries of Europe and is thriving in some segments of its programming. Local and regional television is no longer a marginal, minority phenomenon.

A sign of its vitality is the fact that some European regional television companies have withstood more successfully than some national channels the impact of the recent proliferation of channels and audience segmentation which have resulted from privatization. This has been the case of regional television stations which were conceived as segmented audience television adopting priority programming (news, magazine, sport, debate, etc.), especially those television channels operating in a clearly differentiated cultural and linguistic context.

The viability of television ventures in the regions will increasingly depend on a balance between the supply and demand of 'proximity programmes'. At present, the main feature is news programmes. This does not mean that there are not other genres capable of satisfying the social demand for regional and local media, but it is in the sphere of news that this balance is most clearly perceived. In some extreme cases, moreover, regional programming is exclusively confined to news programmes.

In the early stages of television decentralization, news programmes adhered rigidly to the parameters of the 'television news' genre (Telediario, Telegiornale, News, Journal, etc.). Not only has their format now become more flexible, but they have introduced separate sub-sections for weather reports, sport, miscellany, etc., thus moving nearer to the magazine format.

Moreover, these regional news programmes achieve very competitive audiences. For example, the magazine programme of N3 (third channel of the German NDR) in 1993 obtained an average share of 22 per cent; the 7 p.m. news programme of France 3 Aquitaine that same year achieved an average share of 40 per cent in its region; RTL's news programme *Hei Elei* in Luxembourg achieves average audiences of up to 35 per cent in a country which has around 40 cable TV channels reaching 85 per cent of homes.

This interest on the part of audiences relates not only to what is going on in their own region, but also how external events affect it both directly and indirectly, as for example the impact on the region of EU measures in agriculture, industry, the environment, etc.

The need to satisfy a potential proximity communication demand cannot be confined to the news genre. In fact, and as broadcasting stations achieve more and more autonomy and increase their hours of programming, their references to their local or immediate context are extended to other genres, especially reports, debates, humour, music, sport, teleshopping, live transmission of political debates ... thereby producing an increase in regional advertising.

One case which deserves special mention is sport which, at least potentially, is undoubtedly of the utmost interest for television in the regions. This potential is at the moment curbed by the highly competitive situation in the purchase of television rights and exclusive broadcasting rights for the most popular events, particularly league football. However, this very competitiveness may lead to a form of programming diversification which will in future be an advantage to television in the regions, since they will be able to specialize in the coverage of matches played by their regional teams. In Catalonia, for example, almost every month for several years now, the highest audience ratings have been achieved by the Autonomous channel TV3 with its transmission of matches played by the Barcelona Football Club, obtaining a share of around 35 per cent. This audience level for autonomous television has been possible, thanks to the fact that the various autonomous Spanish television companies have founded a programme purchasing consortium (FORTA), and also, no less importantly, because these television companies are fully independent and therefore fully competitive in relation to the State television networks.

Another special case is that of regionally produced fiction. Fiction is the main problem area of the European audio-visual industry and the one in which the market is the most important dimension. Home produced fiction is the genre which has the most difficulty in adapting to the real potential of television in the regions.

Nevertheless, this genre is also present in the more 'competitive' television channels, such as Sianel Pedwar Cymru (S4C) in Wales, in which a fiction programme, the serial *Pobol y Cwm*, has made its mark in the programming and audience ratings of a limited coverage television channel. For its part, the Catalan channel TV3 in 1994 began daily lunchtime broadcasting of its first home-produced television drama series *Poble Nou*, achieving audience levels until that time only won by the major genres (news and sport), reaching 38 per cent of the share during those months in which the series was broadcast.

In the two cases referred to above (Catalonia and Wales), there is a second factor which must not be forgotten: the existence of a separate language in each of these communities (Catalan and Welsh), which is used by the respective TV channels, together with an important cultural and national consciousness. These factors are decisive in the creation and survival of certain television channels serving limited geographical areas. It is even the case of Italy, where the bilingual regions (in which French, Slovene, German or Ladin are spoken, in addition to Italian) are those in which the regional broadcasts of RAI3 have continued to inspire most interest.

Four reasons for a European regional communication policy

One of the chief problems facing a communication policy which favours the development of television in the regions is, quite apart from doubts concerning its economic viability, the belief that such television does not satisfy any social demand or fulfil any basic and necessary function in our democracies. This belief, or lack of it, is to be found to a greater or lesser degree in politicians, professionals, cultural agents and even communications experts.

We believe that there are four arguments justifying policies favourable to television in the regions, and that they derive from four principle functions: political, cultural, economic and technological development.

The existence of communication spaces in the immediate proximity of citizens' experience – urban and regional – fosters their participation in politics, in that it allows the circulation of information relevant to the reality and political problems of their immediate surrounding area. This type of information, produced in the region, cannot be confined to the printed media, ignoring the visual features which are inherent in our culture and which have already come to dominate in the major communication spaces (State and international).

In this context, television programming in the regions can enjoy a competitive edge over State and transnational television, in as far as it is able to offer exclusive coverage in the following:

(a) representing local reality as different from national and transnational reality;

(b) presenting and interpreting news and current affairs concerning politics, culture and the national and international economy, selected and discussed on the basis of the region's specific character and interests;

(c) highlighting and giving prominence to the region's relations with other regions within the same State and with other nations, as well as the projects stemming from those relations.

Communication policies must consider direct information from the immediate environment as an indispensable feature of modern democratic participation.

There are also strong cultural reasons for communication policies recognizing and supporting the existence of television in the regions. In the modern communications system it is impossible to maintain small cultural identities (and their respective languages) without the corresponding local media of the regions in which they exist. Regional cultural spaces (and the market for their products) form part of, and are always smaller than, the cultural spaces which correspond to the State as a whole. The regional dimension must, therefore, be considered when trying to establish policies in support of the weaker cultural industries. Moreover, just as, in modern communication, cinema and television are inextricably linked, so in the future it will be impossible to separate the audio-visual industry and other sectors as important to culture as theatre, music, festivals and art.

It is a fact that some large regions constitute cultural spaces as large as or larger than some small States in the European Union. These cases illustrate even more clearly the influence of politics and the market on the survival of cultural identity. Generally, we see in these cases the important role played by the political dimension and authority in this survival and development.

The transformation in the communications system and the increasing importance achieved by television have led the audio-visual sector (film, television, video) to become a major sector of the services economy in Europe, with a strong potential for creating employment and with a growing turnover.

The existence or otherwise of a television space in the regions also has repercussions on the revitalizing of their economies. Regional television should not be considered as an exclusively cultural activity, but rather as a key sector bringing together both culture and industry. Moreover, this link which occurs in the audio-visual sector is precisely what makes it a driving force behind global development within society.

Nevertheless, it is often this economic viability of television in the regions which is threatened by the situation of the television market. Changes which have occurred in the audio-visual media in recent years have stimulated growth in the number of television channels and in the programmes available. The result of these changes has caused a great increase in the competition between television channels, which now need to define their programming in greater detail and to adapt more readily to the tastes and interests of their audiences. This transformation offers television in the regions the chance to become an increasingly important element in the new pattern of supply and demand of television programmes.

Regional television companies can find their own space if they succeed in making their programmes different from those of the great national and international networks, and if they also make the most of opportunities opened up by the process of segmentation which is taking place in the European and international audio-visual space.

Television in the regions must now face up to the critical factors in audio-visual production by seeking its own solution in new formats and different television genres, characterized by their regional interest value. Television in the regions is not in a position to compete with the scale economies of large TV channels in the purchase or production of fiction programmes, but it can, at least partially, compete with new formats and genres involving accessible costs, which are essentially different from those provided by the national and international channels (Richeri, 1993). This means being able to rely on a network of relations between regional and local television and other institutions or organizations (newspapers, theatres, universities, sporting associations, public administration, etc.) in order to establish permanent forms of co-production and co-operation.

This co-operation makes it possible to provide services (education, training, professional refresher courses, health education, etc.) aimed at specialist audiences, and at the same time to generate funds. In this way, television in the regions can ensure its own business viability, at the same time as contributing to the overall development of the community. However, it should be pointed out that there does not yet exist an electronic communication and audio-visual culture capable of leading regional and local institutions to use the new media to make institutional and collective interest services more efficient and economical.

It may be said that a region which lacks an audio-visual space of its own, which has no audio-visual production capacity and no inter-sectorial co-operation programmes is doomed to a gradual loss of potential as regards its development as a whole.

European audio-visual policy must understand that the way out of the crisis is to be found not necessarily and exclusively in transnationalization, in the macro-market, but that the answer may lie in a dual solution, both global and local. It is necessary to study ways of making State and regional diversity compatible with the construction of a common market which some, perhaps too hastily, define as the only (competitive) market possible. Scarcely any importance is given in the experts' analyses and in official statements to the economic value of diversity.

Our analysis of television in the regions leads us to believe, however, that a full defence of the audio-visual market and, therefore, the viability of European cultural identity, will only be possible if a balance is struck between the defence of our common space and that of our diversity. In other words, nobody doubts the cultural and economic importance of the creation of large markets, but we still have to assess the cultural and economic importance of small markets.

As we shall see in the last chapter of this book, many statements and documents by the European Union stress the need to redress Europe's trade balance with the United States in the audio-visual field. Moreover, these documents insist on the fact that this sector (in which personnel costs are as high as 47 per cent) is vital, not only from the cultural point of view, but also as regards the creation of employment. The White Paper *Growth, competitiveness, employment* of the European Commission states that up to 2,000,000 new jobs could be created in the European audio-visual sector over the next few years, if the right policies are established.

This hope is related to the need to obtain a return on production costs in large internal markets, that is to say in the larger common market. However, our belief is that this objective will only be viable if the reality (diversity) of the European cultural market is accepted. Diversity must not be considered as simply an obstacle to the economy; diversity can also be considered as a market asset, especially if all the possible synergies between the communication spaces are maximized.

Regionalization should not be seen as an obstacle, nor even a necessary lesser evil in the defence of identity, but rather as a new opportunity for the European audio-visual market. The main challenge now facing communication policies in Europe is to achieve a harmony between the dual concepts of 'identity space' and 'cultural market'.

Finally, we should also mention the regions in the context of technological development.

The regions (and this is also true of States) cannot apply an industrial policy in the telecommunications sector in an isolated fashion. It is precisely these sectors which reveal the greatest need for a common European policy. This does not mean, however, that the regions cannot, or should not, plan the use of telecommunications in their territorial, cultural, social (education, health, etc.) and ... television policies.

It is the distinctive contribution of modern technologies to have put an end to the scarcity of communication channels, which in the 'Marconi era' could be seen as justifying, to some extent, the need for exclusive control and regulation on the part of State governments. Nowadays, with the new cable technologies, this justification has ceased to exist. We are now in a new era, which is characterized by the technical multiplication of channels. This multiplication makes a more direct form of management of telecommunications in the smaller areas of city and region not only possible, but also desirable.

Technological means may represent as much of a risk as an opportunity for the overall development of the media in the regions. The risk may be determined both by economic aspects, for example the high cost of equipment affordable only by the large television channels, and by political and institutional factors, such as the existence of disproportionate Community aids, or the approval of regulations or standards which are detrimental to television companies with a limited broadcasting capacity.

On the other hand, however, technological means also offer new opportunities which can be beneficial to the regions. Low costs involved in transmitting television signals, in the production of certain programmes, or the new telecommunications networks, offer new possibilities to television companies broadcasting on a limited scale.

The new technologies allow a new *intelligent exchange* between the regional level and the rest of the world. This is the case, for example, of the new *videocommunication* techniques, which enable television to make better use of a network of *permanent sources* (banks, chambers of commerce, archives and museums, companies, local organizations, schools and universities, research centres, trades unions, etc.), which can encourage the integration of television channels into their area of reference.

The new information networks, which in the year 2000 will account for 6 per cent of Europe's GDP (Commission of the European Communities, 1993), will require a high trans-European capacity, but at the same time will also require regional and local capacity in order to satisfy the new needs of institutions, companies and individuals who wish to have access to databases, telecomputer terminals, tele-administration, tele-information, or tele-medicine.

Apart from other changes (interactivity, development of multimedia services, multiplication of communication channels, technification of communication processes, etc.), the new communications system (satellite-cable) is determining the re-dimensioning of distances and the appearance of new communication spaces (world-wide, continental, national, regional, local). Thus, changes are brought about in political borders of communication spaces, or at least changes in their political and cultural significance (trans-border world television, transnational regional television, regional television, metropolitan television, municipal television, neighbourhood television, etc.).

A European communication policy will be complete only if it is capable of meeting the challenges posed by these various communication spaces; spaces which, instead of disappearing as a result of technological change, seem to be strengthened as a result of what we have referred to as 'decentralization in the global era'.

References

CIRCOM (1983): *Première Conference des télévisions régionales.* Lille: CIRCOM.

Commission of the European Communities (1992): *Pluralism and Media Concentration in the Internal Market. An Assessment of Need for Community Action.* COM (92), 480 fin, 23 December 1992.

Commission of the European Communities (1993): *Growth, Competitiveness, Employment. The Challenges and Ways Forward into the 21ts Century.* COM (1993) 700 fin, 5 December 1993.

Commission of the European Communities (1994): *Communication from the Commission to the Council and the European Parliament Follow-up to the Consultation Process Relating to the Green Paper on 'Pluralism and Media Concentration in the Internal Market'.* COM (94) 353 fin, 5 October 1994.

Council of Europe (1987): *El rol de la comunicación en el desarrollo regional.* Ref. CC-GP 10 (87) 17. Strasbourg: Council of Europe.

Council of Europe (1993): 'Symposium Presse, Télévision et Régions d'Europe'. Cracow: Council of Europe.

Charon, J.M. (1991): *L'état des medias.* Paris: La Découverte/Médias-Pouvoirs.

Davies, J. (ed.) (1993): *The Mercator Media Guide.* Aberystwyth: University of Wales Press.

EBLUL (1991): *Policy Document on Lesser Used Languages in Radio and Television.* Dublin: The European Bureau for Lesser Used Languages.

Garitaonandía, C. (1990): 'Políticas de comunicación de las regiones y nacionalidades europeas', in RTVV: *Las radiotelevisiones en el espacio europeo.* Valencia: RTVV.

Garitaonandía, C. (1993): 'Regional Television in Europe', in *European Journal of Communication*, vol. 8.

Miguel, J.C. de (1993): *Los grupos Multimedia.* Barcelona: Bosch.

Moragas Spà, M. & Garitaonandía, C. (eds.) (1994): *The Role of Regional Television Stations.* Document presented at the Public Hearing held with the Committee on Regional Policy, Regional Planning and Relations with Regional and Local Authorities and the Committee on Culture, Youth, Education and the Media of the European Parliament, March 1994. Brussels.

Moragas Spà, M. de (1986): 'Lingue meno diffuse e mezzi d'informazione nella Comunità Europea: problemi della radio-televisione. Documento di base'. Sassari: Istituto di Studi e Programmi per il Mediterraneo.

Musso, P. *et al.* (1991): *Régions d'Europe et télévision.* Paris: Editions Miroirs.

Richeri, G. (1993): *La tv che conta. Televisione come impresa.* Bologna: Baskerville.

Robins, K. & Morley, D. (1992): 'What Kind of Identity for Europe', in *Intermedia*, 20, 4–5.

Sánchez Tabernero, A. *et al.* (1993): *Media Concentration in Europe*. Düsseldorf: European Institute for the Media.

Various (1985): 'L'Audiovisuel en Région', in *Dossiers de l'Audiovisuel*, 4 (November-December).

Various (1990): 'La télévision régionale en Europe', in *Dossiers de l'Audiovisuel*, 33 (September-October).

Vasconcelos, A.P. *et al.* (1994): *Rapport de la cellule de reflexion sur la politique audiovisuelle dans l'Union Européenne*. Luxembourg: Office des Publications Officielles des Communautés Européennes.

Zimmermann, P. (1990): 'Las televisiones regionales en Europa', in *Las radiotelevisiones en el espacio europeo*. Valencia: RTVV.

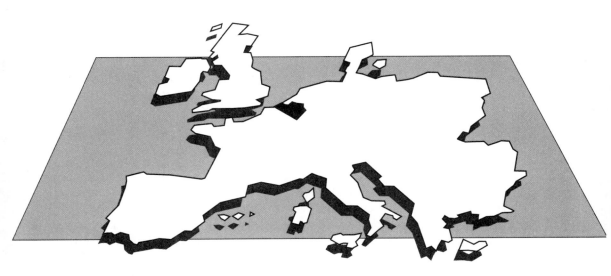

2 Belgium: Federalization of broadcasting and community television

J.-M. Nobre-Correia

The general political framework, the nation and the regions

The state of television in Belgium is, as one would expect, a reflection of the characteristics of the society in which it is immersed. Belgium is a small country covering slightly less than 30,000 km², and with a population of 10 million inhabitants, less than some of the great world and European cities. But Belgium is also a country which lacks its own specific language, sharing those of its neighbours: Dutch (about 55 per cent of the population), French (45 per cent) and some German (about 65,000 people). And to further complicate the matter, the country has not only three unilingual regions (Flanders, Walloon and the Eastern districts), but also a region which is officially bi-lingual (Brussels), although the population is 80–90 per cent French-speaking.[1] In addition to this, the existence of a jealous local control of its important prerogatives, as well as the regional and sub-regional sense of identity, firmly rooted in the mind of the population.

On to this pattern of diversity was grafted a system of State federalization which dates back to 1970. One of the consequences of federalization was that legislation in matters of radio, television and cable broadcasting no longer depended on the nation-state (which, since 1993,

1. The official figures are not available ... to avoid further problems over 'linguistic conflicts'.

has been referred to as 'federal'), but on the Cultural Communities. Since 1971, the Flemish Community, the French Community and the German-speaking Community[2] have legislated in their own respective audio-visual sectors and decided on the budgets they assign to public radio and television. This has caused some problems in the bilingual region of Brussels.

General framework of television: rampant federalization

French-speaking and Flemish-speaking public television stations were created under the auspices of the INR-NIR (*Institut National Belge de Radiodiffusion- Nationale Instituut voor Radio*). This Institute came into being under the law passed in 1930, and, whilst overseen by a single governing body, developed two distinct General Directorates. Since 31 October, 1953, Belgians have had two television channels, one in French and another in Flemish. The law which was passed in 1960 set up three distinct public broadcasting bodies: RTB (*Radiodiffusion-Télévision Belge*), BRT (*Belgische Radio en Televisie*) and ISC (*Institut des Services Communs*). RTB and BRT were each placed under the authority of a board of directors appointed by the national Chamber of Representatives and the Senate. The ISC, constituted by the association of RTB and BRT, was in charge of the management of joint technical services such as the musical and literary libraries, the sound archives and the symphony orchestra, in addition to German language and foreign radio broadcasts (Vertommen, 1980).

The border areas had for a long time been able to receive transmissions from other bordering countries. However, it was not until 26 April, 1961, when the first cable network was inaugurated at Namur (Van Apeldoorn, 1994: 22), that Belgians were increasingly able to receive the majority of television programmes broadcast by neighbouring countries.

The revised constitution of 1970–71 recognized the existence in Belgium of three cultural communities: French, Flemish and German. Each of these communities was granted its own cultural council, constituted by the members of the two houses of Parliament belonging to their respective linguistic communities. Each of these cultural councils was to have authority over the public service radio and television stations within its particular community, as well as the power to legislate in audio-visual matters.

The services guaranteed by the ISC were divided up. Moreover, the law passed on 18 February, 1977 dissolved the ISC, transferring its staff and assets to RTB and BRT (later called RTBF and BRTN, respectively), and created the BRF (*Belgisches Rundfunk und Fernsehenzentrum für Deutschsprachige Sendungen*), in charge of German language broadcasts.[3]

At the present time, and following this pattern, the Belgian audio-visual system is clearly divided in two main geographic areas, with fairly parallel TV systems:

Public television in the French Cultural Community of Belgium is managed by RTBF (*Radio Télévision Belge de la Communauté Culturelle Française*), which operates two TV channels,

2. In fact, the German-speaking community was not recognized until 1 June 1983.
3. To date, the BRF provides only radio broadcasting.

as well as five radio programmes. The general interest RTBF schedules approx. 4,000 hours per year of programming. The second channel, originally called Télé 21, underwent several important changes in 1993, when, following an agreement between RTBF and the Franco-German channel ARTE, the second channel was divided into ARTE 21 and Sports 21. In early 1994, however, this agreement was cancelled and Sports 21 became RTBF 21.The RTBF's budget for 1993 was approximately 8,800 million FB (radio and television), and the staff totalled 2,662 in 1994, of whom 1,333 worked in television. Up to 70.8 per cent of the 1993 budget was secured by the public subsidy of the French Community, which originates in the TV licence fee, while advertising and sponsorship accounted for 18.8 per cent.

Similarly, in the Flemish Community public television is managed under BRTN (*De Nederlandse Radio-en Televisie-uitendingen in België, Omroep van de Vlaamse Gemeenschap*), which operates two TV channels and six radio programmes. BRTN-TV1 is a general interest channel, carrying some 3,400 hours per year programming, whereas the second channel BRTN-TV2, inaugurated in 1977, offers a more specialized schedule (around 1,400 hours per year programming). BRTN has a staff of around 2,700 (radio and television), and a budget of approximately 8,480 million FB (1993). The funding of the Flemish public radio and television is almost entirely based on public subsidy (also partly on the TV licence fee). Advertising is only allowed in radio broadcasts, while sponsorship is permitted in both radio and television.

All of the public Belgian channels, even French and Flemish-speaking, are broadcast throughout the country, even though they are aimed at one or other cultural community.

RTBF has developed a network of regional production centres for radio and television, which provide the different radio and TV channels with a wide range of programmes, as well as news items and reports. There are three radio and TV regional centres (Brussels, Charleroi and Liège) and two regional radio centres (Hainaut and Namur-Luxembourg-Brabant Walloon). Local and regional programming disconnections are only carried out in radio channels; there are no regional disconnections in TV. BRTN did not develop such a dense regional network, so TV production is centralized in Brussels, and only regional radio centres exist in Flanders.

As for private television, the French-speaking Community has the general interest RTL-TVI, an offshoot of the Compagnie Luxembourgeoise de Télédiffusion-CLT (66 per cent) and Audiopresse (34 per cent), a company which includes most of the editors of the French language Belgian daily newspapers. It is widely distributed by cable throughout Flanders. Also addressed to the French-speaking Belgium is the coded Canal + Belgique, which was launched on 27 September, 1989, with a programming schedule largely based on films. Canal + Belgique, whose programming is different from that of Canal + France, is controlled by the latter (42 per cent), the remainder of its capital being held by Belgian shareholders, of whom RTBF accounts for 25.01 per cent. Recognized as the pay channel of the French-speaking Community, it is only available in Walloon Belgium and in Brussels. A fifth channel was launched on 15 February, 1995: the general interest Club RTL.

As for Flemish-speaking Belgians, they are served by the private general interest channel

VTM (an offshoot of various Flemish Belgian daily newspapers and magazines) and by the Benelux version of the coded Filmnet, based on films. Filmnet, recognized as the pay channel of the Flemish Community, is only available in Flanders and Brussels. Another two general interest channels, Kanaal 2[4] and TV 4[5], are due to start operating on 30th January and 1st February 1995, respectively.

Local and community television in Belgium

Federalization of the cultural authorities (specifically audio-visual) in Belgium, was carried out at a time when three important movements were developing. The social disputes which occurred at the end of the 1960s and the beginning of the 1970s gave way to the discovery of 'life in community' and a search for solutions leading to the encouragement of freedom of expression, dialogue and discussion among the members of the community. The new light video camera techniques were becoming popular, allowing them to play the role of catalyst in the community. This was a step which would lead some to attempt to go beyond the state of a simple tool of action on a microsocial scale to try to reach a wider public, questioning the sacred 'monopoly on the air' and thus opening the door to a deregulation movement which would bring about a fundamental change in European audio-visual history (Nobre-Correia, 1992: 285–292).

In the face of Flanders' strong national identity, Belgium's French Community (including the population of Walloon and the French-speaking population of Brussels) urgently needed to form their own cultural identity. This separation would, for that matter, be one of the main factors in the development of the audio-visual scenes to the north and the south of the 'linguistic boundary'.

During the 1970s, the French community of Belgium took Quebec (where the community TV played an important socio-cultural role) as their model for identity affirmation within a nation-state, whereas Flanders would instead wait until the 1990s to take up the question of regional television. Two different histories which would consequently have two different models: one where the socio-cultural problem remained a predominant factor (to the south), the other where commercial considerations seem to have taken control (to the north).

Local and community television in the French-speaking community

French-speaking Belgium, the country with the largest cable density in Europe,[6] started dreaming of community television at the beginning of the 1970s. Some groups, which appeared from nowhere, were using video and doing 'savage injections' in the cable network (Nobre-Correia, 1984). Then on 12 February 1975, the French Community's Minister of

4. Kanaal 2 will be launched by VTM.

5. TV 4 will be launched from the United Kingdom by the American-Scandinavian group SBS and the Belgian newspaper group VUM.

6. In 1975, 41.70 per cent of television owners were connected to cable. In 1991 it reached 105.87 per cent (Communauté Française de Belgique, 1993: 39). This figure, which seems a little abnormal, is due to the fact that each of the TV sets must pay for one subscription to cable, whereas the owner of more than one TV sets only pays for one subscription.

Culture set up an 'audio-visual think tank' and gave it the task of gaining an edge over the 'other television'. He added that: 'we have to convert the new techniques available into instruments of genuine cultural promotion. So that people may express themselves, partici-pate and master their environment; that they may understand the quality of words and the dialogue exchanged, and that they may create living communities'.[7] Wishes in agreement with the times, with the old dreams of permanent education corresponding to traditional left-wing thinking, as well as with the desires for expression and participation on the part of 'post–68' left-wingers.

The minister in charge of the project felt that four rules would have to be respected: '1) management of the venture by a group representing the community; 2) observance of the fundamental rules in use for radio–TV; 3) no advertising; 4) programmes with local contents'.[8] This considerably reduced the operative margin of the future local television. Two other conditions were added, however: 'the other television (l'autre télévision)' must be different from the public national television;[9] the cablecasters are confined to the role of simple signal carriers, and have nothing whatever to do with programming and image production.

A little more than one year later, the minister clarified his options: 'the other television' would be 'responsible for communication, participation and animation'. It would also be 'largely accessible and oriented toward freedom of expression for each and every individual'[10]. Emphasis was therefore given, not to programming with its goals and its level of technical quality and audience, but to greater access by people in the community covered by local television, thereby opening the doors to spontaneity, adventure, imagination and creativity. But also, and more especially, to demagogy, narcissism, banality and boredom...

Legal framework: a tight corset

On 4 May 1976, a royal decree authorized, 'on an experimental basis, and with the agreement of the distributor concerned, the broadcast, through the medium of a distribution network ..., of audio-visual programmes of local interest on condition that these programmes be limited to the socio-cultural field'. The first experiments were to start (Jocquet and Sotiaux, 1981). In the terminology used in French-speaking Belgium, local television was first called Community Television, TVC (*Télévisions Communautaires*) and then Local and Com-munity Television, TVLC (*Télévisions Locales et Communautaires*), whereas in Flanders it was called Regional Television, TVR (*Regionale Televisie*). We will therefore encounter this changing terminology throughout the present paper.

Each local station had to present an agreement signed by four parties: the State of Belgium,

7. *Discours prononcé par le Monsieur le ministre de la Culture française* ..., document duplicated, 12 February 1975.

8. Idem.

9. RTB which, on 12 December 1977, was to become RTBF, Radio-Télévision Belge de la Communauté Culturelle Française.

10. *Discours prononcé par le Monsieur le ministre de la Culture française* ..., document duplicated, 3 March 1976.

the local authority, the association presenting the television project, and the cable-casting company which was to cablecast the programmes. However, it became evident that the cablecasters were not willing to get involved in this kind of experiment: it was therefore necessary to convince some to give it a try.

The agreement recalled that 'the Association's goal is to broadcast audio-visual news programmes, socio-cultural, community and educational animation programmes with local or mini-regional characteristics'. Furthermore, that 'the Association will guarantee that cable access be largely assured, keeping ideological and philosophical pluralism in mind', guaranteeing 'the protection of the philosophical and ideological tendencies' stipulated by the Cultural Treaty (*Pacte Culturel*) of 1972 (Hermanus, 1990: 14).

For the first year of activity of the TVLC, the French Community's Ministry of the Culture allotted them a budget of 8 million FB (Belgian Francs). The minister himself admitted that this amount was too little, and categorically stated that 'we have to start by looking for voluntary help'. In 1983, Vidéotrame, the Walloon federation of local TV, considered that a TVLC should be given a budget of 30 million FB, 'where 15 to 20 million would cover wages, 7 to 8 million would be allocated to operation and 3 to 5 million for write offs' (Vidéotrame, 1983a: 4). However, between 1976 and 1983, it was 'estimated that each of them had operated with one sixth of this budget' (Vidéotrame, 1983b: 1).

The statutory limitations were, therefore, quite pronounced. Statutory and financial dependence on the central and local powers was evident. It was indeed so great that the operating licence 'on an experimental basis', foresaw the possibility of this authorization being withdrawn. The model of the Cultural Treaty – originated in a praiseworthy desire for democratic operation of the institutions – implies a balance of power between different parties (political, trade unions, philosophical and others) more favourable to compromise, levelling-down agreements and stagnation, than to initiatives which might stimulate the creativity of the players and the enthusiasm of the public. And these parties will become involved only if they see some kind of interest in the television station in question. To sum up, the definition of the type of programmes and the broadcasting radius of the television was formulated in such a way that it may have lessened the enthusiasm of those media professionals who had foreseen a different future for the 'other television'.

Results with differences

In the evaluation report on local and community television, carried out by the Ministry of the French Community and which dates from 1981, it was said that 'to the question of whether all the recognized groups had succeeded with community television as planned at the beginning of the experiment, the answer could at times be vague. We can confirm, however, that the Belgian examples have proven that a different television and cablecast approach, inspired directly by the principles of permanent education and community development, was not only possible, but is nowadays in operation' (Jocquet, 1981: 2).

Furthermore, the same report pointed out that 'although the mission to provide local news has been more or less well accomplished by most of the TVLC, we must conclude that the central mission of community television itself, was carried out unevenly' (Jocquet, 1981: 4.).

Indeed this last mission gave way to a 'proliferation of 'narcissistic forums' where the only expected effect was that of the 'visiting card' which praised the merits of such and such association' (Jocquet, 1981: 4). All things considered, more positive results were achieved in the field of permanent education.

In fields which had not been specifically assigned to it, local television showed more initiative. In the perspective of cable use, experiments in television on demand and teletext appeared. On the other hand, cable had also been utilized as a means of remote teaching and professional training. Finally, some TVLCs had rebroadcast foreign films or current affairs magazines. Some had even been experimenting with new audio-visual languages.

In many of these initiatives RTBF, to which cablecasting was forbidden, would become involved by getting around the law by signing agreements with the TVLC of Liège, Verviers and Charleroi from 1981. Arrangements which, justified as 'technical assistance', allowed RTBF to make indirect use of the cable, and which made possible a daily cablecast starting in April of 1982.

This sort of laboratory experiment was positive, taking into account that the equipment and the techniques used by the TVLC were frankly ridiculous: insufficient and inadequate equipment, lack of a proper channel (with the exception of two of them, all the others were using the RTBF2 channel at low audience times) (Jocquet and Sotiaux, 1981: 45), low budget, lack of sufficient technically competent staff.

This lack of means explains the fact that if, in 1983, RTC Télé Liège-Canal Emploi-RTBF Liège[11] was broadcasting a total of around some 25 hours per week, No Télé and Télésambre-RTBF Charleroi was only broadcasting 3.5 and 2 hours per week respectively (without counting the re-broadcasts), while Antenne Centre (which started operating in December of 1982) could only broadcast one hour every two weeks. Leaving aside Canal C, which after broadcasting up to 30 minutes per week, was now idle.

In order to overcome this standstill, Vidéotrame suggested making use of non-commercial advertising[12] (and even commercial) and sponsorship in local television broadcasts, and suggested the introduction of a local tax in their operating areas. But the federation of the TVLCs also asked their members to take care of the pay TV and local data banks, and to associate themselves 'with all projects relating to the development of cultural industries'. Vidéotrame finally proposed to buy back and broadcast more and more films with the objective (which was never really admitted) of pleasing the public and trying to secure a loyal audience.

Following the initial curiosity, the public did indeed turn away from the TVLC, finding their broadcasting dreary, monotonous, moralizing and militant. And, probably, not very enter-

11. Canal Emploi was a unique case of thematic television involved in professional training. Created in 1979, it ceased to function in 1988.

12. This advertising originates from the public institutions, the government, professional, social, cultural or sports associations. It does not promote any product brands or services. The French Community is competent with respect to commercial advertising only since 1988. On 28 March 1990, a decree from this Community allowed TVLC access to commercial advertising.

taining either. A survey carried out in March of 1983 in the town of Liège – within the area where local television was more professional and where the length of the programme was longer – did indeed show that only 38.3 per cent of the people interviewed knew of the existence of RTC Télé Liège, and only 22.7 per cent who recalled having seen one of their broadcasts.

Such a situation gave rise to some important questions, such issues as whether cable had not become too much a matter of socio-cultural associations, political parties, trade unions and other institutions, and not enough a field where media professionals had a role to play. Such as knowing what the specific role of the TVLC with respect to an increasingly regionalized RTBF was. And, finally, knowing whether the private groups already involved with the media should definitely be excluded from local television.

Beginning of the turning point

During the mid-1980s, the local stations of French-speaking Belgium were facing a turning point. With this in mind, a think tank on the future of the audio-visual field was formed in November of 1983.[13] Following that, the TVLC which until then were recognized on an experimental basis, were institutionalized by the decree of July 1985 (Conseil Supérieur de l'Audiovisuel, 1991: 46; Collard, 1994: 5). Among other conditions, this document obliges the cable broadcasters to broadcast local television programmes 'on a specific and reserved channel' (Collard, 1994: 5).

In October of 1985, the coming to power of a centre-right coalition would result in a contradictory policy regarding the TVLC. On the one hand, it refused to extend contracts to its part-time employees, and some stations were thus 'obliged to stop their production' (Hermanus, 1990: 195). And on the other hand, a consolidation of local television is observed, enabling them offer more secure jobs.

Incorporating the main rulings of the decree of 5 July 1985, the decree of 17 July 1987 (modified by the decree of 19 July 1991) stipulates that, in order to be authorized for a period of five years, a local television must:

> (1) 'be a non-profit-making organization' and guarantee 'the protection of the ideological and philosophical tendencies';
> (2) focus its broadcasting on 'local news and events, cultural development and permanent education', with at least one third being domestic production;
> (3) limit its broadcasting zone to one administrative district, where it would have the monopoly;
> (4) 'establish internal rules relative to objective news handling', the responsibility of which must be assured by 'one or several professional journalists' (Conseil Supérieur de l'Audiovisuel, 1991: 46);
> (5) 'institute a programming committee (*comité de programmation*)in charge of establishing the schedules' proposals to be presented to the management body

13. It was replaced in 1984 by the Commission Consultative sur l'Audiovisuel, which on 30 September 1987 was to become the present Conseil Supérieur de l'Audiovisuel (Hermanus, 1990: 17 & 217).

(*organe de gestion*)' and also entrusted with guaranteeing the protection of ideological and philosophical minorities. The two bodies' members cannot include 'more than one third representatives of the public authorities' (Conseil Supérieur de l'Audiovisuel, 1989–90: 37), where the other members represent the associative and cultural sectors (Collard, 1994: 6–7).

As for financing, the decree of 7 December 1987 (modified by the decree of 6 April 1989) put the TVLC in three categories (A, B or C) according to four criteria: quality and nature of the activities, size of the population involved, other sources of finance available to the television and the number of weekly broadcast hours (except for re-broadcasts and the teletext). A second decree made at the same date stipulated that the French Community's subsidies could cover the operating fees, staff salaries and investments.

Financing: low means

In reality, two thirds of the financing of the TVLC is assured by public authorities (French Community, Walloon Region, Brussels-Capital Region and the municipalities): in 1992, the subsidies given by the French Community reached a total of 132 million FB (as opposed to 25.3 million in 1983) (Communauté Française de Belgique, 1993: 131; Collard, 1994: 19). The other third comes from advertisement (some 34 million FB in 1992) (Collard, 1994: 19), pay pages of the teletext, sponsorship and commercial video productions (Conseil Supérieur de l'Audiovisuel, 1991: 47–48; Wangermée, 1993: 33). This leads the TVLC to seek the same formula from which No Télé had long benefited: each cable subscriber in its region pays 300 extra FB per year for it (Wangermée, 1993: 33). Otherwise, assures Videótrame,[14] 'immediate area television would not develop' (Collard, 1994: 21).

Because of their low financial means, the TVLC are forced to operate with a small staff. In total, the eleven TVLC have only '205 employees on a permanent contract basis' and about 'forty free-lance journalists and miscellaneous contributors' (Wangermée, 1993: 33). These figures are really low, also taking into account that looking for alternative resources in itself requires staff and equipment occupation (Collard, 1994: 20). However this does not seem to stop them participating in a 'partnership for the development of new cable services: interactive teletext and videotext, training courses, educational television' (Wangermée, 1993: 34).

While waiting for such problematic diversifications, the TVLC, which have a potential of 'more than 3,400,000 viewers' (Vidéotrame, 1994: (1)), are seeking full coverage of the French Community (Wangermée, 1993: 33). However, this desire to be everywhere gives rise to stations with varied demographic sizes: three metropolitan TV stations (Brussels, Charleroi and Liège), with an audience potential of over 550 thousand viewers; six TV stations for average size towns (La Louvière, Mons, Namur, Ottignies, Tournai and Verviers), with a potential between 160 and 250 thousand; two TV stations for rural and semi-rural zones (Gembloux and Rochefort), with less than 60 thousand (Collard, 1994: 2; Communauté Française de Belgique: 127).

14. Vidéotrame is presently in charge of the documentation centre, programming production and advertising production of the TVLC network (Vidéotrame, 1994: 4).

Table 1. Belgium: local and community television in the French-speaking Community

Name	Start	Office	Number of homes connected (1994)	Potential viewers (1994)	Weekly broad-casting number of hours* (1992)	First broad-cast (% of total) (1992)	Full time employ-ment (1994)
Antenne Centre	18.12.82	La Louvière	62,912	201,318	31h30	15.9	23.00
Canal C	15.04.78	Namur	92,000	257,600	34h00	16.0	23.00
Canal Zoom	22.05.76	Gembloux	10,000	30,000	22h00	9.8	9.00
No Télé	12.11.77	Tournai	678,653	235,959	12h15	70.0	27.50
RTC Télé Liège	26.02.77	Liège	223,641	626,194	37h30	16.7	17.00
Télé Bruxelles	14.12.85	Bruxelles	344,842	850,000	59h00	9.3	27.75
Télé MB	14.11.86	Mons	74,000	236,800	49h00	14.0	16.00
Télésambre	17.12.76	Charleroi	177,341	567,492	32h30	12.7	19.00
Télévesdre	30.06.89	Verviers	59,674	198,000	43h00	12.6	11.00
TV Com	29.09.79	Ottignies	53,629	160,887	30h00	7.1	12.00
Vidéoscope	15.03.77	Rochefort	18,816	60,500	46h00	5.2	11.00

*Not including teletext
Sources: French community of Belgium, Vidéotrame.

Programming: nature of the concepts

But the French-speaking Belgium TVLC are not only different because of their demographic size, but also because of the concepts governing their programming. Some people have established a typology which includes local news TV (for instance RTC Télé Liège, with two daily news broadcasts), general local TV (which covers most of the others) and TV stations located mid-way between these two categories (Télésambre and Télévesdre) (Communauté Française de Belgique, 1993: 128).

In reality the TVLC's schedules place emphasis on 'immediate area television' (*Télévision de proximité*). TV stations with different programming, but which represent at the same time specific local concerns and choices of the people who planned them. Schematically, these schedules are made up of the following main genres: (1) news broadcasts, which achieve a good position; (2) cultural and sports magazines; (3) slots dedicated to cinema and entertainment agenda; (4) debate and encounter programmes; (5) 'files on information and public awareness'; (6) programmes produced in collaboration with associations and local groups ('youth clubs and arts centres, associations, schools, universities, homes'); (7) less frequently entertainment programmes, games or shows. Added to those home-produced programmes, which represent 70 per cent to 95 per cent of the programming from the different stations, are: (8) a monthly and bi-monthly magazine produced by the network and broadcast on all TVLC, and intended for training and reinsertion of socio-professionals; (9) teletext broadcasts with news services (cultural agenda, associations, job offers and classified ads); (10) some foreign productions (now less frequent) (Collard, 1994: 9–11; Communauté Française de Belgique, 1993: 128–129).

Six stations (of a total of eleven) broadcast every day of the week, three are doing so six days a week and two only five days a week. But these broadcasts create a large number of multi-broadcast loops: indeed 'in 1992 there was an average of 83.5 per cent of re-broadcasting out of the total volume of weekly broadcasts from all the TVLC' (Communauté Française de Belgique, 1993: 128).

Nineteen years following their creation, local televisions are still influenced by the principles imposed at that time: 'managed by private associations', they carry out, in reality, 'public service missions' (Vidéotrame, 1994: 2). Even if they have achieved real renown, their audiences are still low ... and are not shown in the surveys made by the specialized organization (CIM, Centre d'Information sur les Média). And this, added to the fact that no attempt was made to join forces with the newspapers and local or regional radio, results in the TVLC's low advertising income.

Local and community television in Flanders: the endless north-south division

In the decree of 17 July 1987, the legislator decided that it would be desirable to create along with the existing local television, 'regional private television'. The lack of candidates to manage of these regional stations has led to the suppression of this possibility in French-speaking Belgium (decree of 19 July 1991).

This challenge of the 'private regional television' was due to the Flemish community in 1991–93. It is true that the situation north of the 'linguistic border' was diametrically opposed to that of the south. For many years, the predominant political attitude in Flanders has been to oppose any opening of the TV sector, controlled by the BRTN (the public Television of the Flemish-speaking Community). The first opening was put into effect to the benefit of VTM, a commercial station covering the Flemish community, owned by the Flemish Press publishers and inaugurated on 1 February 1989.[15]

The success of VTM surpassed all expectations. And, in order to avoid cable penetration from the Netherlands' RTL4 and RTL5, the Flemish community authorized the creation of eleven 'regional TV stations'. As said above, the French-speaking Community call their television 'local', whilst the Flemish-speaking Community call theirs 'regional'. This is only a difference in terminology, since in reality they are fairly similar in size. Nevertheless, three major differences are found between the southern 'community and local television', and the northern 'regional television': the southern ones were created by socio-cultural non-profit-making organizations which still control them, and have year after year sought an increase in the zone their station covered, operating mainly from public subsidies. The northern ones, created only recently, even though awarded to non-profit-making organizations, are operated by commercial societies within zones pre-established by the Flemish community and will have to survive mainly by means of advertising and sponsorship.[16]

15. The French-speaking public TV RTBF was faced, since 1971, with competition from RTL Télévision, which broadcasted from Luxembourg but was aimed mainly at Belgium viewers, and which in December 1985 obtained a Belgian legal status, hence becoming RTL-TVI.

16. Only one exception to the rule regarding resources: TV Brussel, because of the minority position of the Flemish-speaking population in Brussels, would get subsidies from the Flemish government (30 million FB in 1993) and the region of Brussels-Capital (40 million FB).

In fact, four local stations already existed in Flanders, authorized by the decree of January 28th 1987: AVS, in Eeklo (since 19 February 1981), ATV, in Berchem (since 26 April 1986), RTVO;[17] in Courtrai (since 23 March 1987), and RTVL[18] in Louvain (since 10 April 1987). As a matter of fact, only AVS was broadcasting one hour on Saturdays and the rest of the time a teletext was shown on the screen. RTVO was only broadcasting teletext. As for the other two, they had no programmes at all. Such a situation looked strangely like fallow land.

The decree of 23 October 1991 by the Flemish community (modified by the decree of May 1992) defined the structure of a new television scene, which legally was not, in truth, different from the one formed by the southern TVLC. In Flanders as well, the TVR's mission was 'to guarantee news, animation, training and entertainment programmes in order to promote communication among the population of its broadcasting zone, and to contribute to the social and cultural general development of the region'. Also, 'the news programmes must follow the usual standards with respect to the journalistic professional codes of ethics, and assure impartiality and editorial independence'. Likewise, the cable-casters must carry the TVR's programmes 'free of charge, simultaneously and full length, on a specific channel'.

On the other hand, the structure of the stations' management is defined in a more precise and restrictive way than in the south. The structure of the general assembly and the consultative committee must comply with 'representativeness on the political, social, cultural, philosophical, ethnic and geographic scenes'. Whereas the administration council cannot have more than one fifth of its members made up of political representatives, employers' organizations and trade union leaders, mass media, advertising and cable-casting companies' managers, and where legislative or executive public powers' members are completely excluded.

From theory to reality

If at first, from a legal point of view, the northern and southern television scenes had some chance of being more or less equal, the economic and management reality is completely changing this picture. Indeed, whereas in French-speaking Belgium the men and women managing the TVLC come from stations with originally socio-cultural concerns, in Flemish-speaking Belgium we find that professionals coming from the world of media and advertising have taken control of the TVR, in journalistic, technical and commercial aspects.

Under pressure from the political powers of Flanders,[19] groups from the press and northern cable-caster are actively involved in the inauguration of the new regional TV stations. Because, behind the non-profit organizations receiving the licence for such creation, there are hidden operating societies with the technical and equipment support assuring the programme production intended for these stations. Operating societies in which press publishers have made sizeable investments in order to keep their dominant position within the regions where they have often control over the newspaper and/or of the most major free magazines. Press publishers who have taken control of the TVR's advertising departments,

17. RTVO became WTV Zuid in 1993.

18. RTVL became Rob TV in 1993.

19. According to statements made by Rilk De Nolf, director of the Groupe Roularta, to *MédiaMarketing*, 90, October 1993: 24.

by merging them with the newspaper published in their established zone. This explains why the advertisers are worried, even if advertising and sponsorship must originate from the region.

Table 2. Belgium: local and community television in the Flemish-speaking Community

Name	Start	Office	Number of homes connected (1994)	Potential viewers (1994)	Weekly broadcasting number of hours* (1992)
ATV	19.12.93	Berchem	380,000	1,100,000	168h00
AVS	01.01.94	Eeklo	231,000	577,500	n.a.
Focus TV	01.09.93	Jabbeke	280,000	700,000	n.a.
Kanaal 3	26.09.94	Termonde	?	?	122h30
Rob TV	15.11.93	Louvain	250,000	650,000	n.a.
Ring TV	15.02.95	Hal	?	?	n.a.
TV Kempen	01.03.94	Oevel-Westerlo	144,000	400,000	168h00
TVL	15.04.94	Houthalen	230,000	708,000	n.a.
TV Brussel	15.09.93	Brussels	361,198	850,000	n.a.
TV Mechelen	01.11.94	Malines	?	?	n.a.
WTV Zuid	01.02.93	Kuurne	248,000	620,000	n.a.

n.a.: not available; *Not including teletext;
Sources: *Media Plan 1993, télégramme*, January 1994; *Pub*, 10 February 1994.

The programming carried out in TVR, even though designed to 'attract audience', does not really vary from that carried out by the TVLC: local news bulletins, sports magazine, encounter programme, and also games (Galuszka, 1993: 45), with a total of 20 to 45 minutes of daily programme re-broadcast in a loop (Groupe R. Dupuis, 1993: 460–462).

The future of the two models

In addition to these television stations there are, depending on the cable networks, some twenty foreign stations, making a total of approximately 30 national or transnational, general or special interest, free or pay channels. Belgians also enjoy (or soon will enjoy) a 'proximity' local or regional television channel (TVLC or TVR).[20] But here, like in many other fields, the audio-visual landscape will be divided by a linguistic boundary, which will involve a deep gap between two models. Two models that are the result of different cultural and political developments, in French Cultural Community and in Flanders. Two models in agreement with the times that saw their origins: the 1970s, on the one hand, when the notion of 'public service' was still preponderant and people dreamed about 'changing life' and building an 'alternative' society based on participation; and the 1990s, on the other, where private sector and advertisers' drive predominate over the European audio-visual landscape. Will these models be able to achieve a solid enough consolidation to resist the invasion of 'television without frontiers' coming from abroad?

20. At the beginning of 1994, 31 or 32 stations (including TéléBruxelles and TV Brussel) could be received in Brussels via cable.

References

BRTN (1993): *Cahier d'Information* (typed). Brussels: BRTN.

Collard, S. (1994): *Les télévisions de proximité en Communauté française de Belgique*. Namur: Fédération des Télévisions Locales.

Communauté Française de Belgique (1993): *Annuaire de l'audiovisuel 1993*. Brussels: Communauté Française de Belgique.

Conseil Supérieur de l'Audiovisuel (1989–90): *Les avis du Conseil Supérieur de l'Audiovisuel, 1989–90*. Brussels: Direction de l'Audiovisuel.

Conseil Supérieur de l'Audiovisuel (1991): *Les avis du Conseil Supérieur de l'Audiovisuel, 1991*. Brussels: Direction de l'Audiovisuel.

Galuszka, V. (1993): 'Petites, mais ambitieuses', in *Média Marketing*, 86.

Groupe R. Dupuis (1993): *Médiaplan 1993*. Brussels.

Hermanus, A.-M. (1990): *Tempêtes sur l'audiovisuel*. Liège: Editions du Perron.

Jocquet, M. (1981): *Rapport d'évaluation des télévisions locales et communautaires*. Duplicated document.

Jocquet, M. & Sotiaux, D. (1981): 'Au pays où le câble est roi', in *Pointillés, 11*.

Nobre-Correia, J.-M. (1984): 'Rêves et désillusions de l'autre télévision', in *Vidéodoc*, 66.

Nobre-Correia, J.-M. (1992): 'Formes et limites du paysage médiatique européen', in Féron, F. and A. Thoraval (dir.): *L'état de l'Europe*. Paris: La Découverte.

RTBF (1992): *Rapport annuel 1991*. Brussels: RTBF.

RTBF (1994): *Rapport annuel 1993*. Brussels: RTBF.

Van Apeldoorn, R. (1994): 'Les interrogations du câble belge face au numérique', in *Médiaspouvoirs*, 36.

Vertommen, R. (1980): 'Le statut de la radiodiffusion en Belgique, histoire et évolution', in *Etudes de Radio-Télévision*, 27.

Vidéotrame (1983a): *L'avenir des télévisions locales...* Duplicated document. Namur: Fédération des télévisions locales.

Vidéotrame (1983b): *L'information, la diffusion et la publicité non commerciale...* Duplicated document. Namur: Fédération des télévisions locales.

Vidéotrame (1994): *Les televisions locales en Communauté Française de Belgique*. Namur: Fédération des télévisions locales.

Wangermée, R. (1993): *Les Carrefours professionnels de l'audiovisuel. Rapport de synthèse*. Brussels.

3   Denmark: From community radio to regional television

Jørgen Poulsen

Introduction

From a geographical point of view, the Kingdom of Denmark may be divided into three regions: Greenland, the Faroe Islands and the very small southern part, normally referred to as Denmark. The island of Greenland and the Faroe Islands are in the North Atlantic Ocean. These islands have home rule and their own television system where the regional and national programmes (for the separate and autonomous area) fall together. The conditions of these areas I shall discuss at the end of this report, as, from a population, geographical, and historical point of view, each of them diverge from the rest of Denmark.

What in the following will be referred to as Denmark is 43,000 square kilometres, consisting of the peninsula, Jutland, which is part of the European continent, and a number of islands between Jutland and Sweden. Regional television was introduced here during the period from 1983 to 1991. The first service (TV South/ TV Syd) started in Southern Jutland, and the other seven services were established as part of the second Danish national TV channel (TV 2) between 1 January 1989 and 1 January 1991. The eight services broadcast 30 minutes daily, between 7:30 and 8:00 p.m. (except Saturdays) and the national TV 2 programme is interrupted while regional television is on the air. An average of 14 per cent of the population view these programmes which consist mainly of regional news.

Despite the limited usage and hours of broadcasting available for regional television, the political, media, and ideological importance is quite extensive. These conditions will be described in the following sections.

The history of regional television

The history of regional television started with radio. From the beginning of radio in the early 1920s, broadcasting in Denmark has been a strongly centralized business with its cultural and productive centre in Copenhagen, which since the Renaissance has occupied the dominating position in Denmark, culturally and politically speaking. Today up to 2/5 of the population live in the capital area in and around Copenhagen. As a consequence it was a natural thing to situate television here in the beginning of the 1950s as part of Radio Denmark.

Since the 1960s however, there has been an increasing awareness of ideas such as decentralization, pluralism (contrary to the monopoly of broadcasting), and cultural democracy. In 1967 a Broadcasting Commission was set up which submitted a White Book in 1969. It was primarily concerned with the introduction of colour television in order to make the one and only television channel in the country able to compete with television abroad (spill-over from the neighbouring countries, Germany and Sweden, and satellites in a foreseeable future).

The Commission dealt with the possibility of establishing a second national television channel but without mentioning regionalization of the supply. The possibility of establishing 'production facilities (centres) in the provinces' (p. 19) was the only point mentioned. First of all, interest was directed towards an extension of the progressing regional programmes on the radio (15 minutes a day), and the establishment of regional centres for radio broadcasting spread over the country was recommended.

Radio Denmark established such regional units in 1973, and in connection with a structural change of the national radio stations several daily regional radio programmes were broadcast from 4 January 1975. At this point radio had established seven regional units with their own editorial offices. They were later supplemented by an eighth by dividing the very large East Jutland radio into two, establishing Channel '94 in Vejle. After a start, which was rather slack listener wise, the regional radios achieved good listener rates establishing a daily contact of between 40 and 60 per cent with the audience. The capital area was a pronounced exception as only 25–30 per cent of the listeners were reached. The establishment of community radio on a municipality level from 1993 gave the idea of decentralization a considerable boost but was also good competition for the regional radios as well as the national stations.

In the experiment with community radio the possibility of establishing community televisions also became an aspect to be considered. Since 1983 there has been a low viewer rate for the local television stations in ten cities, with Copenhagen as the largest area of coverage, and where the station adopted the ambitious name Channel 2.

The Second National Channel: TV 2

The discussion about the establishment of a second national television channel remained in the background, however, and in 1980 a wide Media Commission was set up in order to find answers to media questions, such as cable television, satellite television and TV 2, in spite of the fact that this was not explicitly mentioned by the Commission. In the fifth White Paper from the Commission on 26 June 1983 it was recommended that a new national television channel be established with public service obligations and a mixed financial foundation: The majority of the financing by means of advertising blocks and the minority by means of licence which was collected beforehand for the financing of television and national radio under Radio Denmark. The commission had evidently been inspired by the enterprise model of the recently established Channel 4 in the UK and the regional possibilities of channels which were known from Germany, Sweden and the UK where one of the national channels was based on regional companies which partly had their own regional broadcasting and partly supplied nation-wide broadcasting with programmes.

On 30 May 1986 the Danish Parliament passed a law on TV 2 where a national commercial public service channel was established, with its own management and headquarters in Odense, in the middle of Denmark, and not in Copenhagen. Furthermore, it was up to the channel to finance a number of independent regional services. As a new venture, these regional services were established from the bottom up as local organizations established a council which elected a board and via a process of hearings in the affected County Councils it was forwarded to the national TV 2 Board and the Minister of Cultural Affairs.

The work of the Media Commission Radio Denmark had already established experiments with a regional television service in Southern Jutland and had, with this, proven what many people doubted; that according to contents as well as talent it was possible to produce daily television programmes outside the capital and that these programmes had the potential of reaching a quite considerable audience. The programme concepts with daily regional news (about 15 minutes) and a supplementary feature programme had already been adopted during the experimental period of TV South from 1983–85 and was since adopted by all 8 regional stations, even though periodically other concepts have been experimented with.

Organizational structure and financing

Regional television in Denmark consists of 8 independent regional stations within the TV 2 system. In order to establish a regional service a representative body consisting of members reflecting or representing a 'plurality of regional cultural and social life' must be formed on a local basis. In practice, the trade unions and employer's associations have played a vital role in the establishment of local councils. Once accepted by the minister of Cultural Affairs, after having received comments by the counties involved and the Board of the national TV 2, the council of the regional services elects a board, which appoints a director who employs his or her staff.

The regional boards have a joint representative in the national TV 2 Board, who deals with the annual budget proposals and proposes to the minister of Cultural Affairs how the economical means and sending period should be divided between TV 2 and the 8 regional stations. From the beginning, the regional stations have been allocated fewer resources than they have asked for and in 1993 they have had over 235 million DKr at their disposal, the equivalent of 28 per cent of the total budget for TV 2 which is 830 million DKr (equivalent to 106 million ECU). The total budget of 830 million DKr consists of three main revenue sources:

1. Commercials   660 million Dkr

2. Licence   143 million Dkr

3. Sponsorships   66 million Dkr

The licence is 6.4 per cent of the total licence revenue in Denmark, which also accounts for the total costs of Radio Denmark (1 national TV channel, 3 national radio channels, short wave services, orchestras, etc.).

The regional stations only cover some 6 per cent of the broadcasting hours (with the exception of re-runs), and 28 per cent may seem like a large amount of money but it should not be forgotten that the regional services produce and broadcast in 8 different areas at the same time. Measured in production time regional stations produce 49 per cent of the programmes and are thus obliged to be 1.75 times more efficient concerning the number of broadcasting hour per money unit than the national TV 2.

Table 1. TV2's broadcasting hours (1992)

	Total	Re-runs	Danish/Scandinavian origin (%)
National service			
News and features	870	49	100
Fiction	1,527	332	26
Factual shows	404	108	58
Programme presentation	171	–	100
Total TV 2/DANMARK	2,972	489	56
Regional TV2 services			
TV 2/BORNHOLM	154	10	100
TV 2/FYN	153	8	100
TV 2/LORRY	156	0	100
TV/MIDT-VEST	152	1	100
TV 2/NORD	153	24	100
TV/SYD	156	8	100
TV 2/ØST	149	0	100
TV 2/ØSTJYLLAND	142	0	100
Total regional services	1,225	51	100
Commercials	164	–	–
Total TV2 service	4,361	540	66

Source: TV-meter survey in Denmark prepared by Gallup for TV 2, Danmarks Radio and TV3.

Contents and audience of the regional services

As stated above, each regional service produces between 149 and 156 hours per year. They broadcast every evening (except Saturdays) between 7:30 and 7:58 p.m. on the national network, each covering 2–4 counties. The programmes consist predominantly of news, usually a news summary with 5–10 features of about 10–15 minutes at first (some days only 3–5 minutes) and thereafter 1–5 features or a studio production.

After a slow start with a very low viewer rate, especially in the capital area, most of the regional services have now achieved a stable viewer rate of around 14 per cent of the total population in the area, with variations of 10 per cent as the lowest in the capital area (TV 2/Lorry) and 24 per cent as the highest in the western part of Jutland. It is obvious, as is also the case with regional radio, community radio, and television, that interest rises with the increase in distance from the capital and other large cities. The rise in percentage of viewers is illustrated in Table 3.

Table 2. Audience of regional shows at 7:30 p.m.
(Daily average ratings in their own regions)

Region	Total viewers (1,000s)	Share
TV 2/FYN	57	13
TV 2/LORRY	157	10
TV/MIDT-VEST	117	24
TV 2/NORD	78	16
TV/SYD	106	14
TV 2/ØST	58	11
TV 2/ØSTJYLLAND	88	15
Total of regional shows	667	14

Source: TV-meter survey in Denmark prepared by Gallup for TV 2, Danmarks Radio and TV3.
Note: TV 2/BORNHOLM's ratings are included in the total average for the shows of the regional services, but the number of measuring units of Bornholm is too small to make reliable reports from this area alone.

Table 3. Viewing of regional services

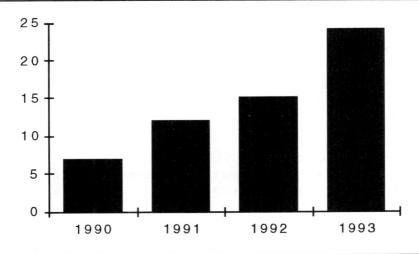

Average rating of persons over 13 years of age. Source: TV meter survey in Denmark prepared by Gallup for TV 2, Danmarks Radio, and TV 3.

Television in Greenland and Faroe Islands

Greenland (with a population of about 50,000 people) has been part of Denmark since 1721, and gained home rule in 1979. While the national language is Greenlandic, both the administration and the educational system are bilingual. Greenland had its first newspaper in the 19th century, and radio broadcasts had already begun in the 1920s. Today, two national, bilingual newspapers are published, and radio, which broadcasts mostly in Greenlandic, can be heard by almost everyone. Television consists mainly of Danish programmes which are sent to Greenland by video a week or more after they are shown in Denmark. There are six hours of broadcasting per day, including only 5–8 per cent of locally produced material, the rest being divided between (in round figures) 30 per cent Danish, 30 per cent American and 30 per cent from other countries (the latter two with subtitles in Danish). Very few programmes are translated into or subtitled in Greenlandic.

By erecting 2-metre-wide parabolic antennas, it is possible to receive Canadian television in parts of Greenland. To my knowledge, however, this is not being done. Videos are more widespread than in Denmark and, despite a lower income for the population, some 60–70 per cent have bought videos. This is considered to be indicative of a considerable lack of television entertainment and films. The arrival of television and video has destroyed an otherwise well-functioning, state-subsidized film distribution network. Television was introduced 'through the back door' when a radio dealer gained permission in 1969 to broadcast cable television by 'camping on the doorsteps of Danish politicians'. He has earned millions by selling television sets and has since given them away to a fund for the preservation of Greenlandic culture. After a prolonged period with private cable network, in 1978 television became a part of the state-owned broadcasting system, KNR, which has now come under government administration.

The Faroe Islands are also part of Denmark, and gained home rule in 1948. A distinct minority of the population wants full independence, but this view is not likely to be adopted by the majority, due (not least) to large financial grants from Denmark. Until 1948 Danish was the official language of the administration and the church, and the introduction of Faroese into all facets of society has been the most important matter for nationalistic groups during the last century. Based on these facts, it is interesting to note that discussions on language have been totally absent since the introduction of the 100 per cent Danish-speaking television broadcasts in 1979.

Television started as a private project, and in the beginning it was based almost exclusively on imported videos from Denmark. Since 1983, an independent Faroese television company has been broadcasting for about six hours daily, including about 15 per cent locally produced material, consisting mostly of daily newscasts. The rest is imported through Denmark in Danish or accompanied by Danish subtitles.

Faroe Islands Radio broadcasts almost exclusively in Faroese, and only one of the seven newspapers is bilingual. The number of newspapers per household is about 3.5, probably the highest in the world, and cultural life is very comprehensive, with many books being published, theatre, musical activities, etc. The introduction of television, and later that of video cassette recorders (which are to be found in perhaps 80 per cent of homes), has posed grave problems for the cinema and resulted in a certain decrease in the otherwise very intensive activities of various associations.

Faroese society is characterized by a tight social network, close family contacts and many activities inherited from the traditional society (sheep farming, small-time fishing, country dancing, family feasts, etc.). The divorce and crime rates are very low, but in recent years, unemployment caused by a crisis in the fishing industry has brought increasing social problems.

References

Mediekomissionen (1970): 'Betaenkning afgivet af Radiokommissionen', in *Betaenkning* 592. Copenhagen.

Mediekomissionen (1985): 'Betaenkning om et Øget dansk tv-udbud. Mediekommissionens betaenkning nr. 5', in *Betaenkning* 986. Copenhagen.

Minke, Kim (1990): 'Media Structures in Denmark, Media Structures in a Changing Europe', in *Innovation*, 3, 2. Vienna.

Mortensen, F. *et al.* (eds.) (1991): *Mediehandbogen*. Gyldendal.

Poulsen, J. (1991): 'Television – Challenge or Threat to Social Identity in Small Language Communities', in *EMI – Educational Media International*. 28, 3.

Siune, K. (1986): 'Denmark', in Kleinsteuber, H., McQuail, D. & Siune, K.: *Electronic Media and Politics in Western Europe*. Euromedia Research Group Handbook of National Systems. Frankfurt: Campus.

Siune, K. (1986): 'Future Media Trends in Denmark', in *Fast II, Com II, Impact of New Communication Technology on Media Industry*. Brussels: EC.

TV 2/Danmark (1992): *Accounts for the Year 1992*.

TV 2/Danmark (1993): *TV 2* (Leaflet).

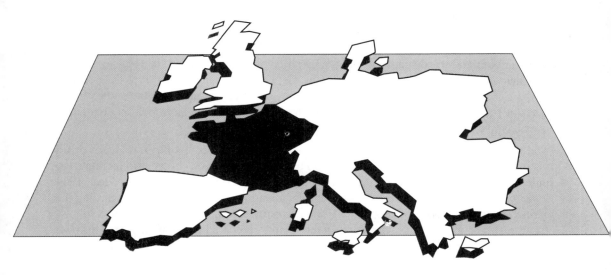

4 France: Identity crisis of regional television and expansion of local television

Gaëlle Canova-Lamarque, Michel Perrot and Bernat López[1]

The general political framework, the nation and the regions

French regionalization was completed tardily. It is only since 1986 that all the regions have been institutionally set up, i.e. they have become administrative institutions with general authority for the management of their own territory, according to the law of 1982. Nevertheless, France has long since had a sort of administrative decentralization, with the existence of the townships ('communes') and departments. In reality, this delay is due to long hesitations in choosing the framework and the scope of authority for the regional institutions with respect to the existing territorial communities. Today, despite this delay, the regions have expanded quite rapidly and have a increasingly important role among the French administrative map, especially in the field of economic development.

The French administrative system consists of five levels: townships, departments, regions, the state and the European Union. This system, which is made up of many compartments, does not simplify the distribution of duties, scopes of authority and financial means between the different levels of administration. Yet, France is not the only European country governed by various levels of administration. However, it is characterized by two original features: the

1. With the cooperation of Marta Civil.

large amount and the disparity of the territorial communities. Indeed, in 1988 the census indicated 36,749 townships. These data show that France has more townships than the rest of the EU countries. At present, 100 departments made up the metropolitan and overseas areas of France, while the regions are in the number of 22 in the metropolitan area and 4 overseas (the so-called 'DOM-TOM').

The present regional division of France has its origins in 1956, but has not received full institutional status until 1982. A law of 1956 delimited the 'region' in order to facilitate the political development and economic planning of the state. The decree of 14 March 1964 instituted a prefect who had the mission of implementing government policy regarding the economic and territorial development of the corresponding district. He therefore administrated planning and public investments in the regions, prepared the plan meant for his own region and followed up its yearly execution. In reality, he was the link between the plan and the budget.

However, the decrees of 14 March 1964 had also instituted a Commission in charge of Regional Economic Development (CODER) in each region. This assembly, which was composed of elected members and professionals, had only a consulting role. It received a report on the execution of the regional plan from the prefect. But the CODER was in the hands of the regional prefect who fixed the agenda and the dates for assembly meetings of which he was the secretary.

In 1969 a regionalization project was submitted to referendum. This project gave the regions the status of territorial communities, and permitted them to be the beneficiaries of a transfer of authority and funding from the state. This regionalization project was submitted to referendum on 27 April 1969. It was rejected by 41.67 per cent of the registered voters and 53.17 per cent of the valid votes. In reality by rejecting the project, it seems that the voters expressed more their repudiation towards the General de Gaulle than their hostility regarding regionalization.

Following the failure of the project, the law of 5 July 1972 set the bases for a decentralized regional institution, but in the exclusive form of a public establishment: the Regional Council. It was composed of the regional members of the national parliament, the representatives of the townships and those of the large towns. The main objective of the Regional Council was to allow for economic and social development of the region. The law of 1972 foresaw the creation of an economic and social committee (for the replacement of CODER) as well. It was composed of representatives of professional and trade union organizations from various sectors. It was responsible for giving its opinion regarding the most important questions involving the scope of authority in the regions. However, the regional prefect kept the regional executive power.

This way the region, with this law in effect, still did not exercise real authority. It was able only to participate in the financing of services, or finance directly but with the agreement and for the advantage of-the local communities or the state. But the law of 1972 foresaw that the Regional Council could benefit from the transfer of the state authority, as well the corresponding state credit. And from 1975 until 1979, the regional public establishment was given the allocation of state authority, especially concerning natural regional parks, sports, sanitary or transport services.

It was necessary to wait for the law of 2 March 1982 for the regions to obtain the status of territorial communities. They were from that moment on administered by a council elected by universal suffrage. According to this law the regions have authority not only as far as economic and social development is concerned, but in terms of cultural development as well. The regional prefect renamed 'commissioner of the republic' lost his prerogatives and particularly his financial control. The executive authority was transferred from the regional prefect to the president of the Regional Council.

The first point to notice concerns the relation between regional distribution and economic development. As mentioned before, the French regional policy has basically followed economic criteria without taking into account the cultural notions such as for example the linguistic phenomenon. Therefore, the maps of the administrative regions do not coincide with the outline of the linguistic regions: the Aquitaine region includes the 'Basques' and the 'Occitans', Britanny is clearly larger than the zone where Breton is spoken (see below, 'Linguistic and cultural dimension'.).

The administrative regions were created from a double imperative, economic and technical, and not from the political willpower to recognize some regional identity. Notwithstanding, in 1982 Corsica obtained a different status than the one given to the other French regions. As a first step, the government recognized the specific political situation of the Mediterranean island and replaced the Regional Council with a Corsican assembly. Secondly, important changes took place with a new law in 1991. Indeed, it details and widens the allocations and the conditions for election of the Corsican assembly and creates an executive council elected by the assembly and under its control. The law strengthens the cultural identity of Corsica (while rejecting the notion of *peuple Corse*). It widens the role of the territorial community concerning economy, planning, development of the territory, fiscality and culture. Finally, it reshapes Corsica into a single electoral constituency.

The four overseas regions (Guadeloupe, Guyana, Martinique and Réunion) have a specific status defined by the law of 31 December 1982. The most important fact is that these regions now consist of one unique department. In other words, one territory consists of a department and a region at the same time.

Administration and economic structure of the French regions

According to the law of 1982, the Regional Council has authority 'to promote the economic, social, sanitary, cultural and scientific development of the region, and the development of its territory, as well as assuring the preservation of its identity while respecting the integrity, autonomy and attributions of the departments and townships'. The regional structure is based on three representative entities: the Regional Council, the president of the Regional Council and the socio-economic committee. The Regional Council, representative body proceeding from the region, is elected for six years by means of direct universal suffrage.

The president of the Regional Council has an essential role since he is the executive authority of the region. He is elected by the Regional Council for a period of six years and is responsible for the preparation and the execution of the council resolutions as well as the regional services management.

The economic and social committee, in charge of representing the economic, social and cultural interests of the region, acts as consulting assembly of the region. This committee gives its advice under strict obligation with respect to the most important issues included in the regional attributions, in particular on planning and the budget, and can, on its own initiative, formulate advice on all questions regarding the authority of the region.

The region has an essential role with respect to economic development. For example, it has the monopoly of the direct distribution of aid packages given to the firms. It can grant direct or indirect aid to a firm in financial difficulty 'when the protection of the economic and social interests of the population calls for it'. Regarding education, the region administers and is in charge of the secondary schools, their buildings and investments. On the subject of professional training, it participates with the state and assures the administration a regional fund

Table 1. The regions of France (regional distribution of the main socio- economic indicators)

	Area (km^2)	Population on 1 Jan. 1991 (1,000s)	GDP (1989) (billion francs)
Alsace	8,280	1,631	180.9
Aquitaine	41,308	2,813	268.2
Auvergne	26,013	1,321	115.7
Burgundy	31,582	1,612	154.4
Brittany	27,208	2,805	243.2
Central	39,151	2,384	235.2
Champagne-Ardenne	25,606	1,348	139.0
Corsica	8,680	251	18.8
Franche-Comté	16,202	1,099	108.1
Ile-de-France	12,012	10,736	1,761.3
Languedoc-Roussillon	27,376	2,138	177.2
Limousin	16,942	722	60.4
Lorraine	23,547	2,304	212.9
Midi-Pyrénées	45,348	2,445	211.5
Nord-Pas-de-Calais	12,414	3,968	346.1
Low-Normandy	17,589	1,395	125.2
High-Normandy	12,317	1,746	186.0
The Loire Country	32,082	3,072	286.7
Picardie	19,400	1,819	164.6
Poitou-Charentes	25,810	1,598	138.4
Provence-Alpes-Côte d'Azur	31,400	4,294	422.6
Rhône-Alpes	43,698	5,391	573.6
Total Metropolitan	543,965	56,892	6,130.0
Guadeloupe	1,702	387	11.0
Guyane	83,500	115	2.9
Martinique	1,100	360	13.8
Réunion	2,510	598	23.7

Source: INSEE, 1992.

for professional training. It exercises authority in the fields of river ports and waterways, and has greater specialized responsibilities for housing and urban management.

The region takes part in the development and the execution of a national plan. For the implementation of the plan, contract documents are exchanged between the state and the region. It is then the responsibility of the region to draw up a regional plan following consultation with the general councils and the important townships.

In terms of media, the region has no power whatsoever. However in some regions, the Regional Council takes some initiative regarding the matter. Hence, the Regional Council of Aquitaine created the agency 'Aquitaine Nouvelles Communications' (ANC). The ANC is a legal society presided by the president of the Regional Council of Aquitaine. Granted a budget of 12 million Francs in 1992, the objective of the ANC is to encourage opinions, projects and actions regarding new technologies. It assures technological monitoring in connecting the expert networks, follows the project in the Aquitaine region and promotes the sector of new information and communication techniques in the Aquitaine region.

Economic structure of French regions

Even if we analyse the population or the gross domestic product as a criteria, the classification of French regions varies very little. Four regions which together account for more than 40 per cent of the French population and half of the gross domestic product stand out. That is to say Ile-de-France, Rhône-Alpes, Provence-Alpes-Côte d'Azur and Nord-Pas-de-Calais. Following is a group of seven regions whose population is within two to three million inhabitants. Among them stand out the regions of The Loire Country, the Aquitaine and Brittany. Eleven regions have less than two million inhabitants and two of them less than one million.

The links between wealth and industry are always very strong. The regions which are classified in first position for their gross domestic product per inhabitant are those whose industrial employment rate is high: Alsace, Nord-Pas-de-Calais, Lorraine, Franche-Comté, High-Normandy and Rhône-Alpes, let us also add Ile-de-France and Provence-Alpes-Côte d'Azur, regions which are also rich with their tertiary sector and their agriculture.

While the North continues to carry out necessary restructuring, the technological South stands out. Agricultural France is located to the west of the line Havre-Marseilles. Population and wealth are not distributed in a consistent manner: the North and the East seem to have an advantage.

Linguistic and cultural dimension

It was King François the First who in 1539 imposed French as 'the one and only language of the French kingdom'. Yet, there are other languages spoken in different regions: Occitan, Catalan and Corsican of Latin origin; Alsatian-Lorraine and Flemish of Germanic origin; Breton of Celtic origin; Basque whose origins have not been already clarified by linguists but which in any case doesn't belong to any Indo-European group.

Those different languages, which had been given up over the past 20 years, are currently regaining importance. This movement is to be included among the various claims made by the regions, who see a symbolic value in rescuing and teaching their languages.

During the period between the two world wars, there were regional movements like the Breton autonomist party or the society for Occitan studies. Since the end of the Second World War, the majority of the regionalist movements are presenting above all a cultural claim. Indeed, the majority of the French population does not support extremist movements claiming the autonomy of a region, because it considers it a utopia. Except for some specific cases like in Corsica and in the Basque Country where separatists are carrying out acts of violence against French interests, regional claims are usually made in a climate of non-violence.

The regions where such claims are made present common characteristics explaining the existence of these movements. As a general rule, they are regions located outside the main centres where the regional languages are still very much alive. With their existence, these movements are more movements of refusal than ones making claims and looking for regional liberation. The sign of recognition is the language and often shows up the desire to tie old links with populations having the same cultural roots, beyond their borders, such as the Basques and the Catalonians in Spain.

In spite of its legal recognition, the presence and use of regional languages in social life is quite low, for example in primary and secondary education, as well as in university education.[2]

With respect to television, France 3, according to its chartered conditions (*cahier des charges*), contributes to the expression of the main regional languages spoken in the metropolitan territory. This has led to the schedule of some regional programmes in regional languages (see 'Minority language's broadcasts', below).

Nation-wide TV broadcasting in France

For a long period of time, French television was dominated by political pressure and confined to a state monopoly. It was necessary to wait for the arrival of the law of 1982 to witness the end of this monopoly which was increasingly threatened by the emergence of cable and satellite. Around that period of time, French television entered a period of 'deregulation' allowing the creation of a private sector. This process has lead French television to a public-private system.

In 1949 'Radio Télévision de France' (RTF) was created, when the television licence fee was also introduced. Television only began broadcasting beyond the capital's perimeter in 1950, the day of the official inauguration of the first regional station in Lille. In 1953 the second regional station in Strasbourg was created. From that date on, covering national territory became important enough for the public to feel encouraged to equip itself – important enough also for the volume of programmes offered to be increased, and enough for this synergy to favour the growth of the level of television development. Ten years later the RTF

---

2. For more detailed information on 'regional' languages in France, see European Bureau for Lesser Used Languages, 1993.

became an 'Établissement public industriel et commercial', under the authority of the Information Minister, and was given budget autonomy.

On 18 April 1964 began broadcasting the second channel. On 27 June, the RTF became the 'Office de Radiodiffusion-Télévision Française' (ORTF). The office was no longer under the authority of the Ministry of Information, but under its supervision. An administrative council was formed but all its members were designated by the government. A general manager and two assistant managers (one for each channel) were appointed by the government. The third channel was created in 1969, and began broadcasting in January 1973.

In 1974 the public monopoly on broadcasting was reaffirmed, but the ORTF as a unitary body, disappeared. Seven different companies were created to replace it:

- four broadcasting companies: TF1, Antenne 2, France Régions 3 (FR3) and Radio-France;
- a public company for technical transmission, 'Télédiffusion de France' (TDF);
- a production company, the 'Société Française de Production' (SFP);
- the 'Institut National de l'Audiovisuel' (National Audio-visual Institute, INA), in charge of storing and exploiting the audio-visual files from the broadcasting companies.

On 1 January 1975, FR3 (the reformed third channel) began broadcasting.

In 1982 the law on freedom of audio-visual communication was passed, which abolished the programming monopoly, allowed the opening of the radio waves to private radios and created the first independent administrative authority, the 'Haute Autorité' (High Authority). The goal of this institution was to 'assure the independence of the public service of radio and television broadcasting and to ensure the respect of pluralism and harmony of the programmes'. It was composed of 9 members, appointed by the President of the Republic, the President of the Senate and the President of the National Assembly.

In 1984 the first French private channel, Canal Plus began broadcasting. In 1986 a new law was passed concerning audio-visual communication. This law created the 'Commission Nationale de Communication et des Libertés' (National Commission of Communication and Liberties, CNCL), replacing the 'Haute Autorité'. Composed of 13 members, it granted the programming and broadcasting authorizations, controlled the programmes and gave out sanctions as well. The law also distributed the authorizations of two new private channels, given to La Cinq and TV6. For La Cinq, the associate groups Chargeurs with 52 per cent and Fininvest with 40 per cent, were chosen. The grouping of Publicis-NRJ-Gaumont was chosen to make TV6 a channel with a musical orientation. At the end of February and beginning of March 1986, La Cinq and TV6 began broadcasting.

The elections of March 1986 brought back a right-wing parliament and the government of Jacques Chirac cancelled the licences granted to the two channels with the decree of 5 August 1986. In 1987, La Cinq was entrusted to the Hersant-Fininvest association, and TV6 to the project 'Métropole TV' (M6). But the most important aspect of the 1986 law was the privatization of TF1. Privatizing a public channel, leader on the market by audience level, was a unique decision in the history of world television. This decision was accepted in spite of the opposition and hostility from the viewers. TF1 was valued at 4.5 billion Francs and the group Bouygues was chosen by the CNCL for its revival on 6 April 1987.

In 1989 the 'Conseil Supérieur de l'Audiovisuel' was created which replaced the CNCL. The CSA has the same attributions, but its control and sanctioning rights are more important.

Ruined by the fight led against TF1 over audience control, La Cinq was forced in 1992 into compulsory liquidation and left a blank screen, stopping all broadcasting in April. Following a decision by the CSA, the fifth channel, left vacant by the disappearance of La Cinq, was given to the Franco-German channel, ARTE.

The 1986 law on audio-visual communication still governs the framework of French television. The decisions taken following this law, have shaped the French audio-visual landscape.

The CSA is an independent administrative authority, which stands between the political world and the world of the media. It is therefore given important administrative prerogatives and even a certain statutory authority. Its scope of authority includes both the public and the private sectors. It has the authority to designate the responsibility for the private channels, grant the audio-visual frequencies to private operators, control the applied regulation and supervise the application of the chartered conditions for each of the TV channels. Among the powers granted it has the power to give sanctions ranging from financial fines to a reduction in the licence duration. All the national, regional and local televisions are under the authority of the CSA. The regions do not have the authority allowing them to grant broadcasting authorization or control the programmes (only the CSA is allowed to do so).

Until now the development of local television did not require, according to CSA norms, opening CSA sections in the regions. However, the growth of independent local radio stations led to the creation of the 'Comités Techniques Radiophoniques' (Technical Radio Committees, CTR). The CTR are assisting the CSA in the provinces with regards to radios. Knowing the local situation, they present the problems and propose solutions. But only the Paris-based management takes the final decision, which the CTR is then charged to execute.

As for the case of television and radio, the region does not have authority over cables and satellites either, which therefore depend on the CSA as well. Yet, the law on audio-visual of 1982 envisaged that regional authority regarding radio and television should be created. This part of the law was never applied.

The public sector

The public audio-visual sector in France is made up of four audio-visual corporations, which carry out diverse activities in the field of programme making and storing, technical transmission, etc., as well as five TV channels.

Public audio-visual corporations

The SPF ('Société Française de Production et de Créations Audiovisuelles') is a company for production and creation of audio-visual material, has as its main goal the production of material and audio-visual documents and the rendering of services, specifically for the national channels. TDF ('Télédiffusion de France') administers the transmission of programmes. The INA ('Institut National de l'Audiovisuel') is in charge of the conservation and promotion of French public television's archives and training the audio-visual staff. It has a team of researchers and occasionally produces audio-visual documents. The principal objective of CFI ('Canal France International'), formed in 1989, was cultural broadcasting to the French region of Africa (four hours of daily broadcasting). This objective spread to include Central and Eastern Europe, the Near and the Middle East, and Asia.

The public TV channels

Since the privatization of TF1, the public service became aware of the importance of its unity. It was therefore decided to bring the two public channels, Antenne 2 and FR3 closer. These two channels are now named France 2 and France 3, and are integrated in the public corporation France Télévision, with a common presidency. Even if France 2 and France 3 try to harmonize their programmes, they have specific characteristics for each of their channels. France 2 is a general national channel, while France 3 carries also a nation-wide programme, but includes disconnected daily 'windows' for regional programming (see below, 'Regional television in France'). Following combined losses amounting to 179.8 million francs in 1990 and 29 million in 1991, France 2 and France 3 have had benefits in 1992 and 1993. This year the net profit of France 2 was 52 million francs, with a turnover of 4,367 million. France 3 had benefits amounting to 22 million, with a turnover of 4,580 million (*Le Figaro*, 14 July 1994). The budget of France 3 for 1994 is 4,703.8 million francs.

'Radio France Outre-Mer' (RFO) broadcasts television and radio programmes meant for the departments and the overseas territories. Initially a subsidiary of FR3 and Radio France, RFO became an independent company in 1986. RFO broadcasts two channels. However the national metropolitan programming is clearly the most important. The first channel shows a variety of programmes from TF1 and France 3, where local production never exceeds 10 per cent of the air time. The second channel shows programmes from France 2.

The French cultural channel, La Sept, was the origin of the cultural European channel ARTE, which first saw the light on 2 October of 1990 in Berlin, following the signing of a Franco-German treaty between the representatives of the French government and the eleven *länder* of the former FRG. Since September of 1992, ARTE has broadcast over the air in France and its programmes have been carried on the German cable. ARTE is based in both Strasbourg and Baden-Baden. In 1994, the French government decided to use the time band not taken up by the transmissions of ARTE on channel 5 (ARTE broadcasts only during the evening) to establish a public channel for study, training and employment purposes, which will probably be called 'La Cinquième'. This channel is due to commence broadcasting in 1995, with a budget of 800 million francs.

TV5 Europe is a French speaking channel which broadcasts by satellite. It broadcasts programmes from French-speaking countries in Europe and North America (Québec).

The budget for the public channels originates mainly from two sources, the licence fee and advertising (except for ARTE which does not have advertising). We can add to that the clear commercial takings coming from, for example, the foreign sales of programmes or the profits made by the television companies from the co-production of films. But the takings from the licence fee are increasingly less important for the public channels, whereas the importance of advertising and other takings have clearly increased.

The private sector

TF1 is the oldest channel in the history of French television. Privatized in spite of all the protest, TF1 is still the favourite channel of the French. Its programming is mainly composed of entertainment shows and films. Since privatization, TF1 has been a profitable channel. For the global exercises of 1987 and 1988 the tax free turnover was about 8 billion francs, and the benefits after taxes, write offs and provisions, about 146.4 million francs. In 1993, TF1 announced benefits amounting to 455 million francs, 4 million more than the previous year. According to TF1 itself, its advertising incomes amounted to 6,540 million francs in 1993 (6,237 in 1992 – *Europe Télévisions*, 118, 27.1.94). In the mid 1994 TF1 launched LCI (La Chaîne Info), an all news channel to be distributed by cable in France.

Canal Plus, a pay TV channel which also broadcasts decoded programmes during the day, first broadcast on 4 November 1984. Facing its first difficulties, Canal Plus was finally allowed to include commercials in its decoded programmes in March 1985. Canal Plus manages its programming along two main lines: sports and cinema. Today, Canal Plus is considered a successful channel, and the number of subscribers has grown from 186,000 at the beginning to 3,700,000 in 1994, with a turnover of 8,675 million francs in 1993. Canal Plus follows a dynamic investment policy involving participation with the TDF1 satellite, cables and creations of scrambled channels in France and abroad. The new satellite TV channels set up in France and participated by Canal Plus are Canal J (created in 1986), Planète, TV Sport and Ciné-Cinémas (1988), Canal Jimmy and Ciné-Cinéfil (1991). The international activity of Canal Plus includes the setting up of scrambled channels in Spain, Belgium, Germany and Poland.

M6 started its programming on 1 March 1987. In May 1988, an agreement between M6 and Télé-Montecarlo (TMC) was signed, where TMC would relay the broadcasts from M6 for the majority of the programmes thus, allowing it to expand its broadcasting network. M6 is mainly a music channel. Indeed, it broadcasts videoseries in the morning, afternoon and at night. These videos are shown intermingled with soap operas, thrillers or films made for TV, especially American material, and by news flashes. In 1991, the estimated turnover for M6 was 820 million francs. The cumulative losses for 1987–1989 reached 1 billion francs.

Cable and satellite broadcasting

The availability of cable television has experienced difficulties and the delay in France in comparison to the more cabled European countries is immense. This is due in reality to the numerous errors regarding the cable network policy. From the start, a technical error was made, France chose an 'all optic fibre' model. But the cost of the optic fibre is three times the one evaluated at first, and a change was rapidly made to a mixed optical/coaxial material, which was much less expensive (the main signal is carried along a fibre optic cable and the home distribution is made using the coaxial system). Furthermore, creation of private Hertzian channels came in direct competition with cable broadcasting.

The 'Plan Câble', which was initiated in 1982 and whose goal was to connect 6 million homes by 1992, was dropped very rapidly since the objectives set were never met. However, the situation improved somewhat during 1990–1993. In March 1994 there were approximately 1.4 million points of connection installed and nearly 1.04 million subscribers (600,000 in 1990). Twenty-five per cent of the reachable households were served by cable in 1994, while only 19 per cent actually subscribed (*Europe Télévisions*, 13.7.1994).

With regard to satellite reception, it is difficult to evaluate the exact number of homes equipped with the installations necessary for it. The Cluzel report of 1990 states: 'In 1988, 650 licences had been registered by the telecommunication administration. Yet, we estimate the number of individual and collective satellite dishes installed to be 10,000. Whatever the case, the real number of subscribers is still low.'

The much more powerful direct broadcasting satellite directly reaches the homes equipped with special satellite dishes. The number of subscribers using direct broadcasting satellites is shown as 'negligible' in the Cluzel report. As is the case with cable, satellite has been a victim of the arrival of the private channels on the Hertzian network and the success of Canal Plus.

Regional television in France

Public regional television[3]

Broadcast across the whole of France, France 3 is the only channel representing regional public television. Except for the recent private initiatives in the regions, this television station has been the only channel broadcasting programmes produced and intended for the regions for more than 20 years.

The origins

In 1969 the decision was taken to form a third nation-wide television network, and in January 1973 the first broadcasts from the third channel started. They were broadcast in colour but only one quarter of the population received them. Jean Louis Guillaud, first managing director of the third network, defined it as a national channel with regional inspiration, despite public regional TV structure not being initially attached to the new channel. In fact, since the end of the 1950s, regional television centres had been created in the main cities of France and, in 1963, Alain Peyrefitte, Information Minister, decided to create regional television news. In September, 1963, the first regional news bulletins were televised. With reference to this early instance of decentralization, it has been said that 'regional television originated in France, as a result of the decision of Gaullist administrations in the 1960s, in order to hit back

---

3. Most of the information on FR3/France 3 presented below has been provided by the channel itself. See France 3, 1993, 1994a and 1994b, as well as the bulletin *France 3. La lettre des Antennes Régionales*.

with the audio-visual system at the supposedly anti-government regional press' (Werder, 1990).

In 1974, the Act which abolished ORTF set up France Régions 3 (FR3, the new name of the third channel) and the existing regional centres were attached to it. However, regional news have been broadcast every evening from 19:15 to 19:30 on the three public hertzian channels, until 1985. At that time, TF1 stopped offering regional news bulletins; from 1989, Antenne 2 (now France 2) followed suit, so that from that moment FR3 became the only national television station in France with regional programming. In January 1983, FR3 was opened to advertising, and one year later advertising was authorized for the regional programmes as well. It was also in 1983 that the first regional broadcasts, besides regional news, were shown.

However, in France, there is no totally regional channel in the public sector. What is evident is a 'short range decentralization, consisting of giving regional authority to one of the national channels. In consequence, the channel creates a network of regional centres with regional "windows" within a national grid of programmes' (Regourd, 1992: 70). There has been much criticism of the lack of political will to develop the regional potential of FR3/France 3. According to F. Werder, the director of FR3 Provence-Alpes-Côte d'Azur-Corse in 1990, 'there is no model of regional television in France ... We have yet to achieve a genuine process of decentralization' (Werder, 1990). Some commentators have even spoken of a re-centralization of FR3, beginning in 1986, coinciding with the most acute phase of private competition. Evidence of this re-centralization was the creation, in June, 1989, of a common chairmanship for the two public channels, and also a diminished presence of off-the-network programming. However, since 1992 there has been a certain amount of recovery of the regional and local dimension on France 3. Since that time, new timetable bands have been added (Wednesday night and Saturday afternoon) to regional programming. In 1993, the 13th Regional Board of France 3 was established in Corsica, and between 1993 and 1994, local off-the-network news bulletins have multiplied and now reach 15 French cities (see below, 'Implementation of local bulletins'). On 18 September, 1994, the government published its new 'cahier des missions et des charges' of public television, which stresses 'France 3's special vocation as local and regional television'.

The map of the regional centres

Regional public television is organized in 13 'Directions Régionales' (regional management centres), set up in the principal cities of France. The limits of their geographical zones correspond to the administrative regions, even though in many cases they cover two regions. Besides their administrative roles, the 'Directions Régionales' are responsible for co-ordinating the production and broadcasting of the regional programming on France 3. Under the co-ordination of the 'Directions Régionales' (DR) there are 24 'Bureaux Régionaux d'Information' or BRI (regional information offices) and 56 'Bureaux Permanents' or news correspondents of the channel, which constitute a network covering the whole of the French territory. Each 'Direction Régionale' has a BRI for every administrative region adhering to it, so that most DRs have two or three BRI, except in the case of the DRs of Aquitaine, Alsace and Corsica, each of which correspond to a single administrative region. Each of the 24 BRIs produce and broadcasts independent regional news bulletins. The remainder of the regional programming, unlike the news, is not 'sub-regionalized': magazines, variety programmes, documentaries, retransmissions, etc., of a regional nature, generally go out to the whole territory of each DR.

Table 2. France 3's network

'Direction Régionale (DR)	'Bureaux régionaux d'information' (BRI) (regional news)	'Bureaux permanents'	Local news bulletins	Production unit
F3 Alsace	Strasbourg	Mulhouse	Strasbourg	Grand-Est
F3 Aquitaine	Bordeaux	Périgueux Cahors Mont-de-Marsan Agen Bayonne Pau	Bayonne	Sud-Ouest
F3 Bourgogne/Franche-Comté	Dijon Besançon	Auxerre Nevers Vesoul Montbéliard Lons-le-Saunier Mâcon		
F3 Corse	Ajaccio	Bastia		
F3 Limousin/Poitou-Charentes	Limoges Poitiers	Guéret Angoulême Brive La Rochelle	La Rochelle	
F3 Lorraine/Champagne-Ardenne	Nancy Reims	Charleville-M. Metz Bar-le-Duc Troyes Chaumont Epinal	Metz	Grand-Est
F3 Mediterranée	Marseille Nice	Gap Avignon Toulon	Toulon	Marseille
F3 Nord-Pas-de-Calais/Picardie	Lille Amiens	Boulogne Soissons Beauvais	Lille Boulogne	Lille
F3 Normandie	Rouen Caen	Le Havre Cherbourg Alençon Evreux		
F3 Ouest	Rennes Nantes	Brest Lorient St. Brieuc Laval Le Mans Angers La Roche-sur-Yon	Brest Rennes Nantes Le Mans	Rennes

'Direction Régionale (DR)	'Bureaux régionaux d'information' (BRI) (regional news)	'Bureaux permanents'	Local news bulletins	Production unit
F3 Paris-Ile-de-France/Centre	Paris Orléans	St. Quentin-en-Y. Chartres Tours Bourges Châteauroux	Tours	
F3 Rhone-Alpes/Auvergne	Lyon Clermont-Ferrand Grenoble	Annecy St. Etienne Aurillac Valence Le Puy		Lyon
F3 Sud	Toulouse Montpellier	Rodez Albi Tarbes Carcassonne Nîmes Perpignan	Albi Nîmes Perpignan	Sud-Ouest

Source: France 3, 1994.

Periods of regional disconnections

In the 1994/95 schedule for France 3, regional disconnections take place at the same time for all the France 3 regional centres. The schedules are as follow:

  – Monday to Friday from 12:05 p.m. to 12:45 (magazine and regional news); 18:58 to 19.09 (local news in 15 French cities); 19:09 to 19:30 (regional news); 19:55 to 20:00 (regional news 'only pictures').

  – Wednesday evenings from 22:45 to 00:30 (magazines, documentaries, current affairs).

  – Saturday: from 12:05 to 12:45 (magazines, regional news); 13:00 to 17:45 pm (magazines, documentaries); 18:58 to 19:09 (local news in some of the 15 cities); 19:09 to 19:30 (regional news); 19:55 to 20:00 (regional news 'only pictures').

  – Sunday: from 12:05 to 12:45 (magazines and live broadcasts); 18:58 to 19:09 (local news in some of the 15 cities); 19:09 to 19:30 (regional news 'only pictures').

There has been an increase in the number and duration of off-the-network programmes on France 3 since 1990. At that time, the regional news bulletins began to be broadcast on Sundays, thus bringing regional news broadcasting to seven days per week. In 1992, the timetable slots for Wednesday nights and Saturday afternoons were 'regionalized'. Finally, since 1990 local news bulletins have been introduced in various French cities (see below, 'Implementation of local bulletins').

Production and programming

With respect to production at the regional level, three levels can be discerned.

(a) Broadcasts of regional interest: apart from the financial control, the regions control this level completely. They choose their own subjects for the magazines and also their processing method. They are fully responsible for their production and broadcast.

(b) Regional productions broadcast both regionally and nationally: these broadcasts are produced regionally but destined for national programming. Starting with a common national theme some regions produce and broadcast programmes which are specific to the region and can be also broadcast at the national level. For example the programmes *La cuisine des mousquetaires* and *Pégase* are a France 3 Aquitaine production, but are also broadcast nationally as well as regionally.

(c) National broadcasts: For its national broadcasts the national programme company France 3 gives work to its six regional production units which are the result of the re-structuring of France 3's production activities. Prior to this reform, France 3 had four 'huge production centres' in Lille, Bordeaux, Marseilles and Lyon. The present production centres are: Lyon, Marseilles, Grand-Est (Nancy and Strasbourg), Lille, Rennes and Sud-Ouest (Bordeaux and Toulouse). This is therefore, material produced in the regions and intended for national broadcasts; final control is carried out in Paris. France 3 does not have central equipment in Paris for large scale productions, and it is therefore left to the regional production centres to manage the national productions following central guidelines.

For the financing of regional broadcasts, each of the regional stations is given an annual assignment from the Parisian management office. This budget generally allows them to pay the staff, the logistics fees and the direct regional costs (the operating fees for programming and especially for the production of the regional bulletin). For production, the regional stations are paid on a cost basis, for each of the broadcast projects.

For the regional programmes, news and magazines are the most important items. Regional-news attracts the main audience of the regional stations. Then, magazines, reports made abroad or live debates represent a large volume of programming for the regional stations. Spread among the regional stations were, in 1993, 9,464 hours of programmes per year broadcast regionally. 5,338 hours were allowed for regional bulletins and 4,126 hours for other regional programmes. In 1994, the total amount of regional broadcasts was 9,800 hours.

Certain regions linked by a theme of common interest, are trying to improve broadcasting quality by multiplying their means. Some European alliances have even participated in the magazines.

European co-operation

The first European co-operation magazine was introduced under the title *Vis-à-Vis* by France 3 Alsace and the German SWF, which France 3 Lorraine/Champagne-Ardennes joined in 1990. Later, it was France 3 Nord-Pas-de-Calais/Picardie which boosted a European trans-border magazine, *Euro 3*, that linked the British station TVS, the Belgian RTBF and the German WDR.

The magazine *Euro-Sud* was created in 1988 with the initiative of the France 3 Aquitaine station, which is involved in co-production with TVE's regional centre in the Basque Country and the Portuguese RTP-Porto. Another 'Direction Régionale' belonging to France 3, Limousin-Poitou/Charentes, also joined the team involved in the production of the magazine. *Zoom* implied the co-operation of France 3 Lorraine/Champagne-Ardennes, three German stations and the third channel from the Netherlands. Through an old common language, *Horizon des Celtes* brings France 3 Bretagne-Pays-de-Loire (at present France 3 Ouest), the Scottish centre of the BBC and the Irish RTE together.

It is clearly seen that French regional stations are playing a key role in European TV co-operation. Those magazines were created out of the will and dynamism of the local people in charge. However, their financial means are very modest, especially those of France 3 regional centres, which are far below the possibilities of the German stations. However, some of the transborder magazines, like *Alice*, the European cultural magazine, take advantage of national broadcasting. It groups France 3 Midi-Pyrénées/Languedoc-Roussillon (at present France 3 Sud), Televisió de Catalunya (Catalonian TV) and the Belgian RTBF together with the recent addition of a few TV stations from eastern countries.

Table 3. Share of audience (%) of France 3 regional programming, 1993[*]

Direction Régionale/BRI		12:00–12:45	19:00–19:30
F3 Alsace	Strasbourg	3.3	27.1
F3 Aquitaine	Bordeaux	10.9	38.9
F3 Bourgogne/Franche-Comté	Dijon	10.6	27.5
	Besançon	4.8	40.1
F3 Corse[†]		19.0	59.6
F3 Limousin/Poitou-Charentes	Limoges	12.9	49.9
	Poitiers	6.5	41.8
F3 Lorraine/Champagne-Ardenne	Nancy	10.0	29.8
	Reims	10.6	44.3
F3 Méditerranée	Marseille	19.0	35.6
	Nice	24/6	30.7
F3 Nord/Pas-de-Calais/Picardie	Lille	13.4	31.2
	Amiens	7.0	23.2
F3 Normandie	Rouen	11.1	31.5
	Caen	12.3	39.9
F3 Ouest	Rennes	14.2	44.1
	Nantes	8.0	39.6
F3 Paris/Ile-de-France/Centre	Paris	11.3	19.3
	Orleans	7.6	30.5
F3 Rhône-Alpes/Auvergne	Lyon	12.1	35.3
	Grenoble	11.7	28.9
	Clermont-Ferrand	10.8	44.4
F3 Sud	Toulouse	14.9	45.5
	Montpellier	20.1	39.9

[*] 15 years and older. April-June 1993; [†] Data from 1990;
Source: Médiamétrie, quoted in France 3: 'La télévision au service du développement régional. Edition 1993–1994'.

Audience and advertising

It is quite difficult to evaluate the figures concerning the audience of the diverse regional broadcasts. However, one factor remains clear: success of the regional news and failure of the other regional broadcasts. According to data from 1993, on the global daily programmes, the audience share for nation-wide programming on France 3 is 14.6 per cent (4 years and older). For the 18:30 to 19:30 period the national average represents a 34.9 per cent share.

Regional advertising was authorized in 1984, and in 1988 the advertising department of France 3 was created. At present it is integrated in the common advertising department for France 2 and France 3 ('France Espace'). Advertising depends on the disconnection schedules allowed to the regional stations. Two windows at midday, one at 12:30 pm from Monday to Friday and one at 12:45 pm from Monday to Saturday. In the evening, four windows are offered to the regions: one at 7:00 pm from Monday to Friday, one at 7:30 pm from Monday to Sunday, one at 8:30 from Monday to Saturday and one at 10:30 on Wednesday only.

To face the regional differences, revenues from regional ads are centralized by the advertising department, which redistributes them to the regional stations. This is done in order to avoid the arrival of a dual speed television. Otherwise, the regional centres with large populations and strong industrial potential would develop whereas those placed in the mainly rural regions with small populations would notice a rapid drop in their advertising incomes. On average, advertising represents 20 per cent of the budget for the 'Directions Régionales' while the remainder comes from the licence fee.

Implementation of local bulletins

France 3's 'Directions Régionales' have recently begun to develop immediate area television ('télévision de proximité') by setting up local news bulletins. This strategy, in line with some commentators (Alessandri, 1992), aims to make use of the decentralized structure of France 3 in order to compete with private local television channels and channel M6 in the French

Table 4. Share of audience of France 3 local bulletins (Monday to Friday)*

Local bulletin	Share	
'Rund Um' (Strasbourg)	27.8	(April-June 1993)
'Euskal Herri' (Bayonne)	56.9	(February 1993)
'Atlantique' (La Rochelle)	49.2	(Nov.-December 1992)
Local bulletin (Metz)	32.4	(Nov.-December 1992)
'Europole' (Lille)	36.4	(Nov.-December 1992)
'Estuaire' (Nantes)	41.2	(Nov.-December 1992)
'Maine' (Le Mans)	40.2	(Nov.-December 1992)
'Iroise' (Brest)	49.5	(Nov.-December 1992)
'Tours Soir' (Tours)	50.7	(Nov.-December 1992)
'Tarn Hebdo' (Albi)	47.8	(February 1993)
'Roussillon Hebdo' (Perpignan)	38.7	(February 1993)

*15 years and older;
Source: Médiamétrie, quoted in France 3: 'La télévision au service du développement régional. Edition 1993–1994'.

local television market. The experiment which started in 1990, seems to be positive and is still being continued. In 1993 a total of 11 local bulletins with fairly acceptable audiences existed in the following cities: Strasbourg (called *Rund Um*), Bayonne (*Euskal Herri*), Perpignan (*Roussillon Hebdo*), Le Mans (*France 3 Maine*), Metz (*France 3 Metz*), La Rochelle (*France 3 Atlantique*), Tours (*Soir 3*), Nantes (*TV Estuaire*), Brest (*Iroise*), Albi (*France 3 Tarnes*) and Lille (*Europole TV*) (*Europe télévisions*, 10.6.1993). In 1994, four new local off-the-network broadcasts were begun in Côte d'Opale (Boulogne), Nîmes, Toulon and Annecy. France 3 has announced its intention to create a further 10 local bulletins in 1995.

In 1994, the bulletins were broadcast between 18:57 pm and 19:09 pm. The regularity of the broadcasts vary according to the region.

Table 5. France 3's broadcasts in minority languages, 1994

Direction Régionale	Broadcast in	Type	Language	Periodicity	Length
F3 Alsace	Strasbourg (Als.)	Local news	Alsatian	Monday-Friday	7'
	Alsace	Magazine	Alsatian	Wednes.	26'
	Alsace	Magazine cult.	Alsatian	(monthly)	15'
	Alsace	Magazine	Alsatian	Saturday	30
				Saturday	
F3 Aquitaine	Bayonne (Aquit.)	Local news	Basque	Monday-Saturday	7'
F3 Corse	Corsica	Magazine	Corsican	Saturday	25'
	Corsica	Regional news	Corsican	Monday-Friday	7'
	Corsica	Magazine	Corsican	Saturday	30'
F3 Mediterr.	Provence-Alpes Côte d'Azur	Magazine	Occitan	Saturday	35'
F3 Ouest	Britanny	Regional news	Breton	Monday-Saturday	7'
	Britanny	Magazine	Breton	Sunday	45'
F3 Sud	Midi-Pyrénées Lang.-Roussillon	Magazine	Occitan/Catalan	Sunday	40'
	Perpignan	Local news	Catalan	Monday–Friday	6'

Source: France 3.

Minority language's broadcasts

France 3's 'cahier des charges' or chartered conditions, as renewed at the end of 1994, establishes the channel's obligation to make broadcasts in the 'regional' or minority languages. According to these obligations some 'Directions Régionales' include in their programming schedules a number of programmes in these languages which, with the exception of the Alsatian language, must be considered as being quite scarce. In 1991, according to the Conseil Supérieur de l'Audiovisuel, the society broadcast programmes in Basque (5hr. 15min., F3 Aquitaine), in Occitan (22hr. 45min., F3 Meditérranée), in Corsican (17hr., F3 Corse), in Breton (64hr., F3 Ouest), in Catalan and Occitan (33hr., F3 Sud) and in Alsatian (78hr., F3 Alsace), hence a total of 220 hours. At the end of 1994, the programmes in minority languages were as shown in Table 5.

Regional private television

The only private regional television venture in France originates from outside France. This is the channel RTL TV, which is owned by the Compagnie Luxembourgeoise de Télévision, CLT. Its programmes are produced in and broadcasted from Luxembourg on a Luxembourg Hertzian frequency, but are aimed at neighbouring Lorraine, thus embodying what CLT understands as 'immediate television'. The audiences achieved within its transmission zone have proved the soundness of this policy of immediate television. RTL TV has existed since 1955, and for many years has been good business. More recently, however, the channel has been forced to expand its potential in France in order to attract more advertising. Therefore, in the early 1990s, the headquarters of RTL TV moved from Luxembourg to Metz. The outlay involved in this move to the centre of the transmission zone was recovered in two years, thanks to the new advertising revenue generated in Lorraine (Hirsh, 1994; see also the chapter on Luxembourg in this book).

Local private television

The M6 disconnections

M6 first went on the air in 1987. It is a musical channel and unlike other channels, it does not broadcast a long news bulletin at midday or during the evening. However the news is offered, but in the 'flash' format of a few minutes in the morning and an 'all pictures' national bulletin in the evening called '6 minutes'.

In 1989 M6 decided to create local news editions. The format chosen was similar to the '6 minutes all pictures' ('6 minutes tout en image'). The local bulletin is broadcasted everyday of the week at 8:35 p.m.

Four years after the launching of the first disconnection at Lille, M6 has now nine local disconnections at Lille, Nantes, Tours, Marseilles, Bordeaux, Lyon, Montpellier, Nancy and Grenoble. The M6 local disconnections reached 11.4 million people in 1994, i.e. 20 per cent of the French population (*Europe Télévisions*, 5.5.1994).

Local private televisions on the hertzian network

In France (mainland) there are 4 local Hertzian televisions: Télé Toulouse in Toulouse, 8 Mont Blanc in Annecy, Télé Lyon Métropole in Lyon and Aqui TV in the 'departement' of Dordogne (Aquitaine). All cannot broadcast for the entire day, and many have now opted to contract a complementary programme. Along with these local televisions in the mainland, we should also mention several channels in the overseas territories (DOM-TOM): Antenne Réunion, Canal Réunion, TCI, Télé Bleue, Archipel 4, ATV, Canal Antilles, TV4, TV Sud.

The four local television stations operating in France were created between 1988 and 1991, at a time when the increase in the demand for local news and a regional and local advertising market (which increased from 50 to 810 million francs between 1985 and 1990, according to the CNCA), seemed to bode well for the future of these ventures. However, the balance of the first few years of management is negative in each case. Between 1989 and 1991, Télé Toulouse made losses of around 38 million francs, Télé Lyon Métropole lost around 45 million, and TV8 Mont-Blanc lost approximately 13.5 million francs. Thanks to a strategy of income diversification and a reduction in costs, these losses have gradually diminished, but the economic situation continues to show a deficit in every case. In spite of these discouraging experiences, projects of local hertzian television initiatives have flourished in France: Télé-Gironde in Bordeaux, RTV in La Rochelle.

Local private cable televisions

At the end of 1992, 21 local channels were in operation on the cable networks, of which six were given authorization by the CSA during the year. These new local services were created thanks to the initiative of the local and territorial communities. Present in small townships and on sites which in time will account for no more than 5,000 connections, they indicate the trend which is developing which favours the 'télévision de proximité'.

Initially with a modest format of half an hour of daily programming, the local channels predict a rapid increase in the programmes offered and are aiming at wider distribution than the one planned for the original areas. According to Geneviève Guicheney, member of the CSA, these channels could be classified in the following categories:

- Channels which offer only local news, in the form of bulletins or short magazines.
- Immediate area channels with 60 per cent to 80 per cent local news and some programmes purchased outside of the region.
- General channels where local news represents only a small part of the programmes (films, magazines, etc.).

The annual budgets for the 21 local channels vary from 200,000 francs to 16 million francs.

Conclusions and outlook for the future

Article 50 of the Audio-visual Act of 1982 provided for the division of FR3 into 12 independent regional television companies, in order to give autonomy to the stations and strengthen their means. It should be pointed out that this part of the Act has not been applied, since the 12 'Directions Régionales' are still answerable to the head office in Paris. According to C. Phéline, the spokesman for the 'Commission de réflexion sur l'avenir de la télévision publique, 1993', this failure to apply the law is due to 'certain reservations, as a result of the unfavourable political balance at that time between interest groups and the regional media, on the part of the central Socialist government' (Phéline, 1994). Nevertheless, the regions are demanding greater independence for the regional stations.

In a document on the future of public broadcasting in France (see Présidence Commune Antenne2/FR3, 1991), Hervé Bourges (former chairman of French public television) suggested different ways of developing regional television. As a first step, France 3 wishes to go on with the experiment of the local news bulletins which are added to the regional news bulletins. Bourges wished that the communities would bring 'their active participation into the efforts of public regional television'.

He also wished 'to give the largest audience to regional initiative programmes'. To reach that goal 'we will have to multiply the multi-regional currents events disconnections taking into account the position and the necessities of the station'. The different European collaboration projects would also go on. In this manner, French regional television would have a greater range of news programmes and improved inter-regional Franco-European collaboration allowing the creation of better quality programmes.

As far as local television broadcast in the hertzian mode is concerned, these channels are now facing serious financial difficulties. For example, 8 Mont Blanc and Télé Lyon are in the process of legal recovery of payments. Aqui-TV came very close to compulsory liquidation. As a general rule, the results of these channels are poor.

Future prospects are not bright. Indeed, Alain Carignon, former Information and Communication Minister, stated his opposition to local advertising for television. He commented that it was impossible to cause an imbalance in the advertising market without putting some of the regional dailies in danger. Even if Aqui-TV continues with the help of a rescue plan chosen by the Trade Court of Sarlat, and even if the Compagnie Luxembourgeoise de Télévision is interested in 8 Mont Blanc, the local channels broadcasting in the hertzian mode have great difficulty starting up in France. Today they participate with local communities. Their support represents the only hope for the local Hertzian televisions.

The local cable televisions also have financial difficulties. Geneviève Guicheney mentioned that the investment in these services could be difficult to pay off. Moreover, this phenomenon is linked to the poor penetration level of cable in France. Without a rapid increase in cable penetration, the problems will continue.

The local channels wish to receive the help of the various social, economic and cultural entities in order to develop sponsorship. They also wish to take advantage of the existing advertising potential. The local channels are also demanding help from the state in order to drop the professional tax and lower VAT (TVA) from 18.6 per cent down to 2.1 per cent, as for the press.

There are very few institutional links between television and the regions. For example, there is no existing law ruling the relations between the Regional Council and the media. But according to their status, nothing forbids the regions having closer ties with the local media world. And this is being done on an increasingly frequent basis.

In most cases help is offered in the form of financial or material aid. For example, the Regional Council of Aquitaine gives a grant to France 3 each year, and Aqui-TV received financial support from the General Council of Dordogne. The territorial communities also have the responsibility of sponsoring programmes or giving the local media access to a recording studio. Created in 1982, the Regional Councils still have not discovered all the steps which could possibly be taken in this field.

References

Alessandri, P. (1992): 'Les télévisions locales sont-elles viables?', in *Dossiers de l'Audiovisuel*, 46.

Balle, F. (1992): *Médias et societés*. Paris: Editions Montchrestien.

Bec, P. (1986): *La langue occitane*. Paris: Presses Universitaires de France.

Cayrol, R. (1991): *Les médias*. Paris: Presses Universitaires de France.

CSA (1992): *Bilan de la Société Nationale de Programme France Régions 3 1991*. Paris: CSA.

CSA (1993): *4ème rapport annuel 1er janvier–31 decembre 1992*. Paris: La Documentation Française.

Dargnies, S. (1991): *Les chiffres clés de la télévision française*. Paris: INA.

Dayries, J.-P. & M. (1986): *La régionalisation*. Paris: Presses Universitaires de France.

European Bureau for Lesser Used Languages (1993): *Mini-Guide to the Lesser Used Languages of the EEC*. Dublin: EBLUL.

France 3 (1993): 'La télévision au service du développement régional', 1993–94 edition. Paris: France 3.

France 3 (1994a): 'La télévision au service du développement régional', 1994–95 edition. Paris: France 3.

France 3 (1994b): 'Historique tv' (typed).

Gardena, J. & Lacroix, C. (1992): *Chiffres clés 1991. Annuaire statistique de la culture*. Paris: La Documentation Française.

Hirsh, M. (1994): 'Luxembourg', in Moragas Spà, M. & Garitaonandía, C. (1994): *Le rôle des télévisions régionales*. Document presented at the Public Hearing held with the Committee on Regional Policy, Regional Planning and Relations with Regional and Local Authorities and the Committee on Culture, Youth, Education and the Media of the European Parliament, March 1994. Brussels.

INSEE (1992): *La France et ses régions*. Paris: INSEE.

Michel, H. (1989): *La télévision en France et dans le monde*. Paris: Presses Universitaires de France.

Phéline, C. (1994): 'Un récent rapport sur la télévision publique ... et quelques autres qui l'avaient précédé', in *Médiaspouvoirs*, 33.

Présidence Commune Antenne 2/FR3 (1991): *Télévision publique, la télévision pour tous; plan strategique 1991–1994*. Paris.

Regourd, S. (1992): *La télévision des européens*. Paris: La Documentation Française.

Remond, B. & Blanc, J. (1989): *Les collectivités locales*. Paris: Presses de la Fondation Nationale des Sciences Politiques.

Rosier, C. (1993): *Télévision, mode d'emploi*. Paris: Dixit.

Tudesq, A.-J. (1992): *L'audience des médias en Aquitaine*. Edition de la Maison des Sciences de l'Homme d'Aquitaine.

Ulrich, R. (1985): *Pour une nouvelle politique de développement régional en Europe*. Paris: Editions Economica.

Werder, F. (1990): 'Las televisiones regionales en Francia', in RTVV: *Las radiotelevisones en el espacio europeo*. Valencia: RTVV.

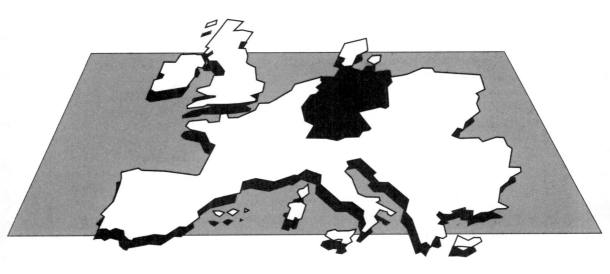

5 Germany: The initiative in the hands of the *Länder*

Hans J. Kleinsteuber and Barbara Thomaß

The general political framework, the nation and the regions

Region is not a prominent term in German politics; it certainly shows little connotation of the repression of minorities and protest movements or the resistance of peripheries to the centre. If it is used, it refers mainly to the administrative dimension of sub-national politics, how to define a regional unit and build a respective administrative infrastructure to serve it. The term region also refers to historical, cultural and folklorist particularities of parts of the country.

The reason for this understanding of region is twofold:

– Germany has a very long tradition of extreme political and economic decentralization, which is reflected today in the federal political system and the fact that there is no economic or cultural centre in the country;
– Germany has a rather high cultural homogeneity; with very few exceptions there is only one undisputed language, one accepted culture (regional variations are mainly folklorist) and the strong identification with a region does not clash with the feeling of belonging to the German national state.

In the European Union, Germany tends to represent the element of decentralization, it has also introduced the idea of subsidiarity in the European process of integration. The adherence to these principles is not without contradictions: In certain parts of Germany elements of centralization and strict exclusion of small-scale initiatives may be found. During the last quarter of a century Germany has also become an immigration country; today nearly ten per cent of the population are (at least this is what they are called) foreigners. But as they are spread all over the country, the mosaic of ethnic minorities has no dominant regional dimension.

Historic origins

Germany happened to be one of the 'late' nation states in Europe. The 'German Empire' was founded only in 1871 after a war against France which was seen at that time as the 'arch-enemy'. Looking back into history we realize that a feeling of belonging to a German culture is much older than any German state. In fact the geographical part of Europe that is called Germany today looked like a patchwork of a large number of mid-sized kingdoms, small principalities and independent republican cities. They claimed state sovereignty, but were at the same time members in a rather weak old German Empire that finally vanished in 1806. This old Empire covered much larger territories than today's Germany and was at times governed by emperors who were not even of German origin.

The old Germany was based on a clear separation of culture and politics. The Germans were culturally united by the use of their common language. The space, where German is spoken today, was much determined by the use of the German language Bible that goes back to Martin Luther's first translation. Politically, this part of Europe was administered by a combination of rulers from quite different backgrounds. Let us take the example of Hamburg (which will be the prime example in this contribution): the port city itself is an ancient republic, going back to the times of the Hanse, dominated by a trade aristocracy. The agglomeration Hamburg included more independent towns: one was Altona, governed by the Danish king (like all territories north of Hamburg) until 1864. This decentralization supported Hamburg in becoming an early media centre, not just because of the port communication lines, but also because the publishers could easily escape censure by moving to one of the neighbouring towns.

For a long time being German meant that a person identified with cultural achievements like poetry and philosophy, music and science as they had developed around the German language. As a political entity, a united Germany had to be created against the old reigning dynasties, creating a nation state was seen as a subversive, politically leftist goal. Unfortunately, the national revolution of 1848–49 failed and the modern German state of 1871, was instituted 'from the top', the German Empire was founded by its old crowned leaders. The king of Prussia was chosen as the new emperor. The resulting political structure accepted the realities of existing strong dynastic states. These states survived the revolution of 1918 which ended the monarchy and became *Land* (plural: *Länder*) an integral part of the present federal system. Quite a few important jurisdictions remain with these *Länder*, the most important being that of culture, referring e.g. to schools, universities – and later to broadcasting.

The specificity of the regions in Germany

A special characteristic of the German type of federalism is a unique two chamber system on the national level that includes the usual national parliament (Bundestag) and a second body (Bundesrat), consisting of representatives of all *Länder*-governments. The *Bundesrat* represents an accumulation of considerable power. Through the *Bundesrat* the *Länder* always share power on the national level; as opposition parties in Bonn tend to be strong on the *Länder*-level, they are always involved in national politics as well. Due to the federal system, the country is somehow continuously governed by a Grand Coalition.

The Basic Law of 1949, the present German constitution, requires an examination of the existing federal system and redistribution of the *Länder* territories to move away from artificial borders and introduce a more balanced system in terms of size and population. As consent about the *status quo* is widespread and politicians profit from the existing system, the chances for change are negligible. Only the *Länder* Brandenburg and Berlin (being an island inside Brandenburg) announced some plans to eventually merge.

The *Länder* system is well established and based on a national consensus. This appreciation is enforced by the fact that the last attempt to establish a centralized state (together with a centralized broadcasting structure) was made by the Third Reich. The federal system is written into the constitution (Art. 20 of the Basic Law), protected by a guarantee that it may not be abolished, not even by the procedure for changing other sections of the constitution (Art. 79). The process of unification in 1990 took place after the federal principle was reintroduced in the former GDR, subdividing its territory into the five historical *Länder* that had been taken away by the Communists in 1952. These *Länder* then joined the Federal Republic individually and adopted the Basic Law.

Today's 16 *Länder* see themselves as main representatives of the regions (and therefore claim exclusive representation in the newly established Council of Regions of the EU). Partly they are historical entities being centuries old (e. g. the former Kingdom of Bavaria), partly they have been artificially created to succeed Prussia after the Second World War (like North Rhine-Westphalia). Some of them cover a large territory, e. g. Bavaria is twice the size of Belgium; some are densely populated, like North Rhine-Westphalia which has more inhabitants than the Netherlands. Other *Länder* are relatively small, especially as we have three City states (Berlin, Hamburg, Bremen), the smallest of them, Bremen, having less than 700.000 inhabitants (and with Radio Bremen the smallest broadcasting corporation in the country).

In Germany people identify with their local or regional home or native place (for which they use the term *Heimat*), where they grew up and developed a strong feeling of belonging. Besides the three city states, most of the *Länder* are too large to be seen as *Heimat*. Instead the *Länder* comprise a number of different regions. The Eurostat *Portrait of the Regions* of Europe subdivides Bavaria into seven regions, Lower Saxony into four. The *Land* of Hamburg is seen as one region. Also historical regions might be administratively divided (like Swebia in the South). Inside the *Länder* a relatively high degree of centralization may be found, being a cause for complaint: Franconia lost its independence roughly 200 years

67

ago to Bavaria and the people around Nuremberg still feel somehow 'colonized' by the Bavarians of Munich.

The concept of a region is not clearly defined in Germany. A common definition separates the functional regions (fulfilling economic, planning functions etc.) from the historical and/or the political regions. Functional regions usually reflect the territorial changes that came with the processes of industrialization, urbanization, and modernization.

The most often quoted example for a functional region is the Ruhr Valley, one of the large industrial agglomerations in Europe, located inside North Rhine-Westphalia. To cope with common problems of planning, infrastructure, environment etc. the communities involved established a rather powerful and well respected association, called *Kommunalverband Ruhrgebiet*. Functional regions of this type may be found all over the country.

The political region is a territorial authority and characterized by borders. Most definitions see the region in size below the *Länder* but above the level of local communities. The political level above local communities is usually the district (*Kreis*), having an elected parliament and an administrative superstructure. Several districts are bound together and constitute a *Regierungsbezirk*, a purely administrative entity. The German understanding of region mostly refers to this intermediate level. A different case are the three city states that in themselves come close to the concept of a region or a very small *Land* like the Saarland.

Media and the region

If Germans were asked about the region they live in, they would probably describe their narrow environs, often quoting more than one region they adhere to. To give an example: Many of the people that call themselves Hamburgers actually live in suburbs that belong to neighbouring *Länder* in the North and South (the largest 'city' of Schleswig-Holstein is also Hamburg, they say). Politically they might identify with their suburban hometown, belonging to Schleswig-Holstein, they read either a local or a Hamburg newspaper or both, they probably listen to a Hamburg radio station and watch regional TV either from Hamburg or from Kiel, the capital of Schleswig-Holstein. In terms of broadcast ratings they are seen as part of the market of Hamburg. They have a choice between Hamburg and Schleswig-Holstein media and may decide either way. This can be seen as a reflection of the somehow split regional adherences that come with today's multi-spaced living.

The traditional media of the region are the daily newspapers. Newspapers have a high distribution rate; about 90 per cent of them define themselves as being local or regional (called *Heimat*-press). Even a nationally available paper like the tabloid BILD is edited in regional editions. National papers also demonstrate their regional affiliation like the *Frankfurter Allgemeine Zeitung* (Frankfurt) or *Süddeutsche Zeitung* (Munich) by referring to the place they come from. This reflects the fact that media activities are not concentrated in one metropolis in Germany. Instead a number of media centres (Hamburg, Munich, Berlin, Cologne) fiercely compete with each other. The (old) capital Bonn was always a media wasteland, only housing correspondents working for outside media.

Cultural and linguistic dimension

Germany has no relevant minorities to speak of. This is mainly the outcome of two wars started and lost by Germany and the resulting rearrangement of national borders. An established minority is that of a little more than 30,000 Danes in the very north, south of the Danish border, kept together by a Danish language newspaper. Another group are the 40,000 to 60,000 Sorbs in the Lausitz, speaking a Slavic dialect, enjoying some autonomy and again having a newspaper of their own. There are few complaints of their minority rights not being respected.

A new element in German society are the approximately 6.5 million people, that are legally described as 'foreigners', even though they may have lived in the country for more than a quarter of a century. The term foreigner refers to the fact that German nationalization laws make it difficult for these people to gain German citizenship. Culturally they may have already adopted the German way of living. It makes more sense to call them German-Turks, German-Arabs etc. Many of them were invited to come as workers, others came seeking political asylum. For the larger foreign groups, special editions of domestic papers, modified for the German market, are offered, e. g. three major Turkish newspapers for Turkish-German citizens. For many years the fact that Germany is a country with high immigration has been virtually ignored by politicians. With the increase of hostilities against foreigners, often initiated by Neo-Nazi-elements, a discussion of their rights and the way to integrate them into the German society has just begun. As they come from a large variety of ethnic backgrounds and are dispersed over most of the country, their problems are certainly those of minorities, but should not be interpreted in terms of regional politics. So far the German media system has not taken much interest in them: foreign households have only recently been included into the national TV-rating system.

The largest group are about 1.85 million Turks that have established a media network of their own, including newspapers, video libraries and TV-programmes that come via satellite from Turkey and are offered on cable systems. The public broadcasters also offer some TV-programming for the larger migrant groups (including the Turkish, Greek, Spanish, Portuguese and Serbo-Croatian languages). Foreigners especially use the public access channels, as is described below.

The socio-economic framework

Economic development in Germany in the last few years has been overshadowed by the unification process and the many resulting problems. Though there had been the hope – and even the promise by the government – that the standard of living in the East would rise, there are still significant differences between the economic potential of Eastern and Western Germany at present. Table 1 demonstrates the main socio-economic indicators as they appear in the states (*Länder*).

While the industry of Western Germany could profit from the growing demand in Eastern Germany it was the prospering economy of the West that had to transfer vast amounts of money to the East. In 1993 about 150 billion DM (German Marks) have been transferred from West to East, so that every citizen in the East received 10,000 DM in subsidies. The present economic crisis increased tension between both parts of Germany and makes future agreements of this kind more and more fragile.

Table 1. Socioeconomic indicators of the *Länder*

	Population (in 1,000s)*	Area km² †	GDP‡	Rate of unemploy- ment¶	Population as %	Share of GDP as %
Baden-Württemberg	10,148	35,751	457.5	6.1	12.5	15.2
Bavaria	11,770	70,554	509.5	5.7	14.5	16.9
Berlin	3,465	889				
West			105.0	12.0	2.7	3.5
East			25.2	13.0	1.6	0.8
Brandenburg	2,548	29,107	39.0	15.0	3.1	1.3
Bremen	685	404	36.3	12.3	0.8	1.2
Hamburg	1,688	755	123.9	8.3	2.1	4.1
Hesse	5,922	21,114	299.0	6.6	7.3	9.9
Mecklenburg-Vorpommern	1,864	23,369	27.4	16.8	2.3	0.9
Lower Saxony	7,577	47,348	270.8	9.6	9.4	9.0
Northrhine Westphalia	17,679	34,068	697.0	9.3	21.8	23.2
Rhineland Palatinate	3,880	19,848	136.4	7.0	4.8	4.5
Saarland	1,084	2,570	39.9	10.8	1.3	1.3
Saxony	4,640	18,338	65.8	14.0	5.7	2.2
Saxony-Anhalt	2,796	20,444	43.5	16.6	3.5	1.5
Schleswig-Holstein	2,679	15,730	96.6	7.7	3.3	3.2
Thuringia	2,545	16,251	34.4	15.4	3.1	1.1
Germany	80,980	356,957	3007.3	–	–	–

*Date: 1.8.1992; †Date: June 1992, in %; ‡In billions DM, 1992; ¶Date: 31.12.1992;
Source: Fischer Weltalmanach, 1994.

Consequently, the most apparent differences between the regions of Germany are to be found between the so-called old and new *Länder*. Each of the five *Länder* in Eastern Germany contributes considerably less to the gross domestic product than it should, based on its population. The East has the lowest rate of productivity, the highest rates of unemployment, and highest percentage of people living on welfare.

Another main feature of the socio-economic situation of the *Länder* is an incline from the South to the North. The Southern *Länder* are strong in industrial production while their unemployment rate is relatively lower. The northern *Länder* do not have a comparable and stable industrial structure and struggle with high unemployment rates.

To reduce the differences in the economic potential of the *Länder* a so-called reallocation of revenues (*Länderfinanzausgleich*) between rich and poor *Länder* is required by the constitution and has to be performed by the federal government. This is part of the federal system, based on the Basic Law and has been practised in Germany since the foundation of the Federal Republic and continued after unification. Until now Baden-Württemberg, Hesse and Hamburg have been the giving *Länder*, while Lower Saxony, Schleswig-Holstein, Bremen, Rhineland-Palatinate and Saarland obtained allocations. North Rhine-Westphalia and Bavaria neither paid nor received any funds. Until the new *Länder* are fully integrated into this system of financial reallocation in 1995 they are paid out of a special fund called 'German unity' to which different sources of the Federal Government, the *Länder* and the local communities contribute.

Considering the economic structure of the German *Länder*, it is obvious that they differ very much in their contribution to the Gross Domestic Product. Putting all aspects together: Besides the general gap between West and East we find quite strong regional variations that do not always follow the borderlines of the *Länder*. So even a wealthy *Länd* might have quite poor regions as the socio-economic structure reflects the general decentralization of the country.

Legal framework of television in Germany

The *Länder* system has been analysed in detail here, as it is absolutely crucial for the understanding of the German broadcasting system. The constitution renders final authority on all cultural matters to the *Länder* (there is no Ministry of Culture in Bonn) and all questions of broadcasting are legally seen as falling into this category. This interpretation of the Basic Law was upheld in a key decision of the Federal Constitutional Court of 1961 (and repeated several times thereafter), outlawing a commercial TV-company licensed by the Bonn government. The national government is not totally excluded: One means of influence in broadcasting is the public company *Telekom,* which handles most of the technical side of broadcasting. Another exception is broadcasting directed towards the rest of the world: *Deutsche Welle*, a federal institution, which is in charge of this aspect. All other broadcast activities, public or commercial, are based on laws, passed by the *Länder* parliaments or written down in agreements that were signed by some or all of the *Länder*.

Public television

The most common case is that one *Land* established one corporation (*Anstalt*) for public service broadcasting (like WDR in North Rhine-Westfalia or BR in Bavaria). In a number of cases several *Länder* agreed to maintain one joint corporation (like NDR for Schleswig-Holstein, Hamburg, Lower Saxony, later incorporating Mecklenburg-Vorpommern). The actual structure is often determined by political events of the past; the French occupation zone still lives on in SWF, covering Rhineland-Palantine and parts of Baden Württemberg. North Rhine-Westphalia's WDR was cut out from the Hamburg based NWDR (now NDR) by the ruling CDU-party as it was considered as being too close to the rivalling SPD- party.

The rule is, that the *Länder* corporations are under heavy political pressure by the governing party of the respective *Land* with some proportional representation for the opposition party. This political approach has often been attacked, but it guarantees that the *Länder* Minister Presidents have a stake and vital interest in the well-being of 'their' broadcast corporations. After the unification of Germany, three eastern *Länder*, all controlled by the CDU-party, established the new MDR; the SPD-government of Brandenburg founded the small ORB.

Public broadcasters, being a creation of the *Länder*, are required by law to report on the respective *Land*. The statutes of North German Broadcasting (NDR) for example require the corporation, to provide 'an objective and comprehensive overview of international, national and *Länder*-related events' and 'the regional pattern has to be properly taken into consideration'.

Table 2. Public Broadcasters of the *Länder* (1994)

Full name	Starting date	Initials	*Länder* covered
Bayerischer Rundkunk	1948	BR	Bavaria
Hessischer Rundfunk	1948	HR	Hesse
Mitteldeutscher Rundfunk	1991	MDR	Saxony, Saxony-Anhalt and Thuringia
Norddeutscher Rundfunk	1955	NDR	Lower Saxony, Hamburg Schleswig-Holstein and Mecklenburg-Vorpommern
Ostdeutscher Rundfunk Brandenburg	1992	ORB	Brandenburg
Radio Bremen	1948	RB	Bremen
Saarländischer Rundfunk	1957	SR	Saarland
Sender Freies Berlin	1953	SFB	Berlin
Süddeutscher Rundfunk	1950	SDR	North of Baden-Württemberg
Südwestfunk	1950	SWF	Rhineland-Palatinate and south of Baden-Württemberg
Westdeutscher Rundfunk	1955	WDR	North Rhine-Westphalia

Source: ARD

The public corporations already offered *Länder*-wide radio programmes before the advent of television. In fact there never was significant national public radio in Germany. In 1954 the first TV-channel was started as a joint venture of all existing broadcasters, called ARD (*Arbeitsgemeinschaft der öffentlich-rechtlichen Rundfunkanstalten Deutschlands*). The federal structure was built into ARD as all *Länder*-corporations offer a fixed share of the national TV-programme, based on a quota system. Very little programming (news, sports) was produced jointly, the center of this decentralized system was established mainly for transmission purposes. This principle is still working with ARD, ensuring that TV reporting and entertainment is produced in different regions of the country and reflects regional differences; for instance an established detective-series (*Tatort*) is produced by different corporations and uses cities in the different *Länder* as background of its regionalized stories.

The second channel ZDF (*Zweites Deutsches Fernsehen*), established in 1961, was legally based on an agreement, signed by all *Länder*. The national headquarters was built in Mainz, the capital of Rhineland-Palantinate and until then no place of any media significance. The programme of ZDF is not regionalized, but *Länder* politicians are heavily represented in its supervising TV- council. Also, beginning in the early 1960s, the *Länder*-broadcasters started to introduce regional Third Channels that today represent the main regional element in television.

Historically the first channel (ARD) carried a 'window' for a daily *Länder*-wide regional news and entertainment magazine. This has recently been moved to the Third Channels, to offer ARD as a national advertising medium. The multi-*Länder*-corporation split up their Third Channel to offer regional programming for each *Land*. Public television is rarely regionalized below the *Länder*-level. In some parts of the country, public radio offers special programming for smaller spaces, but public local radio is the exception.

Commercial television

The *Länder* also have final responsibility for commercial broadcasting. For this purpose, 15 new supervisory bodies (*Landesmedienanstalten*) were established by the 16 *Länder* (Berlin and Brandenburg maintain one joint body) since the 1980s, that hand out licences and regulate the activities of broadcasters based inside their borders. Referring to more local media like radio this form of decentralized supervision makes sense, but obviously television tends to be a national medium. Therefore, the directors of these supervisory bodies closely co-operate and decide which of them licences national TV-producers. In addition, they forced national broadcasters in a kind of bargaining process to offer some *Länder*-wide programming in exchange for the use of (much sought after) terrestrial frequencies. But this worked only in parts of the country and excludes satellite-TV that transmits direct-to-home (which is widely used in East Germany). In Berlin an attractive regional frequency was given in 1993 to an international consortium *IA Brandenburg*.

It has been claimed that this system of 15 supervising bodies, which is unique in the world, is much too fragmented and each body is too weak to check large media companies. The process of licensing also turned out to be heavily politicized, the *Länder*-governments supporting TV-producers of their political affiliation and those that promise to work out of their *Land*.

Regional TV in Germany

Public service regional TV

Until the middle of 1993 the regional TV-programmes of the *Länder* were offered on the First (ARD) Channel that was split up for this purpose. They consisted of a 'magazine' of about 30 minutes reporting on general interest topics like regional politics, economics, culture, and weather but also 'soft news' and entertainment with a regional accent. In two respects they played a crucial role in the broadcasting system of Germany. The Federal Constitutional Court had demanded that the public broadcasters provide the country with a 'basic supply'. Therefore, the *Länder*-corporations are obliged to offer a comprehensive and integrated programme. This was interpreted as meaning that even minorities of audiences have to be served if that is not done by any other broadcaster, including reporting about the *Länder*. Public broadcasters saw their regional magazines as one of the ways to fulfil this demand.

Secondly regional programming on the First Channel was important for the revenues of the ARD-corporations. They get most of their income from monthly user fees, but about 20 per cent (this share is going down because of commercial competition) of all income is derived from 20 minutes of advertising each weekday. These advertising spots are broadcast during intermissions of the programme between 17.25 and 20.00. As regional programming was not as attractive to viewers and advertisers as pure entertainment material, the ARD-corporations decided to move regional programming away from the First to the Third Channel (which is free of advertising). This move made it possible for the ARD-corporations to offer a comprehensive nation-wide programme and become a national advertising medium. This decision was interpreted as implying a decline in the significance of regional reporting, as the Third Channels of the *Länder* traditionally had audiences mainly interested in culture and education there ratings were relatively low. According to recent data though, the audience decline because of the shift to the Third Channel seems to be low.

The presence of regional aspects on the First Channel is now limited to ten minutes of regional information as 'window' in an otherwise nation-wide programme at 17.40. Some of the entertainment series however, which – harmonized for all *Länder* – fill the programme of the First Channel during the time between 17.40 and 20.00, are produced with a regional background and story in mind.

The second national channel (ZDF) does not offer special programmes for regions or sub regional territories because of its centralist structure. Nevertheless, it has programmes with reports from different regions which are broadcast nation-wide: *Länderspiegel*, *Länderre-port*, *ZDF regional* etc. are specialized on regional and/or local subjects.

As was pointed out, the Third Channels were created to serve a *Land* or a combination of several *Länder* with television. Since the middle of 1993 they provide practically all of regional programming, the daily 'regional magazine' being the most important contribution. The Third Channels start their broadcasting time in the morning with educational pro-grammes and end late at night. WDR started to offer a 24-hour-programme beginning in 1994. News programmes are concentrated in the time before 20.00.

Regional TV-magazines

The landscape of regional TV-magazines is quite diverse. NDR for example broadcasts a magazine of 45 minutes, starting at 18.45, called *DAS! – Das Abendstudio*, which contains not only themes from the four Länder which NDR has to serve, but also topics of nation-wide interest. The following 30 minutes are dedicated to magazines for each of the four *Länder*, coming from studios out of the *Land*-capital: Hamburg (*Hamburger Journal*), Schleswig-Holstein (*Schleswig-Holstein-Magazin*), Lower Saxony (*Hallo Niedersachsen*) and Meck-lenburg-Vorpommern (*Nordmagazin*).

WDR as another example broadcasts five minutes of North Rhine-Westphalia news each day (*NRW-Nachrichten)* and later a general interest magazine of 40 minutes, called *Aktuelle Stunde*, which also contains sports. Following this, WDR offers 20 minutes of information in 'regional windows' to different parts of North Rhine-Westphalia (*Fensterprogramme der Landesstudios)*.

To give an example, the *Hamburger Journal* is described in more detail. This 30 minute per weekday programme for the City/*Land* of Hamburg, is produced in a special subsection of NDR, the *Landesfunkhaus Hamburg* that enjoys rather large independence from the main NDR organization. The regional magazine is produced by a staff of about 30 fully employed journalists, including some secretaries, assistants etc. and another 30 free-lancers. According to NDR sources the average market share of the *Journal* has been 22 per cent in 1993 (of all viewers 6 years of age and older). Because of increasing competition in a multi-channel environment this market share is gradually going down. In the mid-80s, when the *Journal* had a virtual monopoly and only three public channels were available, the market share reached about 40 per cent. In addition, the *Landesfunkhaus* produces some occasional programming for the Northern German Third Channel (N3) like *Rund um den Michel* (around the St. Michaelis-church, a famous symbol for Hamburg) or *Profile*, a talk show.

The other three *Landesfunkhäuser* of the four *Länder* corporation NDR offer similar services. The construction of these *Funkhäuser* also serves a political function, as they are usually controlled by the party that is in power in the respective *Land*. By far the largest of the four NDR-*Länder* is Lower Saxony, that consists – according to Eurostat – of four regions (Braunschweig, Hannover, Lüneburg, Weser-Ems) that are only reflected in regional studios contributing to the *Land*-magazine, not in any regional programming. Providing such a large area with a magazine might contribute to the fact, that *Hallo Niedersachsen* has considerably lower ratings than the other *Länder*-magazines.

Other regional programming

Besides these daily magazines, the Third Channels broadcast other types of more infrequent programming which represent aspects of the region. This includes programmes with typical music, talk shows, which invite prominent guests of the region, or documentaries on regional culture. Another aspect are special shows that support regional speech, produced for example in Low German (*Plattdeutsch*), as it is typical for Northern Germany. Many of these programmes with a regional accent reflect somehow a folklorist view of the *Länder*. Their attraction for audiences and their appeal concerning regional identity is therefore limited.

A special service of regional information plates is offered by all Third Channels on teletext (in German: *Videotext*). NDR's *Nordtext* on N3 provides some daily information on Northern German politics and the economy, culture (schedule of theatres), the environment (latest data on air pollution) etc. Even the audience ratings of N3 from the day before are presented.

The Third Channels of WDR (West 3), NDR (N3) and BR (BFS) are transmitted via satellite and may be received via cable or satellite antenna in other parts of Germany and Europe. But this has little significance in terms of ratings. It implies however, that people living elsewhere have the chance to receive some information from their home region, if they should wish to do so.

While the shares of audiences of public broadcasting have fallen drastically during the last

Table 3. Share of audiences of the public regional TV 1994 (Jan-Oct, as %)

	%
Hessen3 (Hessia)	9.3
MDR-Fernsehen (Saxony, Saxony-Anhalt, Thuringia)	9.9
Bayerisches Fernsehen BFS (Bavaria)	9.0
Fernsehen Brandenburg (Brandenburg)	10.7
Südwest 3 (Rhineland Palatinate, Saarland, Baden-Württemberg)	9.5
N 3 (Schleswig Holstein, Bremen, Hamburg, Lower Saxony, Berlin, Mecklenburg-Vorpommern)	9.1
West 3 (Northrhine Westphalia)	7.2

Source: *ARD-Werbung/GfK-Inmarkt*

years, suffering under competition with commercial TV, the Third Channels audiences did not lose to the same extent. While the First (ARD) and Second (ZDF) Channel lost nearly half of their audience, the Third Channels declined from 11 to 8,3 per cent. Within the *Länder*-corporations the Third Channel of Hessia was the most successful in 1992.

Until the beginning of the 1980s, the *Länder*-corporations offered a comprehensive programme for the *Länder* as such, not considering the regions below that level or local entities. They tended to recognize the so-called 'division of power' in the media between public *Länder*-broadcasters and commercial print media which controlled regional and local markets, often as monopolists. The dawning of commercial broadcasting since 1984 with its possibilities of local radio and television brought an end to this mutually recognized division. It intensified plans within the public broadcasters of moving into smaller regions.

Offering TV and radio programmes *Länder*-wide was considered as not being sufficient for the regions. The public broadcasters commissioned a number of studies on how to subdivide their service area, therefore most of the research results on regionalization were produced during the 1980s. As a result, public radio in some parts of the country now offers special programming for smaller areas, but public local radio is the exception.

To provide the same in the TV programmes was estimated to be too expensive. Consequently there is only little regionalized TV-offering below the *Länder*-level. WDR in North Rhine-Westphalia, being the most populous *Land*, maintains a number of regional studios which make it possible to offer real regional programmes besides the daily *Land*-magazine. Multi-*Länder*-corporations like NDR and MDR split up their Third Channel to offer regional programming for each *Land*.

Private regional TV

Commercial broadcasters in Germany are licensed (with few exceptions) for nation-wide transmission and are interested in serving markets as large as possible. They started out as cable programmers, but as they could not reach enough audiences by cable they sought terrestrial frequencies, which are franchised by the *Länder* supervisory bodies. When RTL and SAT.1, the two main commercial TV companies in Germany, applied for terrestrial frequencies in the *Länder*, they were asked to offer a regional TV magazine in return. But following the commercial logic, regional programming was considered by the broadcasters as a burden rather than a chance. It seemed to be too expensive and too unattractive in terms of costs and advertising income. Today we find regional programming by commercial companies only in a number of *Länder*. Mostly in the attractive markets of densely populated regions they opened regional 'windows' where they report during 30 minutes about current affairs of the region.

These magazines, called *Regionalreport* within SAT1 and *Hessen live, Nord live Hamburg* etc. within RTL emphasize infotainment and prefer human touch stories referring to the region. Again Hamburg is the example: Adding all regional magazines up, each weekday three programmes (by NDR, SAT1 and RTL) are offered.

SAT1 has developed a rather dense network of regional magazines. Its 'Regional report' is produced in eight versions throughout the old *Länder* . For the new *Länder* there is only one magazine broadcast. The 'Regional Report Hamburg', which is the only one covering one town, is produced by a subsidiary company of SAT1, the *SAT1 Norddeutschland GmbH*. Started in 1988 the length was until 1994 reduced from 35 to 30 minutes. Within this half of an hour between three and eleven minutes of advertising are broadcast. The magazine is produced by a staff of 7 fully employed journalists, two assistants, four presenters working half a day and two free-lancers. They reached an average market share of 10.3 per cent in the first half of 1993 (of all viewers 6 years of age and older).

Most of the regional magazines of RTL are concentrated in the north: *Nord live* is broadcast for Hamburg, Lower Saxony and Schleswig-Holstein. These three magazines are produced in Hamburg by an independent company, the *Kommanditgesellschaft HRB Hamburger Rundfunk Beteiligunsgesellschaft mbh & Co*. Started in 1988 and 1989 they reduced their length in the beginning of 1994 from 45 to 30 minutes. Within this half hour three minutes of regional advertising and three minutes of nation-wide advertising are broadcast. The three magazines are produced by a staff of 27 fully employed journalists (Hamburg: 17, Schleswig-Holstein: 5, Lower Saxony: 5) and another 20 free-lancers. They reached an average market share of 22 (Hamburg), 11.1 Schleswig-Holstein) and 7.2 per cent (Lower Saxony) in 1993 (of all viewers 6 years of age and older).

In some areas, e.g. in the north, the time schedules of all regional magazines are co-ordinated by the supervisory bodies of the *Länder*, so that the companies do not compete during the same time slot for the regional advertising market. Together with programmes of Schleswig-Holstein, that may be received in Hamburg as well, regional programmes amount to three hours every day.

Besides these regional offerings that were forced upon them, the important media companies more or less ignored the region as an area for television activities. The main reason is that

Table 4. Share of audiences of private regional TV (as %)

		Oct. 1993	Oct. 1994
SAT1	Berlin/Brandenburg	13.3	14.1
	Hamburg	11.0	12.6
	Schleswig-Holstein	16.5	11.6
	Lower Saxony/Bremen	6.9	8.3
	Bavaria	6.1	9.2
	Baden-Württemberg	6.9	8.1
	Rhineland-Palatinate (Hessia)	6.0	7.5
	North Rhine-Westphalia	–	11.0
RTL	Hamburg	22.0	20
	Lower Saxony	7.2	8.5
	Schleswig-Holstein	11.1	15.8
	West	7.6	8.1
	Hessia	5.9	6.7
	Munich	16.0	–

Source: *GFK Fernsehforschung*, November 1993; *GFK Fernsehforschung / RTL Medienforschung*, November 1994.

according to what the companies say, programmes with regional content cater to small audiences, produce only limited advertisement revenues and are highly unprofitable. Based on this argument, RTL in Hesse even managed to reduce its time for regional programmes to half an hour, although its licence obliged the broadcaster to offer one hour of programming.

A new trend: regional commercial broadcasters

Recently the situation has changed as new terrestrial frequencies have been made available for local and regional programmes. As a consequence, ten years after the beginning of commercial broadcasting, the big media companies started a run for licences of regional TV. The most attractive places for regional TV are big cities and regions with a dense population.

The first regional programme based on this new concept – *IA Brandenburg* – started in February 1993 in Berlin and its environs. But after one and a half year problems seem to be bigger than expected. The ratings are low and so are the incomes of advertising. The concepts of programming are restructured and the chief manager was dismissed. Discussions about use of another terrestrial frequency for similar purposes have started. Munich was the second city to put regional TV on the air. Nuremberg, Stuttgart, Halle and a still to be selected city-region in North Rhine-Westphalia are other places where plans for local or regional TV offers have been developed.

In Hamburg the invitation of tenders for a regional TV-licence attracted 13 applicants. Hamburg 1, with the participation of Time Warner (24 per cent), Springer (24 per cent) DFA (a television news agency, 24 per cent), Frank Otto (successful in radio broadcasting in Hamburg, 24 per cent) and two small share holders, was supposed to start in autumn 1994, but did not do it until the end of the year. The concepts of programming are still unknown, but there is the contradiction of the promises of seven hours of local programmes daily and a very small budget for this purpose.

Nevertheless, the transmission of these programmes promises to be a lucrative business and media experts estimate that it should be possible for broadcasters in those densely populated areas to gain a share of ten per cent of national advertising expenditures.

So far, the first station of this type *IA Brandenburg* shows very little regional programming, the main diet consisting of films, shows, soap operas etc. This is the field where big film companies find a new market for selling their stock of programmes. CLT negotiates with applicants in Hamburg and Stuttgart, the Kirch group does business with the Munich local station and tries to enter markets in Berlin and Hamburg.

The viability and future of these regional stations is still unclear. One model sees a network of independent broadcasters, which operate jointly to buy their necessary programmes. Another device proposes a 'mantle', regional reporting provided by the local newspapers. New forms of co-operation between public and commercial broadcasters may also develop on the regional level; for example, Bavaria's public corporation BR is interested in offering parts of its Third Channel as a 'mantle' to future regional commercial stations.

Public access channels

The introduction of cable TV during the 1980s brought proposals to use this new media not just for professionally produced programmes, but to reserve one channel as a forum for individuals and groups of amateurs to produce and distribute their own programmes. This concept of public access was taken from the US and introduced as Open Channel (*Offener Kanal*) in Germany. As the public access channel is physically related to local cable systems, all programming is *per se* local and/or regional. In fact, the content of programmes is often concerned with local/regional developments, experiences and problems.

The Minister Presidents of the *Länder* recommended its introduction, and now the laws of 12 of the 16 *Länder* provide for some kind public access channel, although they are not yet operating in the Eastern part of Germany. Usually the supervisory body which is responsible for the licensing of the commercial broadcasters (*Landesmedienanstalten*) is also the sponsor for public access channels.

At present, 27 public access channels are run in eight *Länder* of Germany. They are offered in areas of very different sizes and potential audiences including for instance the (new) capital and largest city Berlin, Hamburg and small villages like Kirchheimbolanden in Rhineland-Palatinat. In most cases they serve a local area rather than what we would call a region.

The main idea of the public access channel is to be a medium of nonprofessional users who contribute to the communication of a municipality or a region. In terms of ratings, the audiences of these channels are microscopic, as they have to compete with many other channels, provided by cable. Nearly half of the cabled households never switch to a public access channel; only one to two per cent can be counted as regular viewers.

Also in relation to the active users, the public access channels seem to disappoint the expectations once created. It was hoped, that politically motivated individuals and groups, especially of lower formal education, would use this do-it-yourself television to promote communication and discussion in a local/regional area. It turns out though that only 20 to 30 per cent of the programmes include a local or regional aspect. Furthermore, the typical user of the facilities of a public access channel is a young man from 20 to 30 years of age with a high formal education.

Conclusions and outlook for the future

As was demonstrated, the regional dimension is very alive in German culture and history; among many other things it may be found in the strong federal state, based on the *Länder* and their dominant role in broadcasting. The *Länder* are leading actors in public service television and some *Länder*-wide television has always been present. In addition, commercial broadcasters offer regional TV in some parts of the country. Because of the effects of the so-called 'dual system' and increased commercial competition regional TV has declined in importance as well as in ratings. Public broadcasters moved the daily regional TV magazine from their First (ARD) to the Third Channels.

Taken the German concept of region, most of the *Länder* include a number of regions. In most cases only the large-scale area of the *Land* is served, not the small-scale regions inside the *Land*. Exceptions are the City-*Länder* (like Hamburg), small *Länder* (like Saarland) and large *Länder* that subdivide some of their programming (North Rhine-Westphalia). In many cases the structure inside one *Land* can be quite centralist (like in Bavaria or Lower Saxony).

Regional TV-programming, usually as a *Länder*-magazine is available in all parts of the country, offered on public broadcasting, sometimes additional commercial programming is available. They are usually transmitted as general interest magazines during early evening (before 20.00 h). Interest in these regional programmes is limited and tends to go down, mainly due to the multi-channel competition at the same time of the day.

An additional source of regional programmes are the public Third Channels that provide some programming with a regional flavour, including political reporting and debate, culture, language and folklore from the region. Additional demand for more regional broadcasting seems to be low. The small-scale regions below the *Länder*- level are either served by public and/or commercial radio or all together ignored by broadcasting. In all cases, newspapers (the *Heimat*-press) represent the backbone of reporting in the local–regional sphere.

We may conclude that regional television does not rank high on the agenda of German media policy. The reason is rather simple: The region is being served relatively well, mostly by local newspapers and local or regional radio, some larger regions also by television. Demand for additional services is limited and there are not foreseeable tendencies that this is going to change in the near future. What is happening in the region, does not support the establishment of more regional media, not in terms of reportable events, not in the amount of financing available and not in terms of audience demand. But it has to be emphasized that the situation differs very much in the different parts of Germany.

Länder-regulations for electronic media make sure that at least some regional programming is available, always in radio and to some extent also in television. Recently the licensing of TV-stations for large urban agglomerations ('Ballungsraum-TV') started, Berlin IA being already on the air; similar projects start in 1995 or are under planning in large cities like Munich, Hamburg, Cologne, Nuremberg. Even though these stations will be licensed for the region they serve and will be required to offer some regional programming, regional content will be limited. These licences are the last ones for terrestrial television to be handed out and as such interesting for investors. It is foreseen though, that they will join a national network (following the American example) and much of the programming will be centrally provided.

The German example underlings that a traditionally decentralized political culture provides a fertile ground for extensive regional reporting. Limits are mainly provided by the market and, concerning broadcasting, regulations. Complaints about to little regional reporting are rarely heard, criticism is more concerned with the fact that news is biased because of regional monopolies (e.g. local newspapers being co-owner of radio and TV-stations as well). Also there is a definite lack of small, community oriented radio and/or TV-stations that are run by non-commercial initiatives and enthusiasts, as they flourish in some neighbouring countries and provide a forum for local information and exchange.

The question remains how regional TV will survive in the age of digital multi-channel and interactive television. One option may be that regional reporting will flourish because it is widely available, another that it will enter hard times due to the increased competition by non-regional material that is considered to be more attractive by the viewers.

References

ARD (1993): *Jahrbuch.* ARD: Frankfurt.

Buss, M. (1979): 'Regionale Medien und Bürgerinteressen', in *Media Perspektiven* 12.

Darschin, W. & Frank, B. (1993): 'Tendenzen im Zuschauerverhalten', in *Media Perspektiven* 3.

EUROSTAT (1993): *Portrait der Regionen. Vol. 1: Deutschland, Benelux, Dänemark.* Luxembourg: EUROSTAT.

Först, W. (ed) (1984): *Rundfunk in der Region. Probleme und Möglichkeiten der Regionalität.* Köln.

Heidinger, V., Schwab, F. & Winterhoff-Spurk, P. (1993): 'Offene Kanäle nach der Ausbauphase', in *Media Perspektiven* 7.

Hinrichs, E. (1987): 'Regionalgeschichte', in Carl-Hans Hauptmeyer (ed.): *Landesgeschichte heute.* Göttingen.

Jarren, O. (1989): 'Lokaler Rundfunk und politische Kultur. Auswirkungen lokaler elektronischer Medienangebote auf Institutionen und institutionelles Handeln', in *Publizistik* 4.

Jonscher, N. (1991): *Einführung in die lokale Publizistik.* Opladen.

Lange, K. (1970): 'Regionen', in Akademie für Raumforschung und Landesplanung (ed.): *Handwörterbuch der Raumforschung und Raumordnung.* Hannover.

Lerg, W.B. (1982): 'Regionalität als Programmauftrag'? in *Rundfunk und Fernsehen* 1.

Lindner, J.-U. (1993): 'Kampf um die TV-Provinz', epd *Kirche und Rundfunk* 87.

Niemeyer, H.-G. (1979): 'Regionale Informationen im Fernsehen', in *Media Perspektiven* 5.

Rühl, M. (1982): 'Auf der Suche nach dem systematischen Regionalprogramm', in *Media Perspektiven* 1.

Schuler-Harms, M. (1992): 'Das Rundfunksystem der Bundesrepublik Deutschland', in *Internationales Handbuch für Hörfunk und Fernsehen.* Baden-Baden.

Schütte, W. (1971): *Regionalität und Föderalismus im Rundfunk. Die geschichtliche Entwicklung in Deutschland 1923–1945.* Frankfurt.

Teichert, W. (1982): *Die Region als publizistische Aufgabe.* Hamburg.

Walendy, E. (1993): 'Offene Kanäle in Deutschland – ein Überblick', in *Media Perspektiven* 7.

Wirth-Patzelt, S. (1986): *Regionale Fernsehberichterstattung in Bayern. Inhaltsanalyse ausgewählter Sendungen des Bayerischen Rundfunks.* Frankfurt.

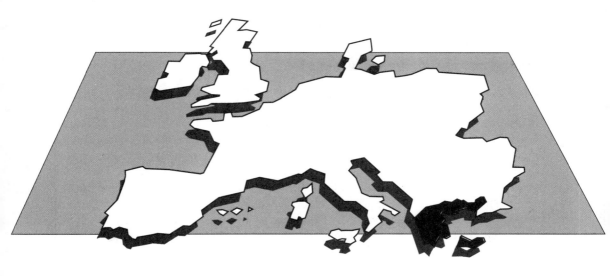

6   Greece: Unbridled deregulation

Panayote Elias Dimitras

The general political framework, the nation and the regions

The modern Greek state dates from 1830, when a small 'matrix-state', confined in the southern continental part of today's state and the adjacent islands (one third of the present state's area), was officially recognized as independent. As was the case with all other Balkan 'matrix-states', (or Piedmont states), products of secessions from the centuries-old empires, the new Greek state assigned itself an 'irredentist' mission to conquer all as yet 'unredeemed' territories: the related struggle lasted for one century, ending with the post-World War I border arrangements, which, with minor changes, have survived to this day. One consequence of that irredentist mission was that the matrix-states had to be centralized and, ethnically, as homogeneous as possible: their cohesiveness was perceived as a necessary condition for a successful 'irredentist' (i.e. expansionist) struggle. Another consequence was that minorities in the new states, in considerable numbers in the early twentieth century, were the victims of assimilationist repressive policies or of ethnic cleansing by elimination or expulsion (Dimitras, 1993b).

Through 1987, therefore, Greece's administrative sub-divisions, above the municipalities and the communes, were the *nomos* (district) and, within the latter, the *eparchia* (county). The heads of each district, and each county when there was one, were appointed by the central government and had relatively little power, compared with the similar administrators in other European countries: all major decisions about each district were made in the respective ministries in the state's capital, Athens. In 1987 Greece was finally compelled to introduce administrative regions for the needs of the EEC's regional planning policies.

Political and administrative dimension

Although Greece had never been divided into administrative regions, there was a 'natural' division, included in every geography textbook, into eight regions (although that term was not used, the term geographical districts being preferred instead): Thrace, Macedonia, Epirus, Thessaly, Continental Greece, Peloponnese, Ionian Islands, Aegean Islands, with Crete the largest of all islands sometimes perceived as a separate, ninth, region, and the densely populated Greater Athens area, part of Continental Greece, as a tenth region. The Greek socialist government in 1987, though, proceeded into a division of the country into thirteen regions: Attica (Greater Athens plus the rest of the old district of Attica), Continental Greece (without its Western district or Attica) Peloponnese (without its North-western districts), Western Greece (the Western districts of Continental Greece and of the Peloponnese), Ionian Islands, Epirus, Thessaly, Western Macedonia, Central Macedonia, Eastern Macedonia and Thrace, Northern Aegean, Southern Aegean, and Crete. This division served in fact the electoral goals of the then ruling government party PASOK (Panhellenic Socialist Movement), as well as the effort to weaken the electoral representations of the officially called Muslim but largely self-determined Turkish minority in Thrace as it was becoming obvious in 1987 that the latter would support independent candidates in the next elections, as in fact it has done (Dimitras, 1993a: 49–50).

The regions were each given a secretary general with some limited powers: nevertheless, in the aftermath of 1987, Greece became less centralized than ever before, although it has remained a very centralized state. 1994 was an important year for the balance of real power between the centre and the periphery, as in October, Greeks elected directly, for the first time in their history, the prefect and the council in each district (the councils were established in the 1980s and were elected indirectly by the elected municipal and communal councils and various other institutions): although the latter may not have more power than now, the fact that they are now directly elected may make at least those opposed to the government, if not all, more independent from it than the appointed ones. It is also expected that there will be pressure for more decentralization from the elected district authorities.

Linguistic dimension

Greece prides itself on being a very homogeneous country with 98 per cent of the population being Greek-speaking and, at least nominally, Greek Orthodox. Moreover, it recognizes only one minority, the Muslims in Thrace, which is officially supposed to be prospering. Reality, though, is different. For example, the EEC report on linguistic minorities recognizes five linguistic groups in Greece, other than the dominant one (Siguan, 1990: 50–61): Turkish-speaking, Pomaks, Slav-speaking, Aromounes (Vlach), and Arvanites. The terms used in that report were the result of a compromise with the Greek authorities, which would have otherwise vetoed its publication (incidentally, the full report was never published, only the summary report was in 1990). In the forthcoming new report, beyond the above five groups, there will be a reference to Roma (Gypsies) and Jews. Moreover, the European Parliament's declaration on linguistic and cultural minorities (the 'Killilea report'), approved on 6

February 1994 was nearly unanimous which also means the votes of all nine Greek European deputies, also acknowledged the presence of these five minority languages.

Official data do not exist on these minorities. Estimates indicate that Greek citizens with a different mother tongue and/or religion make up close to 10 per cent of the population (MRG, 1994). Almost all Turkish-speakers, who also call themselves Turks, live in Thrace, where Pomaks also live: the latter's mother tongue is Pomak – a dialect of Bulgarian – but they speak Turkish too, as this is the language used in education for the Muslims in Thrace, and also call themselves Turks. Thrace borders with Turkey and Bulgaria, the latter also having sizeable Turkish and Pomak minorities. In Bulgaria, however, most Pomaks do not identify themselves as Turks. As the Greek–Bulgarian border in Thrace has been closed, with one exception, since the early days of the Cold War, Pomaks of Greece have had no contacts with the Pomaks in Bulgaria for two generations. This separation, an aim of Greek policy in the 1950s and 1960s when Bulgaria was perceived to be the main enemy, contributed significantly to the Turkification of Pomaks, along with the use of the Turkish language in their schools and the discrimination against the Muslims, especially since the 1970s (Dimitras, 1991: 68–86; Helsinki Watch, 1990 and 1992).

Macedonian-speakers are spread throughout Greek Macedonia. Most appear to have been assimilated after three generations of repression, and only a minority among them feel today that they do not belong to the Greek nation (Minority Rights Group International, 1994). Part of Greek Macedonia borders with the newly independent (since 1991) Republic of Macedonia, where the majority speak Macedonian, although the literary language spoken in the republic is slightly different from the various Macedonian dialects spoken in Greece. In any case, all belong to the Bulgaro-Macedonian linguistic sub-division of the Southern Slavic languages.

Neither Macedonian, nor Aroumanian or Arberor or Pomak or Roma are taught at school. Therefore, the minority languages, except for Turkish, are in decline. This is even truer with the Aroumanian and the Arberor, spoken by people scattered throughout continental Greece (Aroumanians are more concentrated in Thessaly and Arberor than around Greater Athens and the Peloponnese), who have been fully assimilated, usually without the necessity of repressive policies used in the case of Macedonians. Finally, the Roma are also spread throughout the country, and they are probably the country's largest minority.

Socio-economic framework

The main demographic characteristic of Greece is the very densely populated area in the capital and the surrounding area, to the extent that more than one third of the population lives in the Attica region. Another region with a large population and extensive land area is Central Macedonia, where the country's second largest urban area, Greater Salonica, is located. Population dynamics indicate (see Table 1) that the regions with important growth in the 1980s were the ones around the country's three major urban centres: Central Macedonia – around Salonica – (+8.4 per cent); Continental Greece – around Attica – (+7.8 per cent); Western Greece – around Patras – (+7.1 per cent). Attica itself grew only by 4.5 per cent as it had previously reached near-saturation population levels. The southern island regions of

Southern Aegean (+11.8 per cent) and Crete (+6.9 per cent) also experienced an important growth. On the other hand, the regions with stagnant population were Northern Aegean (+1.7 per cent), Western Macedonia (+1.3 per cent) and Eastern Macedonia and Thrace (–0.9 per cent).

Table 1. Regional structure of Greece according to 1991 Census

EU regions	Area km^2	Population	Density per km	PPS* 1990	Unemploy-ment rate (1991)
Northern Greece	56,792	3,331,865	58.7	46.2	6.3
Eastern Macedonia & Thrace	14,157	570,261	40.3	42.6	5.4
Central Macedonia	19,147	1,737,623	90.8	47.7	6.1
Western Macedonia	9,451	292,751	31.0	51.7	8.0
Thessaly	14,037	731,230	52.1	43.1	6.9
Central Greece	53,899	2,416,779	44.8	44.7	7.2
Epirus	9,203	339,210	36.9	35.1	9.8
Ionian Islands	2,307	191,003	82.8	42.9	3.9
Western Greece	11,350	702,027	61.9	38.9	8.7
Continental Greece	15.549	578,876	37.4	58.3	7.0
Peloponnese	15,490	605,663	39.1	44.1	5.6
Attica	3,808	3,522,769	925.1	50.4	9.9
Islands	17,458	992,743	56.9	44.6	4.8
Northern Aegean	3,836	198,241	51.7	33.8	8.9
Southern Aegean	5,286	257,522	48.7	52.5	3.6
Crete	8,336	536,980	64.4	44.8	4.0
Greece	131,957	10,264,156	77.8	47.1	7.7

*Purchasing Power Standard

Northern Aegean (with the lowest EU per capita purchasing power standard – PPS – at 33.8 while the EU average is at 100) and Eastern Macedonia and Thrace (42.6), along with Epirus (35.1) and Western Greece (38.9), are among the poorest regions of the country. Better off are Continental Greece (58.3), Southern Aegean (52.5), Western Macedonia (51.7) and Attica (50.40). Overall, though, Greece is the least affluent country in the EU and only four of the five continental Portuguese regions have comparable relative PPS.

Greece has a relatively low unemployment rate by EU standards (7.7 per cent in 1991- though provisional official estimates put it above 9 per cent in 1992 and 1993). The highest unemployment rate can be found in the state's capital (9.9 per cent), and in the rather poor regions of Epirus (9.8 per cent), Northern Aegean (8.9 per cent), and Western Greece (8.7 per cent).

Regional development and regional media

The country's high centralization has resulted in a tradition of media concentration in Greater Athens. For example, not only are almost all the national newspapers published in the state's capital, but, with the exception of a couple of Salonica newspapers and a handful of local ones, only the Athens-published newspapers have sizeable circulation anywhere in Greece. The same is true for magazines. The state-owned electronic media followed a similar pattern until deregulation: regional radio stations had programmes partly coinciding with those of the national radio stations, and there were only two television stations, both operating out of Athens. Only to face the competition in the deregulation era of the late 1980s and 1990s did the state-owned ERT (Greek Radio and Television) open one regional television station and one local radio station in Salonica: both were predictably unsuccessful ventures.

On the other hand, the electronic media deregulation led to the creation of hundreds of local radio stations and scores of regional and local television stations. The former were very successful, and in most districts one of them tops the ratings. The latter have proved to be no threat for the national private stations, but some have a non-negligible audience. Overall, though, local electronic media have been more successful than the local print media.

The legal framework and the real world of television in Greece

The legal framework

Today, television in Greece officially functions within the framework of laws 1730/1987 (on ERT), 1866/1989 and 2175/1993 (on the National Radio and Television Council), as has since been amended. The state's constitutionally-mandated control over broadcast media is carried out by the National Radio and Television Council (ESR). The ESR is a nine member body appointed for three years by the Minister to the Prime Minister and selected by the Speaker of the House (or its president), and the four largest parliamentary parties (which select respectively four, two, one and one members each). The ESR members must be journalists belonging to recognized journalists' unions, scholars with prestigious reputations in a field related to the media, personalities from the world of literature, arts or information, or personalities recognized for their participation in public life and in particular in education, local administration or the union movement. The two largest parties should select at least one non-resident of Greater Athens each.

ESR's responsibilities are merely advisory: to hold hearings for and express an opinion on the persons appointed by the Minister to the Prime Minister on the ERT board; to recommend to the government the dismissal of members of the ERT board; to advise the government on the procedures of granting licences to non-state owned radio and television stations, of overseeing the coverage of parliamentary activities and of electoral campaigns by the electronic media; and of sanctioning the violations of the laws by the stations; to issue codes of ethics for journalists, programmes and advertisements in broadcast media

Moreover, there is an independent National Commission of Electronic Mass Media (EEIME), appointed by the Minister to the Prime Minister. It is made up of the nine ESR members and one representative from each of the following unions: Athens' journalists, Macedonia–Thrace journalists, Athens dailies' publishers, ERT employees, artists, workers, civil servants, industries, and farmers in addition to local administration and the Church of Greece. The EEIME decides on matters referred to it by the ESR and has a mostly advisory control over ERT; comments on the annual reports on electronic media sent to it by the competent ministries; and evaluates and publicly debates on the functioning of all national television stations and any other radio or television station it may see fit at least once every semester. These reports are then sent to Parliament. As is obvious from the above, the ESR's and EEIME's functions , as they were (re)defined in the most recent law 2175/1993, introduced by the new socialist (PASOK) government and valid since 16/12/1993, are largely ceremonial, with the real power being concentrated in the hands of the government, as was the case before 1989.

A non-transferable, renewable, seven-year licence to operate only one national or local television station can be granted by the government, upon the recommendation of the ESR, to a local authority or to a company. In the latter case, no individual can directly or through his/her relatives own more than 25 per cent of the personalized shares, and foreign capital cannot control more than 25 per cent of the total. The companies must be reliable, and their members should not have been found guilty of press related offences. Local authorities and media related experience of the shareholders are considered advantages for the granting of licences. No shareholder can have shares in more than one station. At least 50 per cent of the programme, excluding news and current affairs, must be European productions, while the licence contract should specify 'a satisfactory quota of national productions per programme type'. Presidential decrees should specify the procedure by which 1.5 per cent of the annual gross income (minus taxes and contributions to state agencies) of the state or non-state television companies is invested in Greek feature films also to be shown in theatres; and 0.3 per cent of the annual gross income is donated to two national organizations for the blind.

The real world

The state-owned ERT has been operating three national television stations since 1987, two (ET–1 and ET–2) out of Athens and one (ET–3) out of Salonica. On the other hand, since 1989, local (and since 1991, national), non-state owned stations could have therefore operated legally in Greece, with licences granted to them by the government on the advice of the ESR. However, after six years of broadcasting anarchy during which more than 100 (mostly local) television stations went on the air, in the second half of 1993, the government finally granted the first licences to television stations. Eight licences for national broadcasting were granted to Mega Channel, Antenna TV, New Channel, Channel 29 (since renamed Star Channel), Seven-X, and New Television (the only one not yet broadcasting) on 23 July 1993 (by the then ruling conservative government), and to Sky and 902 TV on 3 November 1993 (by the new socialist government). Moreover, five stations were licensed for regional or local broadcasting: Tele City, Tele Tora, and Super Hellas (the latter not yet broadcasting) for Attica, TV 100 for Macedonia, and TV Macedonia for Salonica. In early 1994, however, none of the above stations had signed the mandated contracts with the state and over 100 other regional or local television stations were continuing to operate illegally, while awaiting their applications for new licences to be processed: the old ESR had issued favourable recommendations for just a dozen of them. In addition, a dozen international satellite stations were re-broadcast on the air by ERT or by private channels, mainly in Greater Athens and Greater Salonica.

ERT is a public company in the form of a joint stock company: its only stockholder is the Greek state, which gives it the receipts of a special mandatory fee paid by each electricity consumer (regardless of whether s/he owns a TV) and very significant subsidies. The licensed private national television stations are also joint stock companies, whose sole source of income is sales and advertising. The owners of the licensed stations are often major publishers or radio station owners: Mega Channel is owned by five newspaper publishers, Antenna TV by one radio station owner, Channel 29 (now Star Channel) and Tele Tora by one publisher each (although there is a nearly confirmed rumour that a second publisher and shareholder of Mega Channel is also behind Star Channel), Seven X by a radio station owner, Sky by a newspaper and radio station owner (also a shareholder of Mega Channel), New Television by three publishers; 902 TV belongs to the Greek Communist Party (KKE), Super Hellas is a subsidiary of the European satellite Super Channel, while New Channel, Tele City and Macedonia TV belong to the municipality of Salonica. The above information shows that some stations have fewer than four owners, as the law mandates, while some businessmen own shares in more than one station, another violation of the law. Naturally, if one looks at the official share ownership, most of these violations will not be found, as the businessmen legally circumvent the legal restrictions by using 'front persons'.

The 18 to 24 hour programme of the main channels has been determined by the choices of the two main private channels, Mega and Antenna. It is based on the kind of programmes that could attract sizeable audiences, and therefore advertising: series, movies, games, children's shows, music, sports, and news. Educational television or documentaries have no place (the latter can be watched on the state channels or on minor private ones). The main private channels' news coverage is of better quality than the state stations' and more objective, though it tends also to be more sensational (with emphasis on crimes and tragic events). On the other hand, all channels have the habit of starting many programmes later or earlier than announced, or making unannounced last minute changes.

AGB television audience data for urban Greece indicated that the state stations were radically displaced by private competition. In January 1994, the private channels Antenna and Mega led the ratings with shares of 31 per cent and 30 per cent respectively, with ET–1 far behind tied in third place with Star Channel with a 7 per cent share, and ET–2 and Sky tied for fifth with 5 per cent, while the other channels had a total 12 per cent, of which less than 1 per cent for ET–3, satellite channels 1 per cent and videos 2 per cent. On an average day, Greeks watched television for three and a half hours.

From the above description, it is obvious that deregulation in Greece followed a pattern similar to the Italian one, except that, in the Greek case, there was a detailed legislation to begin with. The strength of the media tycoons who own the major private stations, however, made all restrictions inapplicable, with the legislation finally being adapted to reality. For example, most advertising limitations in the 1989 law were never observed and were eventually abolished. So, when the Greek state decided to grant licences in 1993, it just legalized *Ex post facto* the market situation as it had developed in violation of all legal provisions. Besides, as the ESR, initially conceived during the country's rare coalition government interval in mid-1989 as a balanced regulatory body, became, through the amendments legislated by the conservative government in 1990, a government controlled institution, the new socialist government introduced new legislation which gave the government direct authority, similar to that which it had enjoyed before deregulation. Nevertheless, while at the time direct government control meant that all broadcasting output was also controlled by the government, in the 1990s such control is, in practical terms, important only for the negligible ERT.

Regional and local television in Greece

When television was deregulated in 1989, private stations could operate only locally (not even regionally). Nevertheless, the first private stations which opened up in Athens soon extended their coverage to Salonica and then nationally, in violation of the law: relying on the bargaining strength of their owners (publishers of the most important newspapers and/or owners of the main radio stations) and of the inability of the ESR to speedily process their applications for licences, the new stations saw a legal and power void and moved in to fill it. With some delay, ERT's third channel which opened as a regional competitor (in Salonica) of the municipal TV 100, followed the pattern and broadcast nationally, though hardly anyone seems to be watching it.

So today, when we speak of regional and local television, we think of stations which do not aim at covering (near) national audiences. Although some of these stations do not broadcast farther than the respective district's borders, this is the result not only of their poor signal but also of geography. So, most non-national stations can also be seen outside their district, though, in most cases, their largest audience is in the district if not in the city they broadcast from.

The daily media survey Bari, carried out by Focus and covering continental Greece and Crete (so excluding the Ionian and the Aegean Islands), had registered in autumn of 1994, besides the three ERT stations and the seven stations with licences for national broadcasting (of which two, though, Seven X and 902 TV, were operating only in Greater Athens at the time), 13 stations in Greater Athens (among which licensed Tele City and Tele Tora), 13 in Greater Salonica (among which licensed TV 100 and TV Macedonia), and 69 in the rest of the country (naturally all unlicensed). There probably exist another score of stations operating throughout Greece, including the islands not covered by the Focus survey. None of these stations broadcast, even partly, in a minority language, but Turks in Thrace and ethnic Macedonians or Macedonian-speaking Greeks living near the border with the Republic of Macedonia can watch Turkish satellite and Macedonian television stations respectively: naturally, no audience figures for the latter are available.

The most important stations, measured by the percentage of the population in the respective regions who watch them on an average day (autumn 1993 data from the Focus daily day-after recall audience and readership survey), are Power TV (4.4 per cent) and TV Macedonia (3.6 per cent) in Greater Salonica; TRT (6.2 per cent) and Top Channel (4.0 per cent) in Thessaly; TV Delta (4.2 per cent) in Thrace; Echo TV (6.3 per cent) in Epirus; Super B (3.2 per cent) in the Peloponnese; and Crete TV (10.0 per cent) in Crete. Only the latter (Crete TV) was watched by as many as the least popular of the four main channels (ET–1, ET–2, Mega,

Antenna), ET–2 (9.8 per cent). So, except perhaps in the very town or district where these stations are broadcasting from the regional/local stations have a rather marginal audience, and are certainly no 'threat' to the established national stations, just as the local newspapers are no threat to the Athens-based national newspapers, but unlike the situation with the radio stations, where, in almost all districts surveyed by Focus, local stations have higher audiences than the national ERT radio stations or the powerful Athens- or Salonica-based stations.

In terms of programming, the regional/local stations generally imitate the national private stations, except that they do not have 18- or 24-hour programming and they cannot afford either to produce their own series or even run popular series, preferring instead movies. On the other hand, they cover regional/local news and some run current affairs programmes with interviews or round table discussions. In Greater Athens, one such station, Junior TV, specializes in children's programmes with some success, as it rates third in the 7–12 year old range, behind Mega and Antenna, while another channel, Jeronimo Groovy, is a musical channel, a kind of Greek MTV or MCM, but appears less successful than its sister radio station.

As regional television in Greece is recent, chaotic and broadly marginal, in a very centralized country, there have been no studies on it, no measure of its advertising expenditure, or any other information made available even by the stations themselves. There is one notable exception, which may be the only effort to make regional television respectable and viable: TV Net. It is a network of 15 regional stations throughout Greece, co-operating with 60 local radio stations, created in late 1993. The regional television stations cover 85 per cent of the state's territory and include four of the eight channels with significant ratings mentioned above (TV Macedonia, Delta TV, TRT, Crete TV). Their aim is co-production and common acquisition of Greek and foreign programmes; common attraction of advertisements; common representation of the channels towards the authorities (especially the licence granting ones), audience measurement companies, EU programme agencies, concert sponsoring, etc. The hope is that, by 1995, all network channels will have a common programme frame with network productions or distributions, local (opt-out) programmes, and re-transmission of a satellite programme to fill the low audience hours of the day (so that these channels can broadcast on a 24 hour basis) and that their audience share will reach 5 per cent which may make it the fifth, alternative channel (with the other four exclusively Athens-centred) and secure it an equal share of the advertising revenues, sufficient to help the co-operating stations make profit.

Conclusions and outlook for the future

Generally, Greek television has great potential, as it has accumulated nearly two thirds of the total advertising revenue. In the near future, the lead of the two private channels, Mega Channel – the uncontested leader since day one of private television until late 1993 when new channels took away from it more audience than from its immediate rival- and Antenna TV is not expected to be challenged, but their rivalry for first place will be fierce. If the state channels continue their decline, they will quickly find themselves out of the top five, as the private stations launched in 1993, Star Channel and Sky TV will easily better their audience;

in that case, the regional network TV Net has good hopes of making the top five, and so do other new channels. If, on the other hand, ERT awakens from hibernation, given its means and the safe revenue of the licence fee, one of its channels could easily secure more than 10 per cent of the total audience and the other remain in the top five: in that case, new private channels will have a difficult time securing satisfactory audiences, and so will the regional stations, especially if one of the three ERT channels takes a semi-regional structure. If, in the end, Greek regional television remains a marginalized phenomenon, it would only be considered 'normal' in a country that is and will remain highly centralized, not only administratively, but also politically, demographically, and media-wise.

References

Dimitras, P.E. (1991): *Political Background, Parties and Elections in Greece*. Athens: Lychnos (original in Greek).

Dimitras, P.E. (1993a): 'La fabrication du baklava, ou la pâtisserie electorale grècque', in *Espaces Temps*, 51–52, second quarter 1993.

Dimitras, P.E. (1993b): 'Specificities of Balkan Nationalisms and the Case of Macedonian Nationalism', paper presented at the International Conference on the Question of Nationalities and Minorities in Eastern and Central Europe, Budapest, December 1993.

Helsinki Watch (1990): *Destroying Ethnic Identity: The Turks of Greece*. New York.

Helsinki Watch (1992): *Greece: Improvement for Turkish Minorities*. New York.

Minority Rights Group International (1994): *The Southern Balkans*. London: 1994.

Siguan, M. (1990): *Les minorités linguistiques dans la Communauté Economique Européenne: Espagne, Portugal, Grèce*. Luxembourg: Office des Publications Officielles des Communautés Européennes.

7   Ireland: From nation building to economic priorities

Ellen Hazelkorn[1]

The general political framework, the nation and the regions

Historic origins

The island of Ireland is divided into two jurisdictions: Northern Ireland – with an industrial hub centred around Belfast – is part of the United Kingdom, while the Republic of Ireland – Eire, with a capital in Dublin – is an independent state established in 1922 after a war of independence from the British. The latter occupies 26 of the 32 counties into which the island had been divided administratively by the British. Throughout this study, Ireland refers to the entire island prior to 1922, and the Republic of Ireland subsequently.

Irish history, culture and society have been strongly influenced by several invasions. It is believed that the first people arrived from Scandinavia via Britain in 6000 BC. The Celts – around whose customs, skills and language, Gaelic Irish society evolved – came from Central Europe between 450 BC and 250 AD, followed by the Vikings in 795. In political and institutional terms, the Norman invasions of 1169 inaugurated the foundations of statehood by establishing the Lordship of Ireland in 1171, albeit the structures remained 'little more than nominal for several centuries' (Coakley and Gallagher, 1992: 1). In the sixteenth century, the Tudor dynasty subjugated and firmly stamped its authority over the entire island, promoting the Lord of Ireland to the status of King and establishing formal self-governing

1. Other contributors were Ité Ni Chionnaith, Brian O'Neill and Wolfgang Truetzschler.

but non-autonomous political structures. Despite years of resistance, Ireland was formally merged with Britain under the Act of Union in 1800 until independence for 26 of its 32 counties in 1922.

Religion, over-determined by opposing identities and political affiliations, has been integral to recent Irish history and resistance to British rule. But Ireland's internal political and economic structures have also been shaped by domestic political and class forces. While the majority of the island's population is Catholic, the majority in the northern six counties, which constitute Northern Ireland, is Protestant. The roots of nationalism and unionism, respectively, reside in the uneven development of the island. During the industrial revolution, manufacturing flourished in the north, commercially integrating it into the British economy while leading to its isolation from political developments in the agrarian south. By the mid-nineteenth century, Irish nationalism became virtually the sole expression of the Catholic tenant-farmer and burgeoning bourgeoisie of the south, while unionism was identified with the Protestant bourgeoisie and skilled working class of the north. Nationalist pressure for home-rule or limited independence outraged unionist opinion which successfully prevented the passage of three home rule bills and paved the way for the partition of the island in 1920. Political differences continue to be fuelled by economic, religious and social differences between the two states.

The Irish Free State (IFS) was established after a war of independence, 1921–1922. Its constitution reflected the influences of both English liberalism and Irish nationalism, albeit remaining firmly within the British commonwealth – a status which did not threaten key economic linkages between the two economies. Nevertheless, the 1920s–1930s was marked by deliberate and persistent undermining of the IFS's dominion status by the opposition, Fianna Fáil, whose political victory in 1932 heralded a new constitution, *Bunreacht na Eireann*, endorsing a catholic-nationalist concept of Irishness and laying claim to the counties of Northern Ireland. In 1948, the IFS was formally established as the Republic of Ireland. Correspondingly, Northern Ireland was governed in a sectarian manner by the dominant Unionist Party between 1921–1972; political challenge, initially from the civil rights movement, led to the collapse of self-government in 1972, the introduction of direct rule from London and the intensification of sectarian conflict between Protestant/unionists and Catholic/nationalists.

Cultural and linguistic dimension

Ireland is a peripheral society on the edge of Europe. It is a monolithic society with no entrenched minorities and largely untouched by the recent waves of migration. Its economy is comparatively overly-dependent on agriculture, despite state-inspired change since the 1960s. Famine and mass emigration have significantly impacted on an existing small population, revealing a continual decline since 1841; 6.5m lived in the area now designated as the Republic of Ireland compared to 3.5m in 1991. The overwhelming majority – 93 per cent – are Catholic, who, despite the constitution affirming Irish as the official language, speak English; while official statistics reveal a steady rise in the numbers who claim to be able to speak Irish (17.6 per cent in 1911 to 33 per cent in 1993), it has declined as a 'living language' and is primarily concentrated in the west of the country, in areas known as the Gaeltacht. Today over one-third of the population live in Dublin and its environs while only four out of ten are rural dwellers.

The level and extent of educational development throughout the nineteenth century was credited with both the spread of literacy, whereby over 80 per cent of the population were literate by 1910, and the spread of English. More recently, the (tele) communications revolution has been attributed or blamed, depending on one's perspective, with the profound change in public values, morals and the political agenda. Fifty-seven per cent of the adult population read at least one morning newspaper, while 80 per cent read a Sunday paper (1988–89); television viewing in Ireland is high – 79 per cent viewing per night – with British programming particularly popular for those in Dublin and in cabled urban centres (63 per cent of television sets are capable of receiving British including Northern Ireland programmes [1993]).

Internationalization of the economy marked by industrialization and entry into the EEC (now EU) in 1973 have led to a 'sustained and increasing internal assault' on the traditional values of women and the family, religion, sexual conservatism, and 'rural fundamentalism'.[2] Affiliation to traditional nationalist objectives as expressed in a desire for a 'united Ireland' have also weakened. Feminism, in place of historically weak support for a 'liberal-progressive' social and political agenda, has provided the most sustained and comprehensive challenge to traditional values and in support of personal rights. The extent of social fragmentation has signalled a profound transition in the political composition of the state, from one dominated by a traditional, agricultural and nationalist petit-bourgeoisie to one dominated by a modern, commercial and professional Europeanized bourgeoisie.

Politics and administration

The Irish political and administrative system evolved from structures established or copied from the British. The constitution of the 'revolutionary' First Dáil or parliament (1919), written and convened in semi-secrecy, was modelled upon the British-style cabinet government, undergoing little change subsequently. The *Irish Free State Constitution* (1922), obliged by the terms of the treaty with Britain to ensure the primacy of the Monarchy, proffered some populist initiatives but these were removed by a succession of amendments. The subsequent *Bunreacht na Eireann* (1937) reaffirmed a strong cabinet government under a Taoiseach (prime minister). In reality, the Oireachtas (parliament), which is divided into two houses, the Dáil (166 members) and the Seanad (60 members), plays a comparatively minor and passive role, with the latter weaker again. The government dominates all aspects of policy making, supported by a tightly disciplined political party system. The Oireachtas does not govern; rather, government exercises power through it. Power is centralized rather than diffused. Local authorities, organized along a county basis, operate on the prerogative of the national parliament and under the tight control of the Minister for the Environment.

Compared with political parties elsewhere in Europe, the differences between Irish political

2. Desmond Fennell, quoted in *The Irish Times*, 6 February 1967; Commins, 1986: 52.

parties is not always clear. In addition, the politicization of the working class, as a by-product of industrialization, has been particularly weak, despite the Irish Labour Party being the oldest political party in the state. Thus, disagreements over the terms of the treaty with Britain, resulting in a civil war between 1922–23, rather than ideological divergence, have often been credited with the formation of Fianna Fáil (FF) and Fine Gael (FG). A closer examination of the debates of the 1920s, however, would reveal divergent socio-economic objectives and class bases.

Political power in Ireland has been dominated by Fianna Fáil, who constructed its hegemony on an alliance of petit-bourgeois economic nationalism and popular social reform. Sustaining an image of itself as classless, it has successfully appealed to the Irish nation, urban and rural, above class conflict. Politics came to be perceived as a contest between Fianna Fáil and the rest; the Irish nation and the British; Catholicism and socialism. Since coming to power in 1932, it has dominated government whether in or out of office. Fiscal, political and social crisis, and the weakening of nationalist objectives have contributed to the decomposition of Fianna Fáil. Thus, since 1987, it has retained power only as the major partner in a coalition.

Today, the Irish political landscape is complex and fragmented. Predictions that modern-ization and European integration would prompt political realignment, producing a clear left-right divide have proved premature. Instead, the 1992 election, which witnessed the coming-of-age of the Labour Party and its formation of a 'partnership government' with Fianna Fáil, portrayed a growing convergence on the political centre. In the wake of the sudden collapse of that government in November 1994 and negotiations for another, the policy demarcations between Labour, Fianna Fáil and Fine Gael have slowly dissolved. Prior to this, Labour had only considered itself part of an anti-Fianna Fáil alliance. Given this development and the likelihood that Ireland will follow the European pattern of coalitions, there are a myriad of government possibilities. In this scenario, there seems little reason why the centre parties should not be able to forge deeper and longer-term alliances in the future. In turn, this strengthening of the centre reopens possibilities for both the Progressive Democrats and the Democratic Left, the radical right and radical left, respectively.[3]

Socio-economic framework

Irish economic development has broadly seen three contradictory strategy positions adopted since independence in 1922.[4] In the 1920s, the Cumann na Gaedheal government (the predecessor of Fine Gael), representing primarily a pre-industrial exporting and farming elite, chose to retain an orthodox fiscal approach to economic growth, relying on 'access to capital', reducing costs, and maintaining wealth through continued agricultural trade with Britain, without pursuing Ireland's comparative advantage. Political independence with dominion status formally preserved these links.

In 1932, Fianna Fáil's ascendancy, under the tutelage of Eamonn de Valera, moulded a consensus of social and political forces around a matrix of economic, ideological and cultural

3. For an update on the Irish political situation, see Hazelkorn and Patterson, 1994 and Hazelkorn, 1994.

4. For a fuller discussion of these issues, see Bew, Hazelkorn and Patterson, 1989.

nationalism, with heavy reliance on protectionism, exclusion of foreign capital, substantial subsidies to manufacturing, import substitution, and tillage farming. This provoked a limited improvement in the volume of industrial production and employment. An economic war with Britain, 1932–1938, and the international depression impacted negatively on economic growth: export volumes, prices and markets collapsed, and average earnings in 1937 were 9 per cent below the 1931 level. Eighteen thousand people emigrated annually between 1936 and 1946, rising to 42,000 per annum between 1956 and 1961.

In the aftermath of the UK post-war consensus, Seán Lemass promoted Keynesianism. The 'Programme for Economic Expansion' (1958) was highly interventionist, putting liberalization of trade, encouragements to foreign capital, and state subsidization of capital-intensive export-oriented production at the heart of industrial policy. Domestic conditions improved so significantly that Ireland was transformed within two decades from a traditional agricultural society with a class structure based on family property to an urban industrial society with a class structure based on skill and educational opportunity. Population decline registered over the previous 100 years was reversed, and the early 1970s recorded a slight net immigration.

While these initiatives enabled Ireland to take advantage of the long-wave of economic expansion experienced elsewhere – to essentially 'free ride' – they proved inadequate for resolving fundamental problems: little indigenous manufacturing and virtually no commercial exploitation of national resources; small-scale and inefficient agriculture; poor dispersal of resources; and weak infrastructure. High productivity growth was unable to absorb labour surplus and raise living standards. In these respects, the 'boom' was both short-lived and superficial.

Throughout the 1980s, there was a noticeable shift towards new technological sectors, expanding Ireland's attractiveness to telecommunications and financial investors. High-technology export-oriented foreign-owned manufacturing accounted for 34 per cent of manufacturing employment, over half of industrial production and 80 per cent of non-food manufactured exports. This performance explains a 12.9 per cent rise in the value of exports in 1992, putting Ireland way above the EC average balance of payments surplus as a percentage of GNP of –1 per cent. But this sector's strong performance has given a 'fundamentally wrong account of economic health' (Taylor, 1993).

There are glaring contradictions between booming financial indicators and the real economy. Irish growth rates have traditionally been well below those of other Euro-late starters. The unemployment rate has never fallen below 5 per cent even when rates elsewhere in Europe have been 2 per cent or less (Kennedy, 1992: 9 and Mjoset, 1992: 6). By 1994, official Irish growth rates had accelerated to 4.8 per cent per annum, although there is a dispute as to whether the use of GDP rather than GNP overstates this growth due to the inclusion of the multinational sector. Commentators suggest that a combination of extraordinary growth rates, budgetary controls – the current budget deficit is well within the Maastricht Treaty's criterion of 3 per cent – the Northern Ireland peace 'dividend', and declining birth rates proffers a picture of an 'economy which is catching up with its richer brethren' (Huhne, 1994). These figures, however, ignore the fact that the very rapid pace of officially recorded growth is not mirrored in rising living standards (Murphy, 1994). Income per capita is 40 per cent below the EC average and unemployment is the second worst in the OECD. In 1990, the long-term unemployed comprised 67.2 per cent of the total out of work while employment levels were lower than those of 1926. Indeed, the proportion of the population actually employed fell by 26 per cent between 1926–1986, from 41.4 per cent to 30.5 per cent .

This inequality of growth is reflected in the class nature of Irish emigration, which peaked at 46,000 per annum in 1988–89.[5] Since 1981, the collapse in traditional manufacturing employment has disproportionately affected males, in contrast to female labour which has risen sharply in expanding foreign and service sector employment. Over the decade, 25 per cent of graduates left to work in the core economies of the EC and the US. This pattern is likely to persist as the pace of economic growth will be too slack to deal with the numbers looking for work; with 28 per cent of its population under 15 years, Ireland has the youngest western European population with the exception of Turkey. Today, approximately one-third of the population survives solely on state subsidy (Hazelkorn, 1992).

In brief, the abandonment of realizing a national bourgeoisie was replaced in the late 1950s by a strategy aimed at 'importing innovation' (Wickham, 1993) or 'economic development, off-the-peg' (O'Toole, 1993). Coinciding with US domination of the global economy, it sought to encourage forward linkages with the domestic economy through massive state transfers made possible by access to unlimited external (EC) funds. The latter provided sufficient (temporary) shelter for the government against rising unemployment enabling it to respond with public sector expansion and underwriting agriculture. But, the strategy significantly underestimated the extent of global and economic restructuring. By the mid-1980s, Ireland could no longer depend on the migration of (US) capital as a source of employment. Influenced by neo-liberal trends, the strategy shifted to making Ireland competitively attractive to foreign capital by raising productivity and lowering wages. In the context of global-restructuring and the emergence of a new international division of labour (NIDL), Ireland is in danger of becoming a labour-intensive, low-cost, low-wage production centre. The scramble for EC funds is public affirmation of Ireland's failure to succeed as an self-reliant economic entity and frank espousal of the economics of dependency.

At best, the IR£6billion economic transfers via EC structural and cohesion funds (1994–1999) offer the possibility of providing the wherewithal for Ireland to compete. But, the rationale of the single market and the EMU is to transform hitherto autonomous and unequal European economies into a single global player by breaking down barriers to labour and capital mobility. Expenditure on infrastructure and education/training is beneficial to the periphery but it also allows the core to operate more profitably. The Irish Economic and Social Research Institute estimated that structural funds would only enable Ireland to grow apace with its European neighbours, in other words, to retain Ireland's position near the bottom. Essentially, 'infrastructural expenditures *peripheralize* regions in the world-system, rather than decreasing their peripherality' and dependency (O'Hearn, 1993: 169–197).

---

5. See information on the sectorial distribution of employment in Ireland in O'Malley, 1989: 91; "Labour Force Survey', *The Irish Times*, 3.11.91.

Legal framework for television

General model of television

Although Ireland has followed its European partners in attempting to establish a dual system of private and public television services by making legal provisions for private (terrestrial) commercial television (Brants and Siune, 1992), the only television station operating at the end of 1994 is the public service broadcaster RTE (Radio Teilifís Eireann). RTE provides Ireland with two national television channels, RTE 1 and Network 2. There is no regional or local television in Ireland, apart from the occasional campus television of a Dublin university and the local cable television programmes run by the cable TV company in Cork, Ireland's second largest city.[6]

Regarding Irish television, a number of historical trends can be highlighted. As the country is too small and its people too poor to be able to finance a broadcasting service through licence fees alone, Irish broadcasting has since its inception relied both on advertising revenues and licence fees to fund its public service broadcasting service (see Table 1). Secondly, Ireland's geographical location, in particular its proximity to the UK, has been and is of major influence in the development of Irish broadcasting.

Table 1. RTE Income – 12 months ended 31 December 1991 (IR£'000s)

	IR£'000s	%
Licence Fees	48,919	41.3
Advertising: Television and Radio	55,848	47.0
RTE Commercial Enterprises	9,012	7.6
Other Broadcasting Income	3,856	3.2
Long Wave Radio	1,102	0.9
Total	118,737	100.0

Source: *RTE Annual Report*, 1991.

Concerning the development of Irish television, RTE has had to face strong competition from British television since the inception of its television operation. Prior to the establishment of RTE television, approximately 30 per cent of all television households could receive British television off-air. In 1993 around 66 per cent of all television homes are in 'multi channel' areas, i.e. ones which can receive British television either off-air or via cable. The founding of a second RTE television channel 'Network 2' in 1978 was a direct result of demands by 'single channel' areas to equalize the television services being offered in different parts of the country. This decision did not fully satisfy these demands, which were increasingly met over a ten-year period by illegal 'deflector' systems capable of receiving British television. Finally, the Government in 1989 awarded twenty-nine licences to install and operate a network of multipoint microwave (television retransmissions) distribution systems (MMDS) in those parts of the country in which viewers are currently not able to receive cable television.

6. During 1994, the Minister for Communications permitted eighteen limited experiments in cable community television.

Cable TV in Ireland is provided by 43 cable TV operators, the biggest of which is the firm Cablelink with over 80 per cent of all cable TV subscribers. (Telecom Eireann owns sixty per cent of the shares in Cablelink, the remaining forty per cent are owned by RTE.) Cable TV in Ireland began in the latter half of the 1970s as a way of relaying British (and Irish) television signals available 'off-air' – it was not the result of any government policy designed to encourage the 'cabling' of the country.

Licences for MMDS were awarded by the Minister for Communications in October 1989 in accordance with the 'MMDS Frequency Plan' drawn up by the Department of Communications. The plan divides the state into 29 'cells' for purposes of MMDS, and the exclusive licences awarded relate to the retransmissions of television services within these cells. There are seven companies or 'MMDS franchises' each of which has been awarded exclusive licences for MMDS in a number of these cells.

Around two thirds of the population live in 'multi-channel' areas, and a third of the television households have cable television. The latter are able to receive the Irish and British national television programmes as well as between six and ten (mainly) English-language satellite television programmes. Pay TV may be provided on cable TV and to date several cable operators relay the two British movie channels to its subscribers. A number of households can also subscribe to MMDS, but as this system has only been implemented partially, the number of MMDS subscribers is less than 2–4 per cent of TV households. Annual subscription fees for cable TV/MMDS amount to just under.

Public vs. private broadcasting

The size of the advertising market in Ireland, which is relatively small in comparison to other European countries, and the fact that all media in Ireland, including public television, are commercial in the sense that they all rely on advertising revenue (see Table 2), has to date prevented the operation of a private commercial television service. A licence for such a national television service was awarded in 1989 to an Irish consortium but the licence was revoked in 1991 due to the inability of the consortium to come up with the necessary finance for the venture. An October 1993 Supreme Court decision overturned the IRTC's decision thereby reopening speculation of a TV3 venture.

Table 2. Advertising expenditure 1992 (IR£ million)

Media groups	IR£m
National Press	100.2
Regional Press	7.7
Consumer Press	11.0
RTE TV	64.7
RTE Radio	14.2
Independent Radio	7.7
Outdoor	14.0*
Total	219.5

*Estimated;
Source: *Advertising Statistics Ireland 1993.*

Table 3. Market shares of television channels in multichannel homes in Ireland (1992)

Channel	Market share
RTE 1 and Network 2	45.3
BBC 1 and BBC 2	22.5
UTV (ITV)[1] / Channel 4	20.3
Satellite Channels	11.9

[1] The UK channel, ITV (Independent Television) is broadcast via Northern Ireland as UTV (Ulster Television); BBC has regional programming emanating from Northern Ireland and is known as BBC NI; Source: AGB TAM, 1993

RTE has, therefore, no indigenous competitor. RTE's competitors are the British television channels and the various satellite TV services which have become increasingly available to viewers in Ireland. RTE's scheduling of programmes is noteworthy in that RTE has always operated in a highly competitive environment and is therefore very skilled in arranging programmes in such a way that its audiences are higher than those of its foreign competitors (see Table 3).

Basic legislation

According to current Irish media law, there are three main Acts regulating Irish television broadcasting: the Broadcasting Authority Acts 1960–1993, which regulate the public broadcaster RTE; the Radio and Television Act 1988, which contains the regulations applicable to private commercial broadcasting; and the Broadcasting Act 1990, which, inter alia, facilitates the implementation of the EC Directive on Television Broadcasting.

Additional 'regulations' for the private (radio) broadcasters are contained in the broadcasting contracts signed between individual stations and the Independent Radio and Television Commission (IRTC) , the government-appointed regulatory body for private broadcasters.

Cable Television is governed by the Wireless Telegraphy (Wired Broadcast Relay Licence) Regulations 1974, as amended in 1988; the Multipoint Microwave Distribution System (MMDS), is subject to the Wireless Telegraphy (Television Programme Retransmissions) Regulations 1989. Apart from these specific Acts and Regulations, other statutes such as Contempt of Court, Censorship, Defamation, Copyright, Official Secrets Act, Public Order, etc. also apply to broadcasting.[7]

The three Acts mentioned above contain the fairly detailed and explicit regulations for private and public broadcasters. Thus programmes broadcast are subject to impartiality, fairness and objectivity clauses. Programmes must not offend against good taste and decency; they must not incite to crime or undermine the authority of the state. The laws also enable censorship by the government in relation to 'The Troubles' in Northern Ireland: the Minister for Communications may direct broadcasters to refrain from broadcasting interviews or reports of interviews with spokespersons of prohibited organizations, such as the IRA, under Section 31 of the Broadcasting Act, 1960 and 1976. This ban was annually renewed from 1978–1994,

7. See Truetzschler, 1991b for a more detailed discussion of Irish Media Law.

and there was only token public or indeed broadcasting protest at this gross interference in broadcasting by the State although a recent report by the UN's Human Rights Committee obliged its replacement. In 1993, the Supreme Court determined that RTE's implementation of the above Ministerial Directive had been too rigidly applied. In January 1994, against the background of the British-Irish *Joint Declaration for Peace and Reconciliation in Northern Ireland* and in line with the Minister's own criticisms of the ban, the cabinet agreed to allow Section 31 to lapse. In its place, RTE and the IRTC introduced new guidelines under Section 18, and with due regard to Section 9 (1) (a) and (b), of the same legislation to curb the broadcasting of any material deleterious to the 'authority of the State'.[8]

In its programming, the public broadcaster and any future private television service has the duty to be responsive to the interests and culture of the whole community, be mindful of the need for peace within the whole island of Ireland. It must have special regard for the Irish language and for promoting understanding of other countries, especially those in the EC. This duty does not apply to the private radio broadcasting services; instead private radio is subject to the requirement to ensure that 20 per cent of transmission time consists of news and current affairs.

The most recently enacted piece of legislation, the Broadcasting Authority (Amendment) Act 1993 removes the limit ('cap') on advertising revenue that RTE may earn as contained in the Broadcasting Act 1990. The cap was introduced in order to divert advertising revenue away from the public service broadcaster in order to assist the private radio broadcasters and the private television service planned at the time. Not only was this aim not achieved but it lead to severe cutbacks in the operation of RTE. It is mainly for this reason that the 1993 Act was passed by parliament.

The 1993 Act restores the situation with regard to broadcast advertisements on RTE that obtained prior to the enactment of the Broadcasting Act 1990, i.e. that the total daily times and the maximum time in any one hour for broadcast advertisements fixed by the RTE Authority shall be subject to the approval of the Minister. This will probably mean that RTE will once again devote 10 per cent of daily programming time to advertising.

However, the Act also forces RTE to make specific amounts of money available in each financial year for programmes commissioned from the independent television sector. The amounts of money to be made available annually range from IR£ 5 million in 1994 to 20 per cent of television programme expenditure or IR£ 12.5 million (whichever is greater) in 1999. Independent television producers are very clearly defined in the Bill, thereby ensuring that RTE or any other existing broadcaster is prevented from allocating the money to any subsidiary company.

Ireland and Europe

National broadcasting policy is fairly consistent with European tendencies and generally there is much emphasis on the economic and financial benefits of EC membership for Ireland.

8. See Broadcasting Authority Acts, 1960–1993, Section 18(1) Guidelines (20 January 1994) Dublin: RTE, and Interim Guidelines for IRTC Sound Broadcasting Service (20 January 1994) Dublin: IRTC. For further discussion of these issues, see Hazelkorn and Smyth, 1993.

As was mentioned above, the licensing of private broadcasting operations and the regulation of broadcasting in Ireland reflect current European trends, such as abolition of state monopolies, privatization of state enterprises, and commercialization of broadcasting. In fact it can be argued that Ireland has simply copied its European partners and has privatized the airwaves, without developing a specifically thought-out policy appropriate to a small state like Ireland. Concerning the EC Directive on Television Broadcasting and the Council of Europe Convention on Transfrontier Television, existing Irish media law is broadly in line with these. Furthermore, RTE programming is in accordance with the quotas of made-in-Europe non-news programmes and of independent productions.

Teilifís na Gaeilge

Political background

The announcement by the government on 23 November 1993 that it had finally decided to establish Teilifís na Gaeilge -an Irish language television channel- was the most important step taken by any Irish government in decades for the maintenance and development of the Irish language. A unanimous cabinet decision, the proposal had already formed part of the Fianna Fáil and Labour *Programme for a Partnership Government*, 1992. That programme included a section entitled 'Fostering our Language, Culture and Heritage' which stated i) that it was essential to establish a television service in Irish for Irish speakers and the people of the Gaeltacht and ii) that the government was committed to the establishment of such a service as a third channel with limited broadcasting hours.

The decision followed a long and arduous campaign spearheaded by the main Irish language, voluntary organization, Conradh na Gaeilge (the Gaelic League), and an Feachtas Náisiúnta Teilifíse (the national television campaign). Since the establishment of RTE in 1960, Irish speakers had been dissatisfied with the amount and scheduling of Irish language programmes broadcast by the national station. Over the years, the percentage of time given to Irish language programming seldom reached more than 3 per cent, ranging between 5 per cent and 0.5 per cent, with the lowest occurrence during the summer. Programming varied between two and five hours per week, with a low of thirty-five minutes per week (composed of seven five-minute news bulletins) during the summer and about five hours per week during the autumn/winter schedule (see Table 4).

A campaign since the early 1970s called for an increase in Irish language television programmes, highlighting the need for children's and young peoples programming. This took the form of meetings with senior management in RTE, submissions to relevant broadcasting committees, petitions, public meetings, pickets and protests, occupations of RTE offices and studios, mounting the RTE mast, refusal to pay television licences and court cases arising therefrom. Between 1977–1993, fifteen people were jailed for refusing the buy a television licence as a protest against the lack of Irish language television programmes.

Table 4. Irish as a proportion of total output, 1963–1993

	Total output	Irish output	%
1963	43.5 hours	1.85 hours	4.2
1968	51.5 hours	3.26 hours	6.3
1973	52.3 hours	2.8 hours	5.2
1978	72.7 hours	4.2 hours	5.8
1983	109.9 hours	3.4 hours	3.1
1988	126.7 hours	3.7 hours	2.9
1993*	167.3 hours	4.5 hours	2.7

*Figures for 1993 account for January-July only;
Source: Quill, 1993.
N.B. These figures overestimate the amount of Irish language programming because of the inclusion of bilingual programmes, whose content is predominately in English (ed.).

Statutory obligations

As the national broadcaster, RTE has statutory obligations to promote the Irish language in its programming. The reference to the Irish language in the Broadcasting Authority Act, 1960, is not, however, specific enough to ensure any minimum amount of programming. Moreover, the stipulation within the 1960 legislation was watered down in the Broadcasting Authority (Amendment) Act, 1976, as indicated below.

> Broadcasting Authority Act, 1960 17. In performing its functions, the Authority shall bear constantly in mind the national aims of restoring the Irish language and preserving and developing the national culture and shall endeavour to promote the attainment of those aims.

> Broadcasting Authority (Amendment) Act, 1976 13. The Principal Act is hereby amended by the substitution of the following section for section 17: '... In performing its functions the Authority shall in its programming:
> (a) be responsive to the interests and concerns of the whole community, be mindful of the need for understanding and peace within the whole island of Ireland, ensure that the programmes reflect the varied elements which make up the culture of the people of the whole island of Ireland, and *have special regard* for the elements which distinguish that culture and in particular *for the Irish language* ... [emphasis added].

As a consequence, the special section on the Irish language in the initial legislation was subsumed into a general section. There is no longer any reference to 'the national aim of restoring the Irish language' or RTE's 'endeavour to promote the attainment of that aim'. All that remains is the necessity to 'have special regard for the Irish language', but neither 'bearing constantly in mind' nor having 'special regard for' guarantee a minimum number of programmes. The Irish language is given special recognition in *Bunreacht na Eireann* (the constitution) which states in Article 8.1 that 'The Irish language as the national language is the first official language' and Article 1 that 'The Irish national affirms its ... right ... to develop its life, political, economic and cultural in accordance with its own genius and traditions'. Campaigners have claimed that it is impossible for Irish speakers to fully develop their cultural lives without the support of an adequate television service in Irish, and that its absence amounted to a denial of both cultural and linguistic rights, and civil and constitutional rights.

Policy choices and consensus

The campaign for Irish language broadcasting has centred around two sets of conflicting demands: more programming on RTE vs. a separate channel, and a national *vs.* a local channel. Throughout the 1970s, attention focused on providing more Irish language programmes on RTE. In 1980, campaigners shifted to favour a separate, independent Irish language television channel while maintaining the short term aim of at least one adult and one children's Irish programme per night on RTE. The former proposal was initially seen as radical but was significantly strengthened by the establishment of S4C in Wales in 1980, and throughout the decade by television channels in Basque, Catalan, Galician in Spain and Faroese in Denmark.

A parallel campaign emerged in the Connemara Gaeltacht[9] in the mid-1980s. Meitheal Oibre Theilifís na Gaeltachta opposed a national service and demanded a local service benefiting the needs of people in the area. They claimed the service would cost only IR£ 0.5 million and that, if successful, other such services could be established in other Gaeltacht areas. To prove the point, a pirate television station broadcast over a 15 mile radius for a weekend in Connemara in 1987 at a cost of IR£ 4,000. Proposals for such a service albeit covering the entire Gaeltacht area and extended nation-wide as per Raidió na Gaeltachta (state Irish language radio) were formulated.

In 1988, Udarás na Gaeltachta (the Gaeltacht Authority), with government sanction, commissioned the management consultancy firm, Stokes Kennedy Crowley (SKC), to undertake a feasibility study on the establishment of an Irish language/Gaeltacht television service broadcasting nation-wide. In March 1992, Márie Geoghean Quinn was appointed Minister for Communications; she appointed a special advisor on Irish language broadcasting. Specific proposals had been prepared for presentation to government prior to the unexpected general election in November 1992. The new Minister for Arts, Culture and the Gaeltacht with responsibility for broadcasting policy, Michael D. Higgins, a long-time supporter of an Irish language television station and in whose constituency the Connemara Gaeltacht lay, put his proposals to cabinet. A formal announcement to establish Teilifís na Gaeilge was made in November 1993.

Launching in 1996?

Current government proposals expect that Teilifís na Gaeilge will begin broadcasting nation-wide, including Northern Ireland, for three hours per day in April 1996. Its headquarters will be in the Connemara Gaeltacht. One hour of programming per day will be provided free-of-charge by RTE as part of its public service remit. Most of the remaining programmes will be commissioned from independent producers or bought in and dubbed (mainly from

9. A Gaeltacht area is an officially recognized geographical area where Irish is the community language. These areas exist in counties mostly along the west coast of Ireland; the Connemara Gaeltacht is located in counties Galway and Mayo.

languages other than English, and from particularly less used languages), while a small number of programmes will be made by Teilifís na Gaeilge itself. A broad range of programming is intended with emphasis on material coming from different areas of the country. At least one of the three hours will be set aside specifically for children's programming. The concept is a national service, broadcasting to a national audience but with its headquarters in the Gaeltacht.

The independent sector in the Gaeltacht is mainly a fledgeling sector. Presently about twenty independent production companies are registered with Udarás na Gaeltachta and/or Réalt (the umbrella body for independent production companies in the Gaeltacht). The majority of these are about three years old, with only a few operating for more than five years. Most have little experience of producing broadcast material, working only on the RTE series Teilifís Pobail (Community Television) in summer 1993, for which RTE/Udarás na Gaeltachta had commissioned independent companies to make either one programme or a short series of programmes. In contrast, Cinegael has been successfully operating since 1973, while Telegael, established in 1988 by Udarás na Gaeltachta and RTE, has been responsible for dubbing many children's cartoons and animation programmes bought from the Welsh S4C and other television channels.

The start-up costs for Teilifís na Gaeilge are designated to come from advertising revenue accumulated by RTE due to restrictions imposed upon it in the Broadcasting Act 1990; these funds amount to IR£ 17.35 m. The running-costs are estimated at IR£ 15–20million per year, with money expected to come from:

(a) Government expenditure;

(b) National lottery: only 4 per cent of lottery funding is spent on the Irish language at present although it was originally mentioned as one of the main sector that would benefit;

(c) EC Funding: through a combination of structural, lesser used languages or media funds;

(d) Other: including a possible rise in the television licence.

Compared with spending on the Welsh S4C channel, which has an annual budget of Stg£60 million for 30 hours programming per week of which 10 hours are provided free by BBC as part of its public service commitment, the proposed Irish expenditure is quite low.

Since 1989, IR£ 1.6 million has been spent by Udarás na Gaeltachta on employment, training and equipment grants to the independent sector which employs only fifty people at present. In preparation for Teilifís na Gaeilge, which may create an additional 250 jobs, IR£670,000 has been promised for training. By late 1994, £3 million had been allocated by the government; £1 million of that was released for current expenditure on Teilifís na Gaeilge. A staff of six had been appointed, and planning and commissioning commenced. However, Comhairle Theilifís na Gaeilge, the committee appointed by RTE and the government to oversee the establishment of the station, argues that £12 million is required.

Audience

Various statistical data is available on the number of Irish speakers. The 1986 Census of Population reveals that over one million people or approximately 30 per cent of the population speak Irish in the Republic of Ireland, with the highest concentration, 77 per cent, in Gaeltacht areas. These figures are sometimes questioned given the subjective nature of census information although they were supported by reports published by the Committee on Irish Language Attitudes Research (CLAR) 1973 , the Institiúid Teangeolaíochta Eireann (ITE) 1983 and 1993, and MRBI 1985.

The 1993 report showed that a high proportion of the national population has some speaking or reading ability:

(i)   2 per cent native speaker ability (approximately 70,000 people);

(ii) 9 per cent capable of most conversation (approximately 315,000 people);

(iii) 22 per cent capable of some conversation (approximately 770,000 people).

These figures have tended to remain static over the entire period of the surveys, with those claiming the highest level of fluency or competence in Gaeltacht areas.

How do these figures translate into a potential audience for Irish language television? Little research has been conducted on this issue except by Irish language organizations which aggregate Irish speakers in the Republic with the 142,000 Irish speakers denoted by the 1991 Census in Northern Ireland. BBC Northern Ireland devoted only three hours of broadcasting time during 1991; this figure increased by a half-hour in 1992 and extended to six hours in 1993. According to the above figures, the potential audience for Teilifís na Gaeilge could be as high as 0.5 million people. Among those capable of some Irish conversation, there is a further potential audience for language teaching programmes, programmes in simple Irish or bilingual programmes. These people could be catered for in special programmes on Teilifís na Gaeilge or on RTE.[10]

Table 5. Audiences for Irish on television and radio

Do You: (Daily, Weekly, Less Often)	1973 %	1983 %	1993 %
Watch programmes in Irish on TV?	51	72	40
Listen to Raidió na Gaeltachta?	n.a.	15	15
Listen to other radio programmes in Irish?	33	23	16

Source: O Riagáin and O Gliasáin, 1993: 13.

The 1983 ITE report revealed that 72 per cent of the population view Irish language programmes at least occasionally; by 1993, this figure had declined sharply to 40 per cent although the national audience for Raidió na Gaeltachta had remained steady (see Table 5).

---

10. A survey carried out by Bord na Gaeile in May-June 1994 indicates that 46 per cent of respondents were in favour of Teilifís na Gaeilge, an increase from 40 per cent six months earlier. See Uinsionn Mac Dubhghaill, 'Survey finds 46% favours Teilifís na Gaeilge', *The Irish Times*, 6 December 1994.

O Riagáin and O Gliasáin suggest that there may be a relationship between the hiatus of viewership and the availability of Irish language programming on television and radio; in 1983 RTE 1 carried a number of Irish language or bilingual programmes which were fairly popular with viewers in contrast to 1993 when such programmes have been relegated to the less popular Network 2.[11]

Although viewership for Irish language programmes varies depending on time of day, whether broadcast on RTE 1 or Network 2 or the available competition, patterns do emerge:

> *Nuacht/Cúrsaí* (news and current affairs/arts/magazine programme broadcast five nights per week) has a regular audience of 100,000 occasionally peaking at 150,000;

> Children's Cartoons at 3:30pm every weekday have a regular audience of 130,000;

> Young People's Programmes, e.g. *Eureka* (quiz programme for 10–12 year old) and *Jabas* (young people's soap opera translated from Welsh) have a regular viewership of 200,000;

> *Scaoil Amach an Bobailín* (aimed at older teenagers) had a regular viewership of 350,000, peaking at 500,000;

> *Ros na Rún* (six-part pilot Irish soap-opera for adults and older teenagers) maintained a regular 400,000 viewers.

These figures indicate a high core audience for Irish language programmes, particularly those aimed at children and young people. These audience figures should, however, be seen in the context of competition from multi-channel television, and the fact that Irish speakers will not watch Irish language programmes simply because they are in Irish.

The experience of RTE

Ireland's state-sponsored, public broadcasting organization, Radio Teilifís Eireann (RTE), was established in 1960 with the Broadcasting Authority Act. RTE since that time has enjoyed a monopoly in the provision of television. In 1978, a second RTE television channel was established. Known first as RTE2, and now as Network 2, its purpose was to complement the existing single channel service and to strengthen home-produced television against the competition from British channels available in many parts of the country.

Placed in what has been described as the most competitive broadcasting environment in Europe, RTE has faced increased pressure since 1989 with the deregulation of radio broadcasting. While RTE continues to enjoy a monopoly in television broadcasting, increased competition for advertising revenue as well as government measures to curtail the quantity of advertising that RTE can carry has placed its dominant position in the market place under threat. Local radio now successfully competes against RTE's radio service where many stations outperform the national broadcaster at peak times. On a national level,

11. O Riagáin and O Gliasáin, 1993: 12–13.

however, RTE appears to have seen off the challenge to its position with the collapse of private national radio franchise, Century Radio, in 1991, the revision of plans for a third privately-owned television channel, TV3 , and the removal of the 'cap' or ceiling on RTE advertising revenue.

A restructuring of RTE's organization since 1985 has seen a general improvement in its financial affairs, the introduction of new technology, significant reductions in staff, increases in home production as well as diversification into ancillary services and activities. In the five year period between 1985 and 1990, there was a 24 per cent increase in total television hours and a 37 per cent increase in television home production. RTE during this same period recorded a 17 per cent increase in television multi-channel market share.

Production and programming

RTE's television programming mix comprises a range of factual, entertainment and educational programmes typical of public service broadcasting organizations. Like most such organizations, RTE are committed to a policy of retaining popular support by a combination of high ratings entertainment programming, thereby ensuring its advertising revenue base, and a range of public service programming in such minority interest areas as Irish language programming, religious affairs, culture, the arts and educational programming. Given these requirements and limitations on its revenue, RTE has fulfilled this 'public service remit' well. Increased competition and costs of production do, however, pose threats to its continued ability to retain and extend quality broadcasting. One effect of these pressures is evident in the high proportion of studio-based discussion and talk-radio programming which passes as home-produced programming.

RTE has traditionally relied on a high proportion of imported programming in its schedule. This reliance has been gradually reduced in recent years from 65 per cent in 1984 to 53 per cent in 1990. RTE now aims to produce itself or to commission approximately 50 per cent of its programming requirements, as per instructions under the Broadcasting Authority (Amendment) Act 1990. Popular and often quite cheaply produced home programming has been RTE's main weapon to maintain its 48–50 per cent share of all peak time home viewing in multi-channel areas where it competes head on with British television – BBC, ITV and Channel 4 – as well as satellite channels available on cable.

Current scheduling policy exhibits a strong emphasis on news and current affairs programming, which consistently head the TAM (Television Audience Measurement) ratings list. Until the recent introduction of a syndicated news service for private radio, RTE was the only provider of broadcast news in the country. A major reorganization of current affairs programming was undertaken in 1992. The single flagship programme was replaced with a composite strand comprising individual investigative documentary, political analysis, panel discussion and business review programmes. Critics of this redesign argue that the new schedule represents a dilution of current affairs commentary given the significant increase in output with no corresponding increase in resources or staff. It is also seen as inflexible and unable to react in-depth and quickly enough to fast-breaking news stories. This might have been the objective as some argue that the changes were undertaken in response to political disapproval of current affairs commentary.

Drama production centres around the production of two soap operas: the weekly rural-based and long-running popular series and a more recent urban soap opera. *Glenroe*, the Sunday evening rural soap opera has consistently achieved a high audience rating of approximately 47 per cent. It follows in the tradition of a number of successful rural soaps produced by RTE since 1965 and features well known actors and writing talent. There has, however, been much criticism of the failure to encourage new talent in writing or acting or to innovate with new drama production. A number of controversial policies in drama have been pursued including a largely unsuccessful attempt at high profile co-productions with the intention of international distribution. The 1993 and 1994 schedules have attempted to redress this situation including specially commissioned scripts and a new sit-com series featuring prominent Irish comic acting talent.

Daytime programmes broadcast between 10am and 1pm were first introduced on RTE 1 in 1992. This strand which is independently commissioned includes phone-in and access programmes, and advice slots on domestic, legal and current affairs. RTE produces its own daytime programming for the afternoon schedule with a similar mix of talk and advice aimed at an older audience. The bulk of young people's programmes are broadcast on RTE's second channel, Network 2, relaunched and formatted as a 'life-style' channel in 1988.

Irish language programming has been controversial. Its marginalized location in the schedule and on the second channel has suggested a diminution in RTE's commitment to the language. It could be argued that it would be extremely difficult for RTE to provide the type of service demanded by some Irish language proponents. The demands placed upon it as the national broadcaster, with no complementary regional public or private stations, facing strong competition from UK stations, are particularly onerous. These difficulties concern i) RTE's need to attract adequate advertising revenue in order to remain financially solvent; ii) the needs of the majority English-speaking audience in an increasingly competitive market; iii) the scattered linguistic minority with widely varying competence in the language despite it being taught throughout the educational system; iv) the ideological shifts of State policy towards the language; and v) the conflicting demands of various components of the Irish language lobby (Quill, 1993: 46). Opposing demands and changing attitudes towards the Irish language and Irish language broadcasting resurfaced in response to government's decision to allocate funds to Teilifís na Gaeilge in 1993.

The flagship Irish language current affairs programme, *Cúrsaí*, is broadcast five nights a week. This, in addition to the nightly Irish language *Nuacht* or news programme, is the main adult-oriented output of RTE. Recent years have seen the introduction of a number of Irish language young people's programmes (a fuller discussion of the issues involved is found in Section 4 above).

Among RTE's most popular and long-running series are a range of chat show and light entertainment programmes. *The Late Late Show*, now in its 32nd year and presented by RTE's premier broadcaster, Gay Byrne, comprises a mix of serious discussion, music as well as personality and celebrity-oriented chat show items. RTE also produces a number of other shows in this genre. Considerable success has been enjoyed by a range of evening time factual magazine programmes introduced by RTE since 1990. Covering health, fashion, domestic and family issues, these programmes are relatively inexpensive to produce, maximizing the use of studio facilities as well as ENG facilities for features. Many of these programmes provide recurring and crucial anchor points in the schedule while continuing the trend to reduce reliance on acquired programming.

The audience

While the Republic of Ireland is a small state, the broadcasting environment is complex. RTE is available across the country and into Northern Ireland. Television signals from Britain which include the terrestrial channels BBC1, BBC2, ITV (UTV) and Channel 4, are available to 27 per cent of homes in the multichannel areas of the country by virtue of proximity to British transmitters, e.g. in border counties and along the eastern seaboard. In addition, the increase in cable penetration in urban centres in Ireland to 39 per cent of homes as well as sales of satellite dishes has made satellite programming more widely available. In summary, RTE has to compete with British channels or satellite channels in approximately 60 per cent of Irish homes and in this environment has succeeded in maintaining a total RTE audience share of 65 per cent (see Table 6).

Recent research on viewing patterns of Irish TV audiences confirms that like their counterparts in Britain, audiences in Ireland are largely unsegmented, in other words there is little discernible difference in the proportion of time spent watching different programme types between separate social class groupings (Harper, 1993). Young people (15–24) do spend a higher percentage of time (19.9 per cent) watching soaps and sit-coms while older people (55+) spend a higher proportion of time watching news (10.3 per cent).

The average level of programme loyalty among the Irish TV audience is 50 per cent with one half of the viewers of a programme tuning in again the following week. This is also

Table 6. Main channels available and share-viewing in Irish homes, 1991

Channels	Availability (%)	Viewing shares
RTE 1	100	
Network 2	99	65% total RTE
BBC1	64	
BBC 2	63	
ITV (UTV)	53	
Channel 4	53	29% total British
Sky One	34	
Sky News	31	
Super Channel	17	
MTV	13	
Children's Channel	17	6% total satellite

Source: Fahy, 1992.

similar to the British pattern. Significantly for RTE, home produced programmes do enjoy high levels of audience loyalty. *The Late Late Show*, for example, enjoys the highest loyalty factor of 67 per cent. *Kenny Live*, its Saturday chat show equivalent, also enjoys a very high loyalty figures of 60 per cent as does the popular rural soap series *Glenroe*. Weekday magazine programmes all have a 40 per cent loyalty. Frequently broadcast serials like *Coronation Street* (Network 2 and ITV) reach a wide audience in Ireland although few people watch all or nearly all the episodes.

Conclusions and outlook for the future

Looking ahead over the next few years, the most likely changes in the Irish broadcasting scene are the start-up of Teilifís na Gaeilge and the publication of a government green paper on broadcasting structures and issues.[12] Such a paper is anticipated to review all broadcasting legislation, including structures; the relationship between the three statutory bodies: the RTE Broadcasting Authority, the Independent Radio and Television Commission, and Teilifís na Gaelige, may be overdetermined by a new superior broadcasting authority. Other issues possibly under consideration include cabling with particular reference to programme content policy, independent commissioning with reference to RTE and the Irish Film Board, and the regulation of broadcasting transmission. Concern has also been expressed about the cultural implications of trans-frontier broadcasting and threats to RTE's public service remit.

RTE Television is in a fairly secure position under the present government. Although Irish law does enable the setting up of a private television channel, at the moment Ireland continues to be the only European country without domestic television competition. This situation may change because of on-going speculation about the launch of TV3 sometimes in late 1995 (Kenny, 1994 and White, 1994). Negative assessments of the viability of third-channel competition have been predicated upon the relatively small advertising market and audience available for such a channel. Therefore, the suggestion of privatizing Network 2 (and the second radio channel 2FM) and/or granting any potential private channel a slice of a considerably increased licence fee has been floated. Such moves are unlikely in the present political climate. RTE is, however, liable to face increasing competition from foreign TV channels considering the fact that most Irish cable operators are upgrading their systems to enable the relaying of up to 50 TV channels. This may in turn lead to an increase in the average viewing figure which currently stands at 186 minutes per day.

The planned launch of Teilifís na Gaeilge, now anticipated for Easter Sunday 1996 (RTE first broadcast on Easter Sunday 1971), has provoked as much controversy as the campaign for its establishment. The model for the station is Britain's Channel 4, with independent producers and TV companies being commissioned to make programmes. The station's ability to attract an audience will depend on broadcasting innovative, entertaining programm-

12. The timetable for the publication of this green paper is now scheduled for Spring 1995. The Minister announced on several occasions that a 'green' paper, a term used to describe a discussion document on proposed legislation, on broadcasting structures was being prepared and would be presented to cabinet by the end of 1994. For a statement outlining the then minister's, Michael D. Higgins', intentions, see M. Foley, 'Higgins prepares Green Paper on broadcasting', *The Irish Times*, 24 May 1994.

ing for a population with widely differing linguistic competency in Irish in the face of heavy competition from other channels. That funding for the station will be considerably less than anticipated does not augur well. Thus, there is increasing concern about its ability to survive without substantial and permanent state funding, a problem already signalled in the postponement of the station's first transmission form late 1995 until mid-1996.[13]

Both the Broadcasting Authority (Amendment) Act, 1993, and the establishment of Teilifís na Gaeilge will assist the development of the independent production sector. A recent study estimates that over 7,000 people are employed in the media sector with a net value of £155m (co-opers and Lybrand Corporate Finance, 1994 and O'Kane, 1994). Following an intensive period of financial restraint, job shedding and labour restructuring, aided by the introduction of new technology, RTE is being redirected towards commissioning and distributing rather than producing programmes. This trend while beneficial to the independent sector, many of whom previously worked in RTE, is strongly influenced by policies of commercialization, deregulation and restructuring of the public sector and raise questions about 'quality' 'public service' broadcasting, particularly as this criteria does not fall within the ambit of the IRTC. The fledgeling indigenous production sector is likely to face increased competition for a slice of available commissioning funds from other European producers, and from the United States in the aftermath of the GATT agreement.

There are no major changes to be expected in the area of new information and communication technologies. Judging by the trend over the last few years an increase in the ownership of broadcasting equipment such as VCRS and satellite dishes can be expected. Currently there are no plans concerning the introduction of high definition television (HDTV) —in fact RTE has publicly stated that it cannot afford the introduction of HDTV.

References

AGB TAM (1993): *A Report on Television Trends in Ireland 1990–1992*. Dublin: AGB TAM.

Bew, P., Hazelkorn, E. & Patterson, H. (1989): *The Dynamics of Irish Politics*. London: Lawrence and Wishart.

Brants, K. & Siune, K. (1992): 'Public Broadcasting in a State of Flux', in K. Siune and W. Truetzschler (eds.): *Dynamics of Media Politics*. London: Sage.

Campbell, J.J. (1961): *Television in Ireland*. Dublin: M.H. Gill & Son Ltd.

Clancy, P. *et al.*, eds. (1986): *Ireland: A Sociological Profile*. Dublin: Institute of Public Administration.

Coakley, J. & Gallagher, M. eds. (1992): *Politics in the Republic of Ireland*. Galway: PSAI Press.

Commins, P. (1986): 'Rural Social Change' in P. Clancy, *et al.*, eds., *Ireland: A Sociological Profile*. Dublin.

13. The uncertainty about the funding of Teilifís na Gaeilge signalled in the *Donegal Democrat*, 17 November 1994 and *The Irish Times*, 1 and 5 December 1994 appears to be over for the present. Capital funding of IR£16.1 million and an annual Exchequer subvention of £10m for running costs is to be allocated (*The Irish Times*, 27 January 1995). Nevertheless, this represents a scaled down version of the original plan which planned for 3 hours daily broadcasting at an estimated cost of £21m.

Coopers and Lybrand Corporate Finance (1994): *The Employment and Economic Significance of the Cultural Industries in Ireland.* Dublin: Temple Bar Properties.

Chubb, B. (1993): *The Government and Politics of Ireland*, 3rd ed. London: Longman Publishers.

Doolan, L., Dowling, J. & Quinn, B. (1969): *Sit Down and Be Counted.* Dublin: Wellington Publishers Ltd.

Fahy, T. (1992): 'Audience Research in RTE', in *Irish Communications Review* 2.

Farrell, B., ed. (1984): *Communications and Community.* Dublin: RTE/Mercier.

Fisher, D. (1978): *Broadcasting in Ireland.* London: Routledge and Kegan Paul, Ltd.

French, N., Hazelkorn, E. & Truetzschler, W. eds. (1990-): *Irish Communications Review.* Dublin: Dublin Institute of Technology.

Goldthorpe, J. & Whelan, C. (1992): *The Development of Industrial Society in Ireland.* Oxford: Oxford University Press.

Gorham, M. (1966): *Forty Years of Irish Broadcasting.* Dublin: RTE.

Harper, T. (1993): 'Patterns of Irish Viewing', in *Irish Communications Review* 3.

Hazelkorn, E. (1992): 'We Can't all Live on a Small Island': The Political Economy of Migration', in P. O'Sullivan, ed.: *The Irish in the New Communities.* Leicester: University Press.

Hazelkorn, E. & Patterson, H. (1994): 'The New Politics of the Irish Republic', in *New Left Review* (September-October).

Hazelkorn, E. & Smyth, P. eds. (1993): *Let in the Light. Censorship, Secrecy and Democracy.* Dingle: Brandon Books.

Hazelkorn, E. (1994): 'Rotating Round the Centre', in *Fortnight* (December).

Huhne, C. (1994): 'Boomtown Ireland', in *The Sunday Tribune*, November 6.

Irish Broadcasting Review (1978–1983). Dublin: RTE.

Kelly, M. & Truetzschler, W. (1992): 'Ireland', in Euromedia Research Group: *The Media in W. Europe.* London: Sage.

Kennedy, K. (1992): 'The Context of Economic Development', in Goldthorpe, J. & C. Whelan: *The Development of Industrial Society in Ireland.* Oxford.

Kennedy, K.A., Giblin, T. & McHugh, D. (1988): *The Economic Development of Ireland.* London.

Kenny, C. (1994): 'TV3 Tries Again to Rival RTE', in *Sunday Independent*, November 16.

McLoone, M. & MacMahon, J. eds. (1984): *Television and Irish Society.* Dublin: RTE/IFI.

Mjoset, L. (1992): *The Irish Economy in Comparative Perspective.* Dublin: NESC.

Murphy, A. (1994): *The Irish Economy – Celtic Tiger or Tortoise?* Dublin: MMI Stockbrokers.

O Riagáin, P. & Gliasáin, M.O. (1993): *National Survey on Languages 1993. Preliminary Report.* Dublin: Institúid Teangeolaíochta Eireann.

O'Hearn, D. (1993): 'Global Competition, Europe and Irish Peripherality', in *Economic and Social Review* 24, 2: 169–197.

O'Kane, P. (1994): 'Culture and Heritage Unite to Produce 33,800 jobs', in *The Irish Times* , 4 November.

O'Malley, E. (1989): *Industry and Economic Development. The challenge for the Latecomer.* Dublin.

O'Toole, F. (1993): 'Dealing with the Cold Reality Behind the Glossy Hi-tech Images', in *Irish Times*, March 3.

Quill, T. (1993): *From Restoration to Consumerism: Directions in Irish Language Television Broadcasting.* MA, Dublin City University.

RTE (1991): *Annual Report, 1991.* Dublin: RTE.

'RTE', in *Administration* 15:3. Dublin: Institute of Public Administration.

Sheehan, H. (1987): *Irish Television Drama.* Dublin: RTE.

Taylor, C. (1993) 'Poor Indicators Given Fundamentally Wrong Account of Economic Health', in *Irish Times*, July 23.

Truetzschler, W. (1991a): 'Foreign Investment in the Media in Ireland', in *Irish Communications Review*, 1(1).

Truetzschler, W. (1991b): 'Broadcasting Law and Broadcasting Policy in Ireland', in *Irish Comaunications Review*, 1(1).

Truetzschler, W. (1993): 'Irland', in Hans-Bredow Institut: *Handhuch für Hörfunk und Fernsehen 1993/94.* Hamburg: Nomos.

White, P. (1994): 'TV3 Promotors Plan Launch of New Service Next Spring', in *Sunday Business Post*, December 4.

Wickham, J. (1993): 'Industrialisation by Invitation Crashes', in *Irish Times*, February 26.

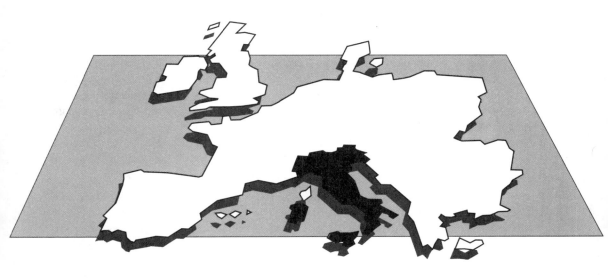

8 Italy: Regional television without a regional vocation

Giuseppe Richeri

The general political framework, the nation and the regions

Italy has a population of 56 million inhabitants and is organized into 8,000 municipalities, 94 provinces and 20 regions. The regions of Italy are generally grouped into three large geographical areas:

- The north, consisting of Liguria, Piamonte, Valle d'Aosta, Lombardy, Veneto, Trentino-Alto Adige, Friuli-Venezia Giulia and Emilia-Romagna;
- The centre, consisting of Tuscany, Marche, Umbria, Lazio, Abruzzi and Molise;
- The south, consisting of Campania, Puglia, Basilicata, Calabria, Sicily and Sardinia.

The north is the richest part of the country and is the part where industrialization began in the 19th century (Liguria, Piamonte and Lombardy) and where an important network of small and medium-sized industries and co-operatives has formed since the Second World War (Veneto and Emilia-Romagna). Milan, the capital of Lombardy, is regarded as the economic capital of Italy, being the financial capital, with the central branches of some of the major Banks and the Italian Stock Exchange. More recent industrialization has taken place in the central regions of Italy, mainly centred on small and medium-sized businesses (Marche, Tuscany, Lazio), although agriculture continues to be significant. The south is the least developed part of the country, where agriculture predominates, where industry is under-developed and concentrated in only a few areas, and which has a high rate of unemployment, many people being forced to seek work in the north or abroad. Generally speaking, all the regions of Italy have a rich historical and local cultural tradition. The majority language is Italian, which has several distinct dialects, but in some regions other languages are also spoken, as is the case of German in the Alto-Adige, French in the Valle d'Aosta, Slovene in Trieste and Gorizia, Sardinian in Sardinia – where also the Catalan language is spoken in one town – and Occitan (*Provençal*) in some areas of Piamonte. There are also scattered communities which speak Albanian, Greek, Occitan and Serbo-Croat and areas where dialects of Rhaeto-Romanic are spoken as 'Furlan' in Friuli or Ladin in Alto Adige.

According to the Italian constitution, 'the Republic, one and indivisible, recognizes and encourages local autonomy; it applies extensive administrative decentralization in State services; it adapts the principles and methods of its legislation to the requirements of autonomy implicit in decentralization' (Art. 5). 'The Republic is divided into Regions, Provinces and Municipalities' (Art. 114); 'The Regions are constituted as autonomous bodies with their own powers and functions' (Art. 115). Although the Italian constitution dates from 1948, the regionalization of Italy did not occur until 1971.

Of the 20 administrative regions into which the Italian State is divided, five have special statutes of their own, according to the constitution, in recognition of their higher degree of differentiation: Valle d'Aosta, Trentino-Alto Adige, Sicily, Sardinia and Friuli-Venezia Giulia. The remainder have ordinary statutes. The difference between the two types of region lies in the fact that in the special regions, the distribution of powers is according to the statute of autonomy, whereas in the remaining regions, it is directly according to the constitution (in a pre-defined, restrictive order), so that the potential for autonomous action is much greater in the former (Fossas, 1990). Regional powers include areas such as health and social services, agriculture, professional training, the environment, etc. In addition, the regions have the authority to intervene in other sectors, such as culture, sport and leisure, industry and transport. The regional bodies are the regional Council, elected by universal suffrage, the regional Board, elected by the Council, and the regional President, elected by the Board.

In cultural matters, the Italian constitution specifies no particular distribution of powers, so that no public body is excluded from the promotion and supervision of culture. The only explicit reference to the delegation of powers to the regions in matters of culture is in Article 117, which confers on regions governed by ordinary statutes legislative powers in the area of 'local authority museums and libraries'. Despite this rather ill-defined and limited constitutional framework, all the Italian regions have adopted in their statutes pragmatic regulations which, among other things, envisages a promotional role of the Region in the cultural sector. It should be pointed out that Italian law makes no provision for any regional powers in the field of the media.

The evolution of the Italian regional structure is uncertain, particularly in view of the growing influence of the federalists of the Lega Nord, one of the partners in the Italian government which emerged from the elections in the Spring of 1994. The Lega proposes a federal Italy, divided into 9 States with ample powers of their own, but these proposals clash with the virtually unanimous unitarianism upheld by the other political groups.

General television structure

As the situation stands at the beginning of 1994, the Italian television channels are organized around a number of bodies which are governed by different rules, depending on the type of ownership (public or private) involved, and on the territorial scope of their activities:

(a) Public television is managed under franchise by RAI, which has 13,000 employees and income of 3,600 billion lire;[1] RAI broadcasts via three national networks, one of which (the *Terza Rete* or RAI3) has daily programming slots devoted to regional broadcasts, specific to each region. RAI is regulated by the 1975 Act 103, which has been partially modified by subsequent Acts.

(b) National private television is organized in nine different channels, managed by private companies;[2] the activities of private television companies are regulated by the 1990 Act 203, which has been partially modified by subsequent Acts.

(c) Local private television has been organized, over the last ten years, around a varying number of broadcasting stations, of which 898 have applied for a licence to the Ministry of Post and Telecommunications; on 8 March, 1994, the newspapers published a 'provisional' list of 463 local television stations which had been authorized to broadcast. However, it seems that other TV stations (both commercial and community – that is to say, non-profit-making) will be added to the initial list. Some stations have regional or semi-regional coverage. Act 203 (1990) also regulates the activities of private local television.

As for the topic in hand, RAI operates substantially the same model of regional television in each of the twenty Italian regions, with some exceptions in the case of regions governed by special statutes (Valle d'Aosta, Trentino Alto-Adige, Friuli-Venezia Giulia, Sicily and Sardinia). As we shall see, in the beginning this model was original in some aspects, but its application has decreased drastically over time. Moreover, the current structuring of public television is due for an overhaul along the lines of the 'restructuring plan' of RAI, published in the autumn of 1993.

Private television companies belong to a sector which has evolved in a spontaneous, disorganized fashion, since it has long lacked regulation. Remarkably late in the day, the Government now intends to apply to it the 1990 Act, which contains regulations for the private national and local TV sector. The Ministry of Post and Telecommunications recently assigned provisional licenses to private local television companies which were selected on the basis of the applications they had submitted. The number of licenses granted formally depended on the availability of frequencies under the national frequencies plan, but there are various suggestions among the mass media that the number of licenses, as well as the way in which they have been granted, has been subject to political pressures. The broadcasting areas of each local television tend to coincide with the various regions, but this does not necessarily mean that the television companies under licence will assume a regional character. Although broadcasts must technically cover a large part of the broadcasting area

1. Last available data, 1992.
2. Each private company may obtain a license for up to three national networks.

to which the licence refers, in many cases the broadcasting station's real area of reference will probably be confined to the regional capital and its outlying municipalities, or to provinces, and even to sub-regional areas. We shall therefore face a situation very similar to the present one, in which only a small number of the existing local television companies operate according to a truly regional vocation. Most local television companies that have operated over the last few years have addressed themselves mainly to the metropolitan areas (Milan, Turin, Rome, Naples, Genoa, etc.), to the provinces, or to parts of regions which had a certain degree of economic or cultural uniformity.

Before embarking on a detailed description of public and private regional or quasi-regional television companies, it is useful to mention some elements which will enable us to understand better the main factors that have helped to bring about the present situation.

The origins of regional television

The idea of creating regional television in Italy emerged from a major institutional change which, in 1970, envisaged the creation of the administrative Regions. This involved a substantial modification in the organization of the Italian State, from the moment that the regional assemblies, elected by universal suffrage, acquired powers of economic organization and territorial planning which involved the direct control of administrative and legislative activities formerly appertaining to central State government.

As said above, the mass communications sector, and particularly radio and television broadcasting (which at the time were under State monopoly), was not delegated to the Regions. However, the statutes of most regions contained an article which referred variously to the role of information as a fundamental tool in the creation of a 'new form of government' based on the participation of citizens and on a direct relationship between those who govern and those who are governed.

Many regional governments rapidly showed special concern and sensitivity towards the subject of information and, in particular, radio and television broadcasting, demanding authority, access and, in general, a new, more decentralized organization of public television, capable of creating region-based production and transmission slots. From a political point of view, the arguments on which the Regions' demands were based may be summarized as follows: 'The Regions are an integral part of the State; as radio and television are a State monopoly, the Regions have an institutional right to participate in the management and control of radio and television broadcasting'.

The mobilization of the Regions around their demands for the creation of regional television coincides with other, divers facts. The first one which contributed to the creation of a 'public' sphere of action on the part of the Regions in this field was the growing response on the part of some political parties, the principal trade unions and mass cultural associations, who criticized the public radio and television service as controlled by RAI, in a way which was not independent of central government, and which was in particular subject to the direct influence of the party with a parliamentary majority. The criticism and the evidence supporting it, together with the expiry of RAI's public service franchise, contributed to the creation of a good opportunity to debate and reform the entire radio and television broad-casting system. The main political, social and institutional platforms, with their various criticisms against RAI, formed the 'reformist front', which drew up a series of guide-lines for the renovation of the public television service that were soon formalized in parliamentary bills. Among the aspects dealt with were the decentralization of television on a regional level, the right of access to national and local broadcasting, and the transfer of the management and control of television from Government to Parliament.

The second element was linked to the availability of new technological resources (television cameras, video recorders and broadcasting equipment) which made local production and broadcasting of television programmes more accessible in economic and professional terms.

These were the elements which provided the bedrock for the growing political pressure and paved the way for the drafting of the television decentralization plan which, after tough negotiations, was included in the 1975 Act 103, and which subsequently resulted in the regional public television network (RAI3).

Before considering the model which served as inspiration to the new regional television services which came into being in 1979, we should recall that, simultaneously with the passing of the RAI reform law, the radio and then the private local television phenomenon appeared and took shape. Initially, the latter operated illegally; in 1976, however, they were legalized by ruling 202 of the Constitutional Court. The legalization of private television referred exclusively to the local level, since the Constitutional Court confirmed the public monopoly of television on a national level. However, the liberalization of private television was not followed by a law defining its regulation. As a result, for a long time the sector was free to develop and operate spontaneously. Some of the stronger or more dynamic companies succeeded in organizing by various means (ownership of local stations, control of programme packages, control of advertising investment, etc.), the same programming on a growing number of local stations, which followed the rulings of the Constitutional Court and confined themselves to the local level, but which at the same time, developed activities similar to those of a network extending far beyond the local level. Thus, in 1980 we begin to witness the dominance of the first national or quasi-national TV networks, based on the co-ordination of local stations. Because the latter were 'technically' not interconnected, they could not broadcast live programmes such as the news or sporting events, and so for a long time this type of programme was exclusively the domain of RAI. This process led to private television in Italy gradually dividing into two different sectors:

(a) The first operates on a national level, in direct competition with the public television networks. After several ownership deals, it was to be concentrated chiefly, in the 1980s, in the hands of a single group, Fininvest, leaving the other private national television networks only a marginal market niche.

(b) The second comprises several hundred stations which operate on a local level (urban, metropolitan, provincial) in various territorial areas, in some cases extend-ing to the regional level.

Public regional broadcasting, conceived during the period of RAI's monopoly, began to operate as such in an unpredictable market situation, characterized by the existence of numerous private local television stations.

This *de facto* distribution among private national and local television companies was not formally recognized and ratified until 1990 in Act 203. The latter, as we have already stated, was provisionally applied in relation to local licenses at the beginning of 1994.

The public regional television model

The public television reform law (no. 103, 1975), in addition to confirming the public monopoly in radio and television broadcasting (rejected a year later by the Constitutional Court, as already stated, with regard to local television), is characterized by a number of new aspects, such as the role in management and control accorded to Parliament (which appoints the majority of RAI's Board of Directors), the decentralization in the creative and production areas, public access, and a new working organization and role for the Regions, even though these were much less far-reaching than the Regions had hoped for.

Decentralization is considered one of the most important and innovative aspects of the new law, ratified in the Agreement between the State and RAI which accompanied the new franchise to the public television company. The Agreement requires RAI to set up a third television network 'of national scope, which at the same time could be used for simultaneous, independent regional broadcasting' (Article 17).

The reform law refers to public television on a regional level on two specific counts:

- The first concerns the role of the Regions: 'Each Regional Council elects ... a regional committee for its respective television service ... The regional committee is the regional advisory body in the field of radio and television, drawing up guide-lines on television programmes destined for regional broadcasting. It also makes proposals to the Board of Directors of the franchisee RAI concerning regional programmes which may be broadcast by the national networks. The regional committee regulates access to regional broadcasts, according to the regulations of the Parliamentary Commission' (Article 5, Act 103/1975).

- The second concerns decentralization: 'The franchise binds the franchisee to organize itself in such a way as to ... promote the development of the service, while respecting the importance and the plurality of opinions, even at the expense of decentralization in the creative and productive spheres within the company, and establishing an effective relationship with the reality of the country as a whole' (Art. 13, Act 103/1975).

It is clear from the documents accompanying the implementation of the Act that the setting up of regional broadcasts is only one aspect of the decentralization it intends to apply to RAI: 'In order to achieve the right proportion of regional and inter-regional contributions to programming, a decentralization process in the creative and production spheres is to be carried out, with a view to encouraging and developing the peripheral structure of the company, by means of an organizational and technical re-structuring plan, as well as a re-deployment of staff and decentralization resources in public television' (Fabiani, 1977).

In other words, the creation of regional television forms part of an ambitious, complex operation which aims to completely reorganize public television on the basis of decentralization, fostering creativity and production skills on a regional level, through human and technical resources, capable of catering to the requirements of local broadcasting as well as contributing to the national programming of the three public television networks.

This is a new approach, which assigns to the dimension of regional television a role not confined to 'localism', but rather designed to project the main news and cultural items of the individual regions on a national scale. At this point, it would be interesting to give a brief analysis of the original programming plan of the new network (Terza Rete), of which the regional broadcasts are an integral part.

Terza Rete's (RAI3) programming

Terza Rete's programmes may have a regional, inter-regional or national origin and target audience. Specifically, these are:

(a) Regionally-produced programmes, which are broadcast regionally, at an inter-regional level (when they are also broadcast to other regions), or nation-wide (when the programme is broadcast on the whole network).

(b) Centrally produced (or acquired) programmes broadcast on the national network or in a single region.

When Terza Rete was launched, it was envisaged that at least 60 per cent of its national broadcasts would consist of programmes made in the regional centres.

The programming plan of Terza Rete, which at the time was not yet in a position to foresee the effects that competition from private television would have on the timing of its broadcasts, refers to a programming structured around a daily two-and-a-half hours of regional programmes, inserted by the regional centres at the beginning, at the end, or at any other time of day, and produced either in conjunction with or at the request of regional and local institutions (on the whole, the intention was to produce service transmissions).

The programming model common to all the regions consisted of regional programmes commencing at 7 pm, with cultural items broadcast on the national network, followed by a 5-minute news bulletin giving a summary of national and international news, and a further 25 minutes of regional news. This would be followed by a cultural programme lasting at least one hour, although in the case of important events, the programme's duration could be extended to provide full coverage of the event.

This programming plan had the support of the regional institutions which had fought for the decentralization of RAI. These institutions were gratified by the creation of a network which had ample programme time not taken up by a pre-determined grid, and which was therefore free to satisfy local and regional needs and requirements.

From blueprint to reality: problems and readjustments

The incorporation of regional structures and broadcasts in the national network constitutes the originality of the Italian model for public regional television, but its actual implementation has operated to the detriment of the regional dimension whilst favouring the national level. To this fact we must add others which explain how an original and ambitious plan has given way to a public regional television whose role and air time have progressively dwindled. These facts may be summarized as follows:

(a) The devaluation of regional broadcasts: the use of resources (human and technical) at the regional level tends to favour programmes and news reporting services designed and produced for national broadcasting, since these enjoy greater prestige.

(b) Competition from private stations: from the very beginning, regional TV has aimed at an audience that has meanwhile discovered and grown used to private local stations offering programmes whose focus is closer to home (city or province), and which place an emphasis on entertainment and fiction, whereas Terza Rete's national programming into which the regional slots are inserted have always had a more 'cultural' vocation.

(c) RAI's financial crisis: the beginnings of Terza Rete and regional programmes coincide with the onset of a major financial crisis in RAI, due to the combined effects of the erosion of its real resources, whose growth was at a rate much lower than that of inflation, and also to increased costs – also due to the effects of competition from the private sector on the quantity and quality of its national programme output.

(d) Lack of interest on the part of the central authorities: regional broadcasts soon came to be regarded as a burden to RAI's programming and its ability to compete with the private television companies which were progressively eroding its audience ratings.

(e) Lack of interest at a regional level: the Regions expressed their disappointment at the results of the new law, which assigned to them a marginal role, and they failed to lobby effectively to ensure that at least RAI's proposed decentralization was carried out.

From the very beginning, all these factors caused Terza Rete numerous problems, especially in its regional programming, which was to undergo several modifications during the 1980s, leading to its present situation. Within the context of a steady increase in the hours of transmission of the third channel, and in tune with what was also the trend, under the pressure of growing competition, in all the other public and private, national and local networks, the regional broadcasts were reorganized into a number of fixed spaces, from which the autonomous regions' initiatives were gradually excluded. These spaces consisted of a daily news programme lasting approximately 25 minutes, plus three weekly broadcasting slots of approximately 30 minutes each, reserved for programmes of regional interest (documentaries, surveys, etc.). In the second half of the 1980s, however, the regional broadcasts were subsequently reduced, leaving only the regional news bulletin, which meanwhile turned into an appendix of Terza Rete's national news bulletin. Notwithstanding, the regional news bulletin, which over the last few years has grown from the original one to the present three daily editions, has recently developed into a landmark item for many viewers, enjoying high audience ratings.

Those regions with special statutes, which in several cases comprise a diversity of language communities (French, German, Slovenian or Ladino-speaking), are an exception to the general rule just described. RAI, according to a specific agreement with the State, earmarks special programming time for these languages.

Table 1. RAI's regional centres

Region	Headquarters
Piamonte	Torino
Valle d'Aosta	Aosta
Lombardy	Milano
Veneto	Venezia
Trentino-Alto Adige (province of Bolzano)	Bolzano
Trentino-Alto Adige (province of Trento)	Trento
Friuli-Venezia Giulia	Trieste
Liguria	Genova
Emilia Romagna	Bologna
Tuscany	Firenze
Umbria	Pregia
Marche	Ancona
Lazio	Roma
Abruzzi	Pescara
Molise	Campobasso
Campania	Napoli
Puglia	Bari
Basilicata	Potenza
Calabria	Cosenza
Sicily	Palermo
Sardinia	Cagliari

Source: RAI

As we have seen, the extent of public regional broadcasting is not determined by law, but rather depends on economic decisions. In view of RAI's recent financial difficulties, and given that the decentralization of television absorb 35 per cent of the total budget of the public broadcasting company, the trend is to modify the present situation.

The evolution of private local television

As already stated, private regional television in Italy belongs to that ill-defined category of local television, which may group together several territorial areas. This phenomenon may be described as follows:

- It first emerged clearly on a continued basis in 1974, although it was not recognized by law at that time.
- It was legalized in 1976, by decision of the Constitutional Court, which based its legitimacy on several articles of the Constitution, the chief of which are Article

125

21 (freedom of expression and information) and Article 41 (freedom of enterprise).

- In the absence of any regulatory law, it has developed according to the rules of free competition, in addition to those dictated by the interests of people in positions of power.

The 'natural' outcome of such a situation was the progressive increase in forms of concentration, which arose in successive stages:

- Initially, this phenomenon affected control over the programme rights (films, TV films, series, etc.) and advertising investment.

- Subsequently, it extended to the control over the ownership or management of a growing number of stations, to such an extent that it co-ordinated their programming to create virtual TV networks capable of covering many of the principal areas of the country, thereby effectively acting on the programme and advertising market as true national television networks in direct competition with the public networks.

- The final degree of concentration is that of a single enterprise which controls three national television networks and the absolute majority of the combined resources invested in private television companies.

This trend has resulted in a proliferation of local TV stations (regarded as excessive by all the parties concerned), most of which have been operating in conditions of structural instability, as regards financial resources, availability of programmes, production and personnel resources.

The local advertising scene, which was, to begin with, under-developed, has been divided up between a large number of stations which have been forced to resort to dumping practices. In most cases, limited resources have prevented their access to the 'quality' products market, to up-to-date production means, as well as the opportunity to work with top professionals, etc.

In this situation, many TV stations have experienced a process of progressive marginalization, surviving in a state of constant precariousness; many more have had to resort to increasingly more passive forms of television production, auctions, and commercial activities, to the point that local television has become synonymous with an unremitting incitement to purchase all types of products, to the exclusion of any other television genre.

The result is that only a small number of stations have managed to achieve a degree of business consolidation that can provide a local service attractive to both advertisers and the general viewing public. Given the speed at which this phenomenon has evolved, we lack the information necessary to specify the exact number of stations belonging to the various categories, but the most reliable informed sources estimate at between 100 and 150 the number of local television stations run along business lines, and capable of providing a quality service, if only in the area of local interest programmes, while remaining financially afloat.

Some of these stations have set up circuits following the American *syndication* model; others have preferred to maintain total independence. In their most sophisticated form, private local television can provide a good standard of local interest news programmes (news, reports, debates, etc.), studio entertainment shows (music, humour, chat-shows, etc.), local sports coverage (football, basketball, etc.) political information services (live broadcast of Assembly meetings), together with a programme of feature films, although in this respect they cannot compete with the national networks. Moreover, it is obvious that there are insufficient resources at the local level to produce locally-based fiction programmes.

It was not until 1990 that the Italian Parliament passed an organic law governing the private television sector, which included some regulations specifically concerning local television companies which have obtained a franchise. The most relevant of these are as follows:

(a) The frequency adjudication plan must, in each broadcasting area, reserve for local television transmission 30 per cent of programmes in interference-free reception conditions (Art.3).

(b) The transmission of local advertising material is reserved for local television companies, while the national networks are permitted to broadcast only national advertising (Art. 8).

(c) Advertisements on local television may not exceed 20 per cent of each hour of programming, or 15 per cent of the day's entire programming (Art. 8), whereas the national networks must observe stricter timetabling restrictions.

Table 2. Local TV stations authorized in 1994

Regions	Number of TV stations authorized
Sicily	77
Sardinia	7
Calabria	22
Basilicata	2
Puglia	58
Campania	48
Molise	4
Abruzzi	20
Lazio	44
Umbria	5
Tuscany	23
Marche	13
Emilia Romagna	22
Liguria	10
Veneto	29
Friuli-Venezia Giulia	6
Trentino-Alto Adige	5
Lombardy	32
Piamonte	33
Valle d'Aosta	2
TOTAL	462

Source: Ministry of Post and Telecommunications.

(d) Central government and non-territorial public bodies must assign at least 25 per cent of their media advertising budget to local radio and television stations.

At the beginning of March, 1994, after due consideration of the applications for licenses, the Ministry of Post and Telecommunications announced that a large number of these had been rejected because of irregularities in the applications they had submitted, or because they did not fulfil the desired requirements, and published a provisional list of 462 stations that had been authorized to broadcast.

A preliminary analysis of this list reveals that the licenses granted so far took little account of the relationship between the number of stations authorized to broadcast in a region and the latter's number of inhabitants, its geographical size, its economic resources, or any other objective factors which might be relevant in justifying the number of stations operating in a given territory. The first result of this is that in 'prosperous' Lombardy, 32 local television stations have been authorized to broadcast, whereas in each of the principal regions of the South – Campania (Naples), Puglia (Bari) and Sicily (Palermo), where the average income per capita, as well as the economic and employment levels are much lower, 49, 58 and 77 local television stations, respectively, have been authorized to broadcast. At the moment, the provisional list of local television stations, region by region (from South to North), stands as Table 2 shows.

The situation of local and regional television: the case of Trentino-Alto Adige

To illustrate the present situation of local and regional television in Italy, we have considered the case of one region, that of Trentino-Alto Adige, and in particular the initiatives in the province of Trentino, taking into account both private television and RAI, the latter in this case having a centre in each of the two provinces of the region (Trentino and Bolzano). The bilingual nature of the province of Bolzano makes it necessary to duplicate transmissions, in Italian and German, within the limits of that territory. By selecting this option, we are able to observe a 'small' region in terms of its geography and population, with a limited number of television stations, which provides us with an overall view which would not be possible in the case of regions where there are several dozens of local stations in operation.

Characteristics of private television broadcasting in Trentino-Alto Adige

The television stations in the province of Trentino cover a basically regional reception area, which is why it is difficult to distinguish between the resources generated in Trentino and those generated in Alto Adige. These stations may be estimated to be based on a total income, consisting of national and local advertising revenue, sponsorships and sale of air time, which amounts, at a regional level, to ten billion lire per year. There are four Trentino television stations which, together with a Bolzano station, share these resources; their respective situations vary considerably. The most characteristic feature of the present situation is the lack of resources available for the number of rival stations. This stems from the financial crisis and the precariousness in which virtually all these stations operate. Current estimations regarding the north of Italy, however, calculate that local television company needs an income of around five billion lire if it is to guarantee acceptable levels of technical quality and programming.

Briefly, this means that the situation in the Trentino province is characterized by an excessive number of private local televisions (a situation common to most other Italian regions) and that this situation generates a negative effect on the whole sector. This situation is made even more complex by the fact that the existence of these stations has generally been hampered by a number of specifically local factors. In Trentino-Alto Adige, essentially an Alpine region, the setting-up and maintenance of television booster stations requires much higher investments than those that television companies in 'flatland' regions need to make in order to reach a potential audience of the same dimension. Moreover, the size of the population of this region is considerably smaller than the average of other regions of Italy. Finally, there are some additional factors which have curbed the development of some stations. The most serious case is that of a Trentino television company which, over the last few years, has repeatedly been bought and sold by owners whose chief interests were political, or related to some other activity. As a result, both the image and the management of the station have deteriorated, while accumulated debts render the task of reorganization and re-launching that much more difficult.

In general, the financial situation of Trentino television companies would appear to be particularly problematic: as statements by their respective spokesmen make plain, three of the four television companies closed the last financial year with a debit balance.

It is probably for this very reason that we have been unable to obtain precise information concerning the companies' balances, turnover, costs and prices.

The small size of the market has forced the Trentino stations to develop a certain degree of product differentiation and, in three cases, to associate with national networks which supply part of their daily programming. In order to achieve this differentiation in the area of news broadcasting, the Trentino stations have placed emphasis, respectively, on the following:

(a) Extensive coverage of local political, social and cultural news.

(b) More in-depth local news than that provided by the other stations, with a 'middle-to-high' target audience.

(c) Strong sports news coverage.

(d) Institutional news, relating to the activities of the elective assemblies of the principal local public bodies.

The search for differential features has not been confined to news, but also applies to the rest of their programming which, in two cases, is linked to two national networks (Cinque Stelle and Junior TV), while in another it is linked to a strong element of commercial broadcasts (teleshopping).

To give some idea of the scale involved, we can take the case of TVA (Televisione delle Alpi), the leading station in the Trentino market. This station has been running for almost 15 years and has developed an unmistakable style and reputation. It has a staff of 25, with a 'strong' editorial board of 5 full-time journalists.

Income is derived, in order of importance, from advertising, sponsorship and the sale of air time for self-managed commercial broadcasts. The main investors are commercial concerns: furniture shops, car dealers, etc. Advertising revenue comes 50 per cent from the provincial capital and the remaining 50 per cent from the rest of the province. In order to provide 80 per cent of the Trentino territory with a fair quality television signal, it needs 110 booster stations. The outreach of the network, as well as the traditional style and the quality of the programmes, has given good results and, according to an official study carried out by the specialist institute Auditel, secured a daily audience of 300,000 viewers.

From the programming point of view, the aim is to guarantee a high standard of general news reporting, leaving aside sports reporting, and as far as possible to develop both local news and the ways and techniques of presenting it, in addition to reporting local history and cultural items. This is an exceptionally well-tended patch, in which neither public and private national networks, nor stations broadcasting from other regions, are in a position to compete.

Characteristics of public television broadcasting in Trentino-Alto Adige

In addition to the private television companies, RAI also broadcasts television and radio programmes to the province of Trentino (there is a separate RAI centre in the province of Alto Adige, which makes the Trentino-Alto Adige region the only one in which RAI has two different centres). It maintains an important presence, both on a technical level, because of the quality of its equipment, and on account of its programming, particularly in the field of news reporting. It is impossible to extract and single out the financial data of RAI's Trentino centre from those of the company as a whole, but it is possible to analyse a few of RAI's organizational aspects which, at the local level, are in fact usually regarded as setting the standard to which private stations should aspire, whilst avoiding some of RAI's 'diseconomies' of scale, which are seen as deriving from the public sector nature of the company.

For its own transmissions, RAI's Trentino centre uses blocks of Terza Rete's national programme, which began broadcasting in the province in 1979. Initially, there was a single general director of regional news, based in Rome, while each of the regional centres, including that of Trentino, had a chief news editor. More recently, there have been two general directors: one responsible for Terza Rete's national news, and another responsible for regional news reporting, both based in Rome.

The RAI programming grid in Trentino is as follows:

- Television news programme from 14.00 to 14.30, which in 1994 has been cut by a third in anticipation of a new news slot at around 22.30.
- Television news at 19.30.
- Two sports programmes which are broadcast following the news on Sundays and Mondays.
- Starting this year, a local programme which goes out on Thursdays from 14.50 to 15.15.

Production equipment and cameras have recently been renewed. The newsdesk has been equipped with a computer system, which provides access to a wide range of services such as databases, networking with the daily newspapers, etc. The introduction of these facilities is designed to improve working conditions and results, by saving time and increasing the speed and flexibility of operations.

Decisions affecting RAI's Trentino centre are taken in Rome, at meetings in which all the heads of the regional centres take part. These decisions are taken on the proposals made by regional chiefs or by RAI's central executive, and then applied in all the regional centres, although their individual circumstances and needs are taken into account when it comes to drawing up a schedule for the implementation of these decisions. The decisions taken in Rome are usually given a favourable reception at RAI's Trentino centre, although they are quick to point out that 'the editor's tendency is to save money, so that our resources are never lavish'.

Programme production and management of the plant are carried out directly at the Trentino centre, while advertising is managed from outside. Occasionally, filming is also contracted out, when internal means are otherwise occupied, or in the case of unforeseen events which occur in areas where access is difficult and there are private filming units nearer the location. This is the case of the programme *Bici & Bike*, produced in Trentino, partly with external support (cutting and editing) but broadcast nationally.

As for the journalists, USIGRAI (RAI's union of journalists) has come to an agreement with the company that there should periodically be public selection contests to fill trainee posts (for student journalists). In the case of professional journalists, however, the method used is direct appointment, although this only occurs when it becomes necessary to fill positions left vacant by other professional journalists (there is currently a freeze on staffing). A few journalists are taken on under temporary contracts to carry out specific tasks.

There is no strict division of tasks between the television and the radio staff: technicians, programmers and journalists are interchangeable. There are no compulsory training courses, but journalists can request to spend time at other RAI centres. This option, however, is not in great demand. As at all RAI centres, there is an editorial committee representing the journalists. The RAI union has traditionally been very strong, although no major conflicts have arisen at the Trentino centre. As for analysis and research resources, the Trentino centre generally uses research already available to which the company has access, although local audience research studies have recently been commissioned from the University of Trentino.

One of the problems RAI generally has to deal with is that viewers do not distinguish between public TV programmes and those of the private TV channels. The first local television company to operate in the Trentino province was TVA (Televisione delle Alpi), and the public frequently identifies other local television broadcasting with that station. The aim of RAI's executive is to maintain their leading position, both in radio and television. In the particular case of television, the spokesman we interviewed assured us, 'RAI presents itself as unique in relation to the other local television companies. What we at RAI do is beyond comparison, on account both of the means at our disposal and the professionalism that the company confers on us'.

The two main objectives of RAI-Trentino in the short term are the introduction of an evening news programme and access to the audience research studies already mentioned. In the medium term, their objective is to obtain more space for regional television broadcasting, which would be possible as soon as RAI frequencies were freed and became available to boost their regional television.

The outlook for public regional television

On 19 October, 1993, the chairman of RAI submitted the public television restructuring plan; this plan contains some indications as to the directions that the transformation of public television will take, involving decentralization and the regional centres of RAI, and new opportunities for each region to exercise influence within its own televisive space.

The first passage which interests us is in the paragraph dealing with decentralization (5.4.3), which considers the possibility of turning one of the three public television channels into a consortium of inter-regional stations. This suggestion is presented as a proposal by the Parliamentary Supervisory Committee, fervently requested by the Conference of Regional Presidents, 'who have gone so far as to back up their demands with the provision of funding for this purpose'.

The document states that 'by decentralization, we mean both a gradual but planned expansion of local broadcasting, and above all the transferring of creative departments and production centres to the local level, wherever there exist the structures and overall conditions necessary for the production of programmes which, whilst reflecting local interest, are considered to be of major national interest'.

A second interesting passage is found in the paragraph concerning the restructuring of the regional centres (7.7): 'we must use our resources to produce more local news, community services, and, gradually, other programmes that can be competitively included in the programming broadcast both on a regional and a national level'.

At this point, the document returns to the hypothesis of transforming one of the three public TV channels into a consortium of inter-regional stations, stating that 'the convergence around RAI of legal persons should be envisaged, representing various local interests, in order to give rise to strong, viable regional or inter-regional stations. The presence of local partners, public and private, could act as the catalyst to create more ambitious objectives in decentralized regional television'.

RAI's restructuring plan, with its above-mentioned transformation of one of the three public channels into a consortium of regional stations, seems to combine two requirements:

(a) To lighten the load of RAI's expenditure by cutting costs in its regional centres, which currently amount to 35 per cent of the total costs of the company.

(b) To meet the 'institutional' demands regarding further decentralization, thus assuming a role traditionally assigned to the public services.

The new channel would be organized as a consortium of regional or inter-regional stations, managed by new regional companies in which other public and private local partners, in addition to RAI, would participate.

RAI's regional centres, which now run the risk of being eliminated in some regions and severely reduced in size in others, would be assigned to these new regional companies as RAI's contribution, and their production would be increased by broadening the scope of their activities (local news, community services, productions for the national channels); their staff intake would be frozen, if not reduced.

Moreover, the presence of local partners in the private sector could increase the company's initiative, while that of public sector partners could lead to the provision of an improved, more direct public 'service'. The risks of the new regional television companies would be shared by their other local partners.

The new scenario put forward by RAI appeals directly to the regions, some of which have taken into consideration the opportunities it offers. The region's opportunities of intervention would now include the possibility of using television with beneficial results in terms of the cost-effectiveness of some services (for example, specialized news in the sectors of farming and tourism, health education, 'open university' education and training, access to study opportunities, the promotion and dissemination of culture, etc.). Moreover, there is the possibility that the region might play a direct role in the new regional television company, in order to guarantee a balanced political and cultural participation in the new forms of political communication, especially during election periods. This possibility would not exist if, alongside RAI, there were only private partners. On the one hand, all the regions need to establish an accessible and 'visible' space for local political communication purposes, in which the various public institutions, political organizations, economic and social forces and cultural manifestations can freely confront one another in a fairly systematic way. On the other hand, it should also be pointed out that the new majority electoral system, which was used in the 1994 national elections, will probably also be adopted in future for use in local and regional elections. In this hypothetical case, the role of local and regional media will be much more important than before, and direct institutional involvement could guarantee the balance and impartiality of regional public television, more than casual shareholder alliances between RAI and private local investors.

References

Bartolomei, A. & Bernabei, P. (1982): *L'emittenza privada dal 1956 a oggi*. Torino: Eri-Edizioni RAI.

Bonomo, B. (1990): *I circuiti nazionali*. Milano: Edizioni rivista de Giurisprudenza Amministrativa.

Debbio, P. del (1992): *Il mercante a l'inquisitore*. Milano: Il Sole 24 Ore.

Fabiani, F. (1977): *Relazione sulla terza rete tv*. Roma: RAI.

Fossas, E. (1990): *Regions i sector cultural a Europa. Estudi comparat*. Barcelona: Institut d'Estudis Autonòmics.

Richeri, G. & Grandi, G. (1976), *Le televisioni in Europa, tv via etere, tv via cavo, videogruppi*. Milano: Feltrinelli.

Richeri, G. (1989): *L'assetto delle televisioni locali in Piemonte*. Milano: Makno media (typed).

Richeri, G. (1993a): *Analisi dei bacini d'utenza televisiva in Lombardia*. Milano: Makno Media (typed).

Richeri, G. (1993b): *L'economia della televisione in Trentino Alto Adige*. Trento: Università di Trento (typed).

Sarli, A. (1994): *Guida alla emitenza televisiva privata*. Milano: Gruppo Editoriale GCE.

Zaccaria, R. (ed.) (1984): *RAI, la televisione che cambia*. Torino, Edizioni Sei.

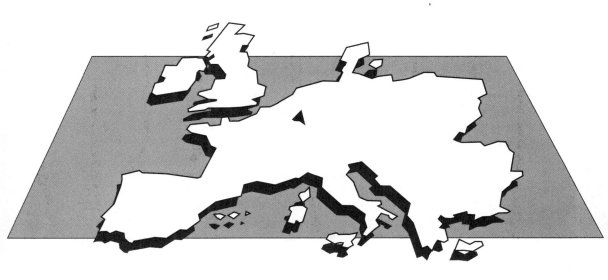

9 Luxembourg: Local, regional, national or transnational?

J.-M. Nobre-Correia

When referring to the Luxembourgian media, which term should be used: 'national' 'regional' or 'local'? For this country of 389,800 inhabitants, the same population as many medium-sized European cities, it is a very good question. And there is an undeniable fact to bear in mind, especially when talking about the media: almost 30 per cent of these inhabitants are foreigners.[1]

In addition to this demographic pluralism, there is also pluralism of a linguistic nature. Although Luxembourgish[2] has been recognized as the official language since 1984, German predominates in teaching and the press, while French predominates in administration, justice and cultural matters.

These diverse 'fragmentations' of such a small population don't favour the existence of an autonomous media landscape, and even less the expansion of media functioning under sheer 'editorial' criteria. This is a weakness which has nevertheless been pointed out as an advantage.

1. In addition to Luxembourg's 30 per cent foreign population, we must also add some 40,000 people who cross the border every day to work in the Grand Duchy. 'If these are taken into account, the proportion of foreigners exceeds 40 per cent.' (Trausch, 1992:12, 227).

2. Luxembourgish is a German dialect, known as Mosellan-francique.

An audio-visual giant

It was indeed in Luxembourg that the Compagnie Luxembourgeoise de Radiodiffusion (CLR) came into being on 30 May 1931 (Nobre-Correia, 1988 and 1992). Created by a shareholding group which was mostly French but included some Belgians, the CLR became the Compagnie Luxembourgeoise de Télédiffusion (CLT) in 1955. Coming under control of the Belgian Groupe Bruxelles-Lambert at the beginning of the 1970s, the CLT is today an important media group whose presence is felt in the sectors of television (with 13 stations), radio (also with 13), audio-visual production and distribution, in addition to magazines (with seven titles) and publishing.[3] It is a group with consolidated positions in Germany, Belgium, France and the Netherlands, and also, though less significantly, in Canada, the United States, the United Kingdom, Ireland, the Czech Republic and other countries (CLT, 1994: 10–11).

Ironically however, this Luxembourgian group has always attached little importance to the Grand Duchy of Luxembourg. As a commercial enterprise, the CLT turned first to those countries where its stations could easily find sizeable audiences and attractive advertising revenues. Between the wars, because of the very make-up of its shareholding group and also owing to the international political situation, CLT radio broadcasts were aimed first and foremost at the Francophone audience (French, Belgian and Luxembourgian). Although there had been broadcasts in German, English, and Dutch since the company's very beginnings, these became less important after the Second World War. From the early 1980s on, however, a shift was to take place within the CLT: the stations broadcast in German and Dutch grew to outnumber and become more financially important than those in French. This was because the political and media context, with audio-visual demonopolization in Germany and in the Netherlands, was favourable to this opening up, whereas François Mitterand and the Socialists remained hostile to the CLT's expansionist designs in France (Chamard and Kieffer, 1992).

In its spread across Europe, this demonopolization movement has clearly reached Luxembourg. Until July 1991, the CLT enjoyed – *de facto* if not *de iure* – a monopoly situation there. And yet it gave little attention to its country of origin. True, as far as radio was concerned, broadcasts oriented toward the Luxembourgian audience had practically always existed and since the 1950s had even had a specific transmitter.[4] In television, on the other hand, CLT's only achievement was the creation of *Hei Elei Kuck Elei* in 1969. This was a broadcast in Luxembourgish, programmed on Sundays on RTL Télévision, the French-speaking Luxembourgian channel, directed above all to viewers in Belgium and eastern France.

Since the mid-1980s, development of CLT activities has led to a decentralization of its implantations towards its neighbouring countries. While this has been the inevitable result of the very geography of the Grand Duchy, such a policy has not pleased the Luxembourgians, who fear that the Company's original site may progressively become an empty shell.

3. Michael Delloye (CLT managing director) in an interview given to *Le Vif-L'Express*, Brussels, 22 July 1994.
4. This radio is now known as RTL Radio Letzebourg.

The CLT has thus introduced a 'compensation' policy, consisting of fomenting new activities in Luxembourg.

From programme to channel

On 21 October 1991, and following an agreement with the government,[5] the programme *Hei Elei Kuck Elei* grew into a Luxembourgish language channel.[6] Broadcast on a daily basis by hertzian waves and also offered by cable, RTL Hei Elei provide a total of some 18.5 hours per week (CLT, 1994: 28). A single team of fourteen journalists sees to a daily ten-minute agenda show, a five-minute sequence of recorded images and a thirty-minute newscast with an emphasis on Luxembourg. Weekly 45-minute thematic magazines have recently been added to this programming schedule and these are focused largely on sports and culture in Luxembourg. Games and shows for young people have also been included and on Sundays in the early afternoon there is even a 60-minute programme in Italian. It should also be mentioned that *Hei Elei Aktueel*, the daily news broadcast, is offered at 7:30 p.m. and later rebroadcast at 8:45 p.m.

In a tri-lingual country where cable TV reaches approximately 85 per cent of the homes and where forty different programmes are offered to television viewers, the audience has been cornered by the German channels and, to a lesser extent, the French. It is nevertheless a fact that, between 7:30 p.m. and 8:30 p.m., 35.5 per cent of the Grand Duchy's population over twelve watches RTL Hei Elei.[7]

With time, the RTL Hei Elei audience has even begun to transcend national boundaries. This is because its programmes are broadcast by Astra satellite 'so that citizens of Luxembourg living abroad may keep abreast of the news of their country of origin (CLT, 1993: 22). Furthermore, in July 1994, Belgium's French Community, which supervises audio-visual matters for French-speaking Belgium,[8] approved a plan authorizing the diffusion of RTL Hei Elei programmes in the south of Luxembourg's Belgian province. 'Some 20,000 homes' will thus be able to pick up these programmes in the Francophone region where older viewers often have a knowledge of the Luxembourgish dialect.[9]

A country in the heart of Europe

Foreign observers may find the existence of RTL Hei Elei to be surprising or even amusing. At a time when cable, satellites and numerical compression forecast a considerable proliferation of television programmes and a vertiginous audience segmentation, can one picture

5. With the upper limit on advertising revenues being established in 1993 at 100 milion Belgo-Luxembourgian francs, the state contributes to the financing of the balance of the cost of the programme (CLT, 1992: 18 and 1994: 26).

6. Luxembourgish is only spoken by some 200,000 people (Frisoni, 1994: 12).

7. Sources: *ILRES TV 94*.

8. See in the same work, J.-M. Nobre-Correia, 'Belgium: Federalisation of Broadcasting and Community Television'.

9. *La Libre Belgique*, Brussels, 13 July 1994, p. 6.

the CLT maintaining a station set up for demographic reasons and whose audience could easily dwindle? Such a question, however, loses sight of two major facts concerning Luxembourgian society. First, unlike the rest, CLT is not a private enterprise: the government of the Grand Duchy, with representation on the CLT's Board of Directors, has always voiced its opinion regarding the Company's future. In exchange, particularly for diplomatic support in its international development,[10] the CLT renders services to the government of Luxembourg which could be classified as political and cultural.

Second is the unshakeable determination of the people of Luxembourg to provide themselves with all the advantages of a modern state, so as to better affirm their sovereignty and their identity. It is a sentiment clearly expressed in the national motto: 'Mir wëlle blaive wat mir sin' (We wish to remain what we are).

References

CLT (1992): *CLT Rapport Annuel 1991*. Luxembourg.

CLT (1993): *CLT Rapport Annuel 1992*. Luxembourg.

CLT (1994): *CLT Rapport Annuel 1993*. Luxembourg.

Chamard, M.-E. & Kieffer, P. (1992): *La Télé, dix ans d'histoires secrètes*. Paris: Flammarion.

Frisoni, C. (1994): 'Luxembourg 95, pays européen de toutes les cultures', in *Le Monde*, 10 June.

Nobre-Correia, J.-M. (1988): 'Une grande-ducale pas très belge', in *Trends-Tendances*, 329.

Nobre-Correia, J.-M. (1992): 'La CLT: querelle franco-belge autour d'une luxembourgeoise', in *Médiaspouvoirs*, 27.

Trausch, G. (1992): *Histoire du Luxembourg*. Paris: Hatier.

---

10. *Le Soir*, Brussels, 23–24 July 1994, p. 4.

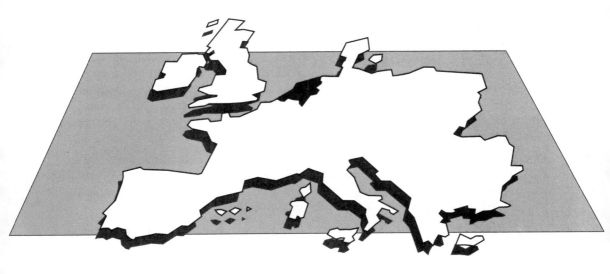

10 The Netherlands: In search of a niche for regional television

Nicholas W. Jankowski

Introduction

Regional television is a new and somewhat uncertain newcomer to the Dutch media scene.[1] Broadcasters in the province of Overijssel claim credit, since September 1992, for distributing the first regional television programming.[2] Since then, a small number of stations have followed with regional television transmissions on a regular basis. This cluster of initiatives is anticipated, depending on the experiences of the 'pioneers', to expand within the coming few years to about seven regional television stations.

Although regional television in the Netherlands is a very recent phenomenon, it should be

1. Many people and organizations have graciously donated their time and information during the preparation of this chapter: Ben Groenendijk (ROOS); Marja van der Leij, Geert de Vries and Marinus de Boer (Omrop Fryslân); Durk Gorter (Fries Academy); Steven Huisman (SALTO); Donja ter Meulen (City of Amsterdam); Jan Kikkert (TV Oost); Marga Peters (Commissariat for the Media); Toshiko Miyazaki; colleagues Coen van der Linden and Ed Hollander, and doctoral student Robert Overvest (University of Nijmegen). I wish to express my appreciation for their input; they cannot, of course, be held accountable for any errors of fact or interpretation which may be present in the text.

2. Such claims are prone to dispute, and Omrop Fryslân in the northern province of Friesland can rightfully issue a counterclaim that it has been engaged in production of regionally orientated television programming, in conjunction with the Netherlands Broadcasting Corporation (NOS) since 1979. And SALTO, officially a local station, has also been producing television programming for a major metropolitan area – one interpretation of 'region' – since 1985.

seen in the context of other small scale electronic media – at both the regional and local level – which have a much longer history. Regional television is, in fact, emerging from a rich heritage dominated until recently by experience with regional radio. In addition, some of the larger local television stations around the country have considered expanding their areas of programme distribution, and these stations now constitute some of the core contenders among current initiatives for regionally-based television.

Another development is that television-based services – such as local teletext and videotext, and cable news services – are often seen as elements which can be integrated into the organizational structures of regional stations. The plans of some stations call for consideration of telematics in the context of regional broadcasting.

This chapter reviews and analyses the place of regional television within this more encompassing landscape of Dutch electronic media at the local and regional level.[3] The central thesis is that current concern for regional television should be seen from two, sometimes conflicting, perspectives: first, the assumed societal value such media can have and, second, the commercial potential they represent. These two perspectives constitute the driving forces behind the development of both local and regional broadcasting, although each perspective has been allotted a different priority at different time periods.

The chapter commences with a review of the issues and statements related to formulation of governmental policy regarding regional broadcasting. Special attention is paid to the functions which have been advanced as 'justifications' or explanations for regional (and local) broadcasting.

In the second section three regional stations currently involved in television production are profiled. These stations suggest, as a group, the aspirations, activities, and concerns of regional television initiatives around the country. The third and final section provides reflection on a number of central developments and notes the most important problems and issues for regional television today. To conclude this section and the chapter, suggestions are made as to where and how social science research may contribute to further understanding of this phenomenon.

Media policy for the regional level

Regional broadcasting has been synonymous with regional radio until the last few years. The first regional television programming commenced in 1992, and as of early 1994 three stations were experimenting with cable-delivered television programming. The rationale sometimes given for this new venture is that television has come to be the primary source of international and national news for most people. It is believed regional television could fulfil that same

---

3. This chapter is not the place for an extended treatment of electronic media in the Netherlands; many other publications are available for readers interested in more detailed information. An excellent and recent enclopaedic reference is Brants and McQuail (1992). Other readily available English language publications, which sometimes emphasize different aspects, include Brants and Jankowski (1985), Van der Haak (1977), Olderaan and Jankowski (1988), Browne (1991), and Stappers, Olderaan and de Wit (1991).

role for news and information at the provincial level. Viewership figures for regional television programming, to the extent available, are presented in the profiles of stations later in the chapter.

Several issues dominate the agendas of the regional stations as a whole, but concern for market encroachment from commercial radio stations – now cable-delivered, but in the near future regulations may permit ether distribution – is perhaps the most important. Also, the relation with stations at both the national and local levels is a frequent issue in discussions. Sometimes the relation is marked by competition for the same advertising market and sometimes co-operation highlights the relation, as in sharing of production facilities. Concern and debate regarding whether the Netherlands is geographically large enough, and financially able, to maintain three levels of broadcasting has also stimulated recent initiatives of co-operation between regional and local stations.

During the 1960s several ministerial white papers and drafts for legislation were produced in preparation of a new broadcasting law, finally enacted in 1967. Regional broadcasting occupied a minor but explicit place in several of these documents. Initially, regional broadcasting was defined as a service intended for residents in outlying regions or provinces. By 1966, this definition had been extended to include cities, and referred to both radio and television. Regional broadcasting slowly came to be seen, then, not merely as a medium for promotion of folk culture in rural and provincial areas, but also as a service for urban residents.

One of the critical issues during this period was which organizational entity was to be responsible for the regional stations – the Netherlands Broadcasting Corporation (NOS) or the regional stations themselves. As a gesture of compromise, both organizational forms were included in the Broadcasting Law of 1967. This situation remained intact until 1989 when NOS responsibility for regional broadcasting was formally terminated.

Whatever organizational form, however, regional stations were intended to fulfil a public service as opposed to a commercial objective. Even with this restriction there was much interest in launching regional stations in the early 1970s. In order to determine how policy should develop the government initiated a regional radio experiment in 1976. Two stations were involved in this experiment, Radio STAD in Amsterdam and SROB in the province Brabant. This experiment with over-the-air regional programming eventually contributed to approval of other regional initiatives. By 1990 the present 13 stations were in operation.

In additional to the organizational form, station objectives occupied a central place in political debates on media policy. During the mid-1970s the governmental minister responsible for broadcasting suggested that local and regional broadcasting should be cast in the framework of community welfare and development. The stations, however, argued for a more professional journalistic objective – providing news and information to the metropolitan regions and provinces which they served. One of the underlying reasons the government wished to see regional broadcasting as an instrument for community development was because the stations would then fall under welfare services, and the funding for such services was being transferred, as part of a general decentralization trend, from the national level to the regional and local levels. With assignment of such a welfare function the national government could absolve itself from further funding of the stations.

Although decentralization of financial support for local and regional electronic media was enacted, the overall strategy of the national government was less successful. By the late 1970s the Ministry of Culture recognized regional radio stations as more than instruments of community welfare. And, in order that the journalistic function of providing independent news and information could be fulfilled with some independence of regional government, an organizational buffer to which the stations are accountable was established.

By 1988, regional broadcasting had come of age in terms of acceptance in policy statements. In the Media Law enacted that year a description and proscription of regional and local broadcasting is provided. Regarding regional stations, they are, in the first place, to produce programming intended primarily for the province or a portion of that geographic area. Secondly, the programming is to be relevant and related to social, cultural and religious life in the province. Finally, the programming in its entirety is to serve the general interest of the province or section thereof. Although tones of community welfare and development are clearly present in these formulations, regional broadcasting had by the time of the enactment of the Media Law been accepted as a professional journalistic enterprise.

Although regional and local broadcasting are indeed anchored in the Media Law, it is by no means certain how secure that anchorage is. In the first half of 1993 the Ministry of Culture, responsible for broadcasting policy, issued a document which strongly questioned the viability of three levels of broadcasting – national, regional, and local – in a country the size of the Netherlands. The Minister proposed dissolving the level of local stations and encouraging mergers between local and regional stations in situations where feasible. The remaining local stations, generally found in small communities, would be degraded to occasional social and cultural 'happenings' on the cable. Several reasons were elaborated for this fusion, but one dominant consideration was the need to secure frequencies for commercial stations to operate at the local or regional level, to conform with European Union media regulations.[4] Although the Minister largely denied any intention to require fusion of stations at the local and regional levels, and spoke of the integrity and independence of local stations, it remains uncertain what may develop after the national elections in May 1994.[5]

Regional television station profiles

In order to appreciate the development of regional television in more detail, the profiles of three stations are presented below: Omrop Fryslân, TV Oost, and SALTO. Each of these

4. This interpretation of European-wide regulations is not shared by all, including the Christian Democratic Party in the Netherlands. As one spokesman for this party noted during a commission debate in late 1993, there is no specific mention of local and regional broadcasting in the regulations under discussion.

5. An amendment to modify the Media Law was submitted to Parliament in late 1994 which is intended to remove restrictions for cooperation in the area of programming and advertising between local and regional stations. Whether the topic of obligatory fusion of regional and local stations will reappear on the agenda depends in part on whether a new Minister is appointed after the elections in May 1994.

stations exemplifies special and generic characteristics of the development of regional television. Together, they provide an overall view of issues and concerns in the current phase of regional television.

Omrop Fryslân

Omrop Fryslân is one of the oldest regional stations operating in the Netherlands, dating from just after World War II when radio station RON (Regionale Omroep Noord) was established. Then, RON provided regional radio broadcasts for the northern provinces of Friesland, Groningen and Drenthe. During the 1950s a specific programme was developed for Frisian speaking listeners. The rationale for this move was that the Frisian language had acquired the status of second national language in the Netherlands and, as such, merited access to the electronic media.[6] Total broadcasting time in that period was no more than a couple of hours per week; cultural events, documentaries, and drama productions dominated the programming formula.

In 1968 a studio was constructed in Leeuwarden, the capital of the Frisian province, and a decade later a separate broadcasting organization for the province had been created. With these developments, the number of programming hours also increased over the years, and by 1992 radio programming was being broadcast an average of eight hours daily. As with other regional radio stations in the Netherlands, Omrop Fryslân has plans to extend its radio service to cover both day and evening listening periods.

Generally speaking, four types of radio programming are currently being produced: news and information, service and public information, background items, and light music. News programmes are presented during the peak listening hours: early in the morning between 7 and 9 am, during the lunch break, and during the late afternoon at the end of the workday. Music and service-oriented programming fill the remaining morning hours.

Financing

As with the other regional stations in the country, Omrop Fryslân receives Dfl. 10 per year from the licence fee for each officially registered radio and television set in the province. This amount is compensated by a contribution from the national government so that the base funding for each of the regional stations in the country is comparable. Another source of funding is through advertising which, since 1992, had been permitted on local and regional stations. Some sponsorship of programmes also contributes to the total revenue.

The television programming Omrop Fryslân produces on the national channel in conjunction with the NOS, described in more detail below, is financed from funding made available by the NOS. The regional television division of Omrop Fryslân, scheduled to start in early 1994, has received seed funding from a special national government subsidy programme for economically depressed regions, from the province of Friesland, and from the European Union. These funds are intended to assist development of this division of the station during

6. Discussions in the national Parliament during the mid-1950s, related to allowing education in the Frisian language, contributed both to acknowledging Frisian as the official second language in the Netherlands and to promoting Frisian programming on national radio and television.

a three-year experimental period. In addition, advertising and programme sponsorship will be solicited to further support the regional television division.

Nationally broadcast Frisian television

Omrop Fryslân has been involved in the production of television programming since 1979 when the station was allocated time from the Netherlands Broadcasting Corporation (NOS) for production of televized instructional materials. This agreement emerged from earlier experimentation with a so-called 'teleboard', initiated in 1973. With assistance from a special pen and electronic tablet, drawings and messages could be transmitted through the ether to television receivers. This equipment was used to supplement Frisian language lessons in schools around the province.

By the end of the 1970s this teleboard equipment was replaced with television equipment and, as of 1979, Omrop Fryslân has received an annual allotment of transmission hours from the NOS. This arrangement has been codified in the Media Law of 1988 which stipulates that the NOS is required to devote programming time to Frisian language and culture. Currently, 31 hours of television programming per year are produced by Omrop Fryslân. About a third of this time is devoted to programming intended to supplement classroom instruction, prepared in co-operation with a school advisory service in the province. The remainder of the programming time is used for general informational programming – documentaries, discussions, and current events. This programming is broadcast weekly on Sundays and repeated once during the week.

Virtually all of the radio and television programming is broadcast in the Frisian language. Since 1992, however, subtitles have been provided in order to make the television programming accessible to viewers who do not understand spoken Frisian.[7]

Audience

The viewership of Omrop Fryslân television programming produced in conjunction with the Netherlands Broadcasting Corporation (NOS) is continuously monitored by the NOS division responsible for audience research.[8] The audience sample for this research, spread throughout the Netherlands, provides an overall indication of viewership. The average percentage of viewers during the 1991–92 television season was less than 1 per cent (equivalent to 96,000 persons) for the most popular Omrop Fryslân programmes.[9]

In order to obtain an indication of viewership among residents of the province Friesland, a telephone survey was held in 1992. Slightly more than half of the respondents indicated they

7. Within the province of Friesland only about 6 per cent of the residents do not understand spoken Fries. The NOS Frisian programme, however, reaches a national audience which is almost entirely unable to understand this language.

8. Data presented in this section are drawn from a NOS audience survey report by Hammersma (1992).

9. As a point of comparison, the most popular nationally transmitted programmes command an audience of several million viewers among the country's 15 million residents.

viewed Omrop Fryslân programmes occasionally. As compared to the results of a similar survey conducted three years earlier, the number of viewers had increased dramatically, from 39 per cent in 1989 to 51 per cent in 1992. This means about 300,000 of the residents in Friesland attended to Omrop Fryslân programming.

Viewers of television programmes listened significantly more to the radio programmes of Omrop Fryslân. They also tended to be more often born and raised in the province than nonviewers. Although viewers were represented in all sectors of the population, older residents with limited education were most prominent among the viewers.

Viewers generally responded positively regarding the television programmes. Some 55 per cent said they found it very worthwhile viewing the programmes. When asked to mention strong aspects of the programmes, various regional elements were mentioned by viewers: that the programmes are about the province, that they are in the Frisian language, and that they provide information about the region.

Regional Frisian television

For several years Omrop Fryslân has wanted to increase the number of broadcast hours allotted by the NOS, but requests were denied. The station then decided to develop its own regional television. And since February 1994 Omrop Fryslân has been producing television independent of the arrangement with the NOS. Initial plans were to broadcast Monday through Friday, between 7 and 9 p.m. The programming format consisted of a half-hour of regional news followed by a general feature on sports or cultural events. This hour block, beginning at 7 p.m. was to be repeated once. As is the case with TV Oost in the province of Overijssel, this programming is distributed via the cable systems in Friesland. In addition, however, Omrop Fryslân has purchased a transmission antenna for over-the-air distribution. This means that residents throughout the province can receive the programming, either by cable or over-the-air.

Before the decision to begin with regional television transpired, much internal discussion and debate within the broadcasting organization had taken place. The station board of directors was generally in favour of the initiative, while personnel affiliated with the national Frisian television service tended to prefer pressing for expansion of this activity. An external advisory commission was appointed to study the alternatives and propose recommendations. A number of observations from the commission's final report (Rapport Adviesgroep, n.d.) highlight many of the central considerations related to the purpose and practice of regional television in Friesland.

The primary reason Omrop Fryslân, along with the provincial government and political parties active in the province, pressed for access to the national television channel in the late 1970s was to strengthen ties of residents with Frisian language and culture. Then, Frisian television programmes were only possible via the national network; co-operation with the NOS was the only option available at the time. The Advisory Commission believed, along with other observers, that the Frisian programming via the NOS was really a form of regional television broadcast nationally. In spite of the later addition of subtitles in 1992, the programming was directed at Frisian residents in Friesland.[10]

One of the particularly troublesome issues was what the relationship would be between the division of Omrop Fryslân responsible for producing the nationally distributed Frisian television programming and the group responsible for programming distributed only within the province, the regional television division. The Advisory Commission recommended integration of the two divisions in order to facilitate efficient use of production facilities and organizational infrastructure. Moreover, the commission felt that eventually changes would be required in the type of programming produced for the national television net, and that producers for each of the divisions should not only co-operate but work toward integration of programming.

Regarding programming, the commission believed a regional news programme should constitute the foundation of regional television. Such a programme, it was argued, would attract the most viewers. Some staff of Omrop Fryslân, however, reacted strongly to this suggestion (as well as toward other commission recommendations) and argued for magazine format and human interest programming as well.[11] The programming format with which the regional division intended to commence service, however, was based on a half-hour regional news service supplemented by another half-hour of programming around diverse subjects in the areas of sports, politics and culture. In addition, plans were to repeat some of the programmes from the national television division.

Future concerns

Although Omrop Fryslân has received considerable financial support for the duration of the three-year regional television experiment from a variety of sources, much of this support is nonrenewable and other sources will have to be found by the end of the experiment. Even with this support, the money available for programme production is substantially less than the amount which the national division receives from the NOS. One division of Omrop Fryslân, in other words, has adequate resources to produce professional television while the other division can hardly make ends meet. This 'rich man, poor man' construction within the same organization will, among other matters, remain on the agenda of Omrop Fryslân during the coming years. Whatever the results of the experiment with regional television, however, programming directed at Frisian residents living in Friesland will remain an objective of Omrop Fryslân, in any event through the weekly programmes produced in conjunction with the NOS on one of the national channels – the national Frisian television division of Omrop Fryslân.

---

10. Interestingly, this construction is unique in Europe, whereby television programming in a minority language, spoken in a single province, is broadcast on the national net and can be received by viewers throughout the country.

11. For reactions to this and other commission recommendations see the international Omrop Fryslân report (Televisiecommissie, 1993).

TV Oost

Interest in establishing regional television in the province of Overijssel can be traced to discussions held in the late 1980s. Then, Radio Oost was becoming increasingly concerned about competition from commercial stations. Two strategies were proposed, intended to counteract this encroachment. First, it was deemed important to increase the amount of the station's own radio programming. Second, it was proposed to explore initiation of regional television. Such a development could provide not only a new television service for the region, but also increase public awareness and use of Radio Oost programming through both announcements and programmatic linkage between the two media.

Another concern during this period was the diminishing number of media 'voices' in the province. There were, only a few years ago, four independent daily newspapers operating in the province. Press mergers have since taken place and one publisher is now responsible for all of the daily newspapers in the region. The thought was that electronic media, particularly television, could provide additional pluriformity in the media at the regional level.

Within a relatively short time, both strategies became policy. Radio station programming was increased from 8 hours per week in 1957, to 12 per day in 1989, 14 in 1993, to a planned around-the-clock service in the course of 1994. Radio Oost was able, much like Omrop Fryslân, to build upon experience with radio programming initiated just after World War II. During those first decades of operation, the station provided programming for several provinces in the eastern section of the country. Since 1985, however, the station has been producing radio programming specifically for the province of Overijssel. As for regional television, a new sister organization was established which began producing weekly television programming in September 1992.

The initial television programming plan was quite modest: a mere weekend of regional television to let residents 'taste' the service. This plan was soon seen as inadequate, and the period was extended to three months. Inasmuch as the television programming was to be distributed via the cable systems in the province (no ether transmitter was available), special governmental permission was required. National regulation only allowed cable distribution of television programming for local stations, and such programming was to be restricted to the municipality where it originated.

In 1992 an amendment to the regulations was proposed and passed by Parliament which allowed for the experimental distribution of regional television programming via the cable. Such experiments could be conducted for a minimum of one and a maximum of three years. The initially modest plans noted above were then transformed into a proposal conforming to the experimental conditions, and in September 1992 the first regional television programming for the province was broadcast.

Programming

The programming format has remained relatively unchanged since the first broadcast. Transmission begins just a few minutes before the six o'clock evening national news programme. The highlights of the regional news are presented in those few minutes. After

147

the 15-minute national news programme, a regional news show is provided which lasts another 15 minutes. Then, an informational magazine-format programme is broadcast. This also lasts around 15 minutes, but can be, when necessary, extended to a maximum of 30 minutes. The programme, in other words, varies from 45 to 60 minutes and is repeated later the same evening. Initially, a single weekly programme was produced with a repeat later in the week. In 1993 two programmes per week were produced, and in early 1994 a programming schedule is planned for five days per week, Monday through Friday.

Financing

One of the central concerns of TV Oost since inception has been to secure an adequate and stable financial base. Until now, the station has operated entirely from advertising revenue. The provincial government has spoken in favour of regional television, but at the same time has made clear that no funding, either grants or loans, is available for the medium. Another possible future source of capital for regional television is a levy on the residents or the cable subscribers in the province, a general option discussed in more detail later in this chapter. It is doubtful, however, whether such a levy will be possible in Overijssel because of public opposition to any increase in the fee for broadcasting services.[12]

Another plan to secure funding through a partnership with a major newspaper publisher in the region did not materialize.[13] These developments, in total, have come to mean that TV Oost is entirely dependent on advertising and programming sponsorship. One of the possible consequences of such financial dependence, particularly for a public service-oriented station, is that concessions may be claimed by, or offered to, advertisers. Editorial independence, in other words, may be jeopardized for attainment of financial solvency.

Audience

Approximately 80 per cent of the residents in the province are connected to one of the cable television systems used for distribution of TV Oost programming. Shortly after the station began cablecasting in 1992 the audience research division of the Netherlands Broadcasting Corporation (NOS) was requested to survey viewer attention and reaction to the programming.

Two telephone surveys were held in October and December of 1992.[14] Researchers were interested in awareness of, interest in, and opinion of TV Oost programming. More than half of the respondents (58 per cent) were aware of the station and about a quarter (26 per cent) had seen programmes on occasion. Some 80 per cent of the viewers assessed the programmes positively. Almost three-quarters of the viewers and 60 per cent of the non-viewers felt TV

---

12. There have already been petitions and letters to the editors of newspapers in the province protesting such a levy.

13. On the basis of a collectively developed business plan and financial prognosis, the board of directors of the publishing firm decided the risk of regional television was too great at that point in time – late 1993. Estimates suggest TV Oost will not begin to make a profit before 1998 and will suffer a loss of Dfl. 5 million during the initial three years of operation.

14. These surveys are reported in Meijs (1993), the source of the percentages noted here.

Oost should continue broadcasting television programmes for the province. A little more than half (52 per cent) indicated willingness to contribute a nominal sum (Dfl. 1 per month) to financially support regional television. Follow-up research, important in determining whether this degree of viewer attendance and opinion remains stable, has yet to be conducted.[15]

Future plans

TV Oost is a young organization and is consequently considering a variety of alternatives for its -admittedly uncertain- future. Initial discussions have already taken place regarding construction of an antenna for ether transmission of TV Oost programming. The necessary preparation for this form of programme distribution, however, will require several years preparation; it is not anticipated this addition in transmission facilities will be available before 1996.

One of the future plans which may help solve the financial problems of TV Oost is extended co-operation with the broadcasting organizations in two neighbouring provinces – Drente and Groningen – and with the primary cable company operating in all three provinces, EDON. This would allow recruitment of advertising from a much larger region. Programming would resemble the current formula with additional news and information input from the other two provinces. TV Oost hopes to have achieved such trans-provincial television by late 1994 or 1995.

TV Oost also has plans to co-operate with local television stations operating in Overijssel. In the course of 1994 the intent is to secure arrangements with one or two local stations regarding programming development and exchange. Finally, the station is considering development of various telematics and interactive cable services. A cable newspaper and local teletext and Videotext system are currently being developed with the cable company active in the province. It is anticipated these services will be operational in the course of 1994.

Realization of these plans rests with securing a stable financial basis, but whether advertising alone can provide that basis is doubtful. It is estimated that one hour of daily television programming on an annual basis costs around Dfl. 5 million, and projections for possible advertising revenue for TV Oost come to no more than Dfl. 2.5 million.

Independent of that problem, a spokesman for the station feels TV Oost has the advantage of emerging from an already existing broadcasting organization, Radio Oost. Another strength of TV Oost, according to this person, is its multi-functional staff, capable of performing a wide diversity of tasks. These characteristics, he believes, are not only important for TV Oost, but for the successful launching of a regional television station anywhere in the Netherlands. However necessary these aspects may be, they offer little compensation for the economic demands of professional television production.

15. Another audience survey was held during a visit by the Queen to the province in the following year. Although viewership was predictably high for such an occasion, there was also some indication that overall awareness and use of TV Oost had also increased somewhat.

SALTO

It may seem peculiar that a local radio and television organization like SALTO is included
in a chapter on regional television. Part of the explanation lies in the debate held in the
Netherlands almost two decades ago around the interpretation of 'region' for broadcasting
organizations (Kuypers, 1977). The upshot of that discussion was that both provincially-
oriented stations – most of the present regional radio stations in the Netherlands – and urban
or major city stations, such as SALTO and Radio Rijnmond in Rotterdam, should be
considered regional broadcasting organizations. The primary reason for this position was
that the audience size of these stations is frequently much larger and more diverse than that
of provincial stations operating in thinly populated areas. A second aspect of consideration
is the sheer size of the cable infrastructures in cities like Amsterdam, that cable system being
one of the largest in Europe. At present, there are more than 350,000 connections, and the
system also extends to a number of satellite cities surrounding the capital.

Perhaps because of this discussion, or because of anticipated extension of the geographic
service area of the station, the word 'regional' was included in the formal name of the SALTO
– Amsterdam Foundation for Local and Regional Television Broadcasting (*Stichting Am-
sterdamse Lokale en regionale Televisie Omroep*). That point aside, SALTO has its 'roots'
in the regional broadcasting organization Radio STAD which was launched in the mid-1970s
as part of an experiment with this level of broadcasting (see description of this experiment
earlier in the chapter). Since the early 1980s, Radio STAD was concerned about developing
a division which would provide television programming, and by 1983 that division, SALTO,
had been formally created.

From that point in time SALTO became the broadcasting organization in Amsterdam with
formal authority to distribute, via the ether or the cable, radio and television programming.[16]
Since 1985 it has provided a public access service on both radio and television channels.
Currently, one television and five radio channels are available for individuals, groups and
organizations. The programming on the radio channels is arranged thematically, and regular
contributors are given specific days and broadcasting times in order to assist listeners in
finding programming.

Programming on three of the radio channels is transmitted both over-the-air and via the cable;
programming on the other two radio channels is only cable-delivered. Programming on the
television open channel, Open Kanaal, is available only via the cable. In addition to the these
channels, SALTO has, since 1992, operated a professionally-run radio and a professional
television channel. The radio station is entirely owned and the television station for 50 per
cent by newspaper publishers, and the stations rely substantially on advertising revenue as a
source of income.[17]

16. National governmental regulations permit one such broadcasting organization per municipality
which is obliged to reflect in its governing body social and cultural life within the city. In 1991, the
SALTO governing body (*stichtingsraad*) had 47 representatives.

17. The open channels, in contrast, do not yet broadcast advertising and rely heavily on a variety of
governmental subsidies and grants for income.

Programming philosophy

The philosophy and programming activities of both the open television channel (Open Kanaal) and the professional television division (AT5) have gained a special place in Dutch media history. SALTO's open channels are based on the public access concept which developed in the United States in the 1970s and is now also present in the station policies of some European initiatives, particularly in Germany.[18] SALTO's Open Kanaal is one of the few examples of stations practising public access philosophy in the Netherlands.[19]

The professional television division of SALTO, AT5, has a similarly unique position in recent Dutch initiatives. The station's programming format has served as a model for other regional television stations, and its staff is frequently consulted by other regional television initiatives.

Open Kanaal

Access can be interpreted and measured in many ways (Jankowski, 1988), but one indicator is the number of persons involved in programming production. Several thousand volunteers are active in producing both the radio and television programming broadcast under SALTO's jurisdiction. Regarding television, the number of productions, broadcast hours and contributing groups has increased during each year of operation. In 1987 some 230 programmes were produced, in 1990 there were 446, in 1993 the number was 1250 and some 1600 are expected by the end of 1994. The number of hours these programmes are made available on the cable, including replays, has increased proportionally: from 2700 in 1987 to 6500 in 1994. The groups which submit programming have, during the same time period, increased from 20 to 65; the current number of regularly contributing groups is 32.[20]

MTV: minority television

Given the number and diversity of groups involved in Open Kanaal television programming, it is not possible to consider them in any detail within the confines of this chapter. One group, however, is singled out as an illustration of SALTO television producers: MTV-Amsterdam (*Migrantentelevisie-Amsterdam*). This organization has been active in the production of television for minority groups in Amsterdam since a national experiment[21] was held around minority television in the early 1980s (see Gooskins, 1992). Initiated in 1984, the objective of MTV is to work toward integration of minority groups in Dutch society. During a decade

18. A recent issue of the journal *Media Perspektiven* sketches these German open channel initiatives; one of the contributions to that issue (Hollander and Renckstorf, 1993) portrays the practice of public access to the electronic media in the Netherlands at various media system levels.

19. In Utrecht and Rotterdam there are also divisions of stations which provide public access opportunities, but the operations are much smaller. In addition, in the early 1980s, a two-week experiment with public access television took place in Utrecht; see Beenen *et al.* (1982).

20. These figures are reported in SALTO (1992:4) and a proposal for an additional open television channel (SALTO, 1993:3).

21. That experiment has, in the course of time, resulted in considerable spin-off. One result is the establishment of a special foundation (STOA, *Stichting Omroep Allochtonen*) funded by the Ministry of Culture to produce radio and television programming for ethnic minority groups in the country. STOA programming is carried out by several local stations, including SALTO's MTV.

of activity, MTV has earned the status of a valued television production company for minority groups in and around the city. Presently, programmes are produced for Turkish, Moroccan, Suriname and Antillian residents of Amsterdam. Employing a magazine programming format, each broadcast generally consists of news, art and culture, public information, and entertainment. The language of the programming corresponds to that of the intended target group; in addition, Dutch subtitles are usually provided for viewers unable to comprehend Arabic and Turkish, the two other languages in which programming is produced. MTV programmes are cablecasted weekly on Thursdays, beginning at 11 a.m. and repeated until around 2 in the afternoon.

Relatively recent audience research[22] around MTV programmes suggests that they are well attended by Amsterdam viewers. About a quarter of the residents of Amsterdam watch at least once a month MTV programming. When account is taken of the intended target groups of particular MTV programmes, viewer attention reaches as much as 80 per cent. Viewers tend to watch programmes in their entirety and, in the case of Moroccan and Turkish viewers, sometimes twice a day.

AT5: professional television

SALTO has been interested in providing a form of professional television since inception, but it was not until 1992 when the financial basis was made possible. Then, advertising was permitted by the national government for local and regional stations. As of April 1992 this division of SALTO, called AT5, began cablecasting programming.

The initial period of the station was exceptionally problematic. The chief editor resigned after the first few weeks of activity and advertising revenue fell far short of the anticipated amount. Particularly this last development stimulated AT5 staff to modify the programming formula – which until then primarily consisted of news and talk shows – to include more entertainment-oriented programming. A cooking programme, a dating show and an American soap series were added to the programming list.

These programming changes created a wave of debate among SALTO board members, as well as among others concerned with the new direction taken by this division of SALTO. The SALTO board of directors (*stichtingsraad*) felt such programming, particularly entertainment such as the American soap series, was not within the guidelines established for AT5 programming. When the AT5 editor refused to modify the programming, the SALTO board took the far-reaching measure of requesting a court injunction. The issue was ultimately resolved outside of court, however; after expiration of the American soap series, the programming format returned to one in which Amsterdam-related programming predominates.

Once these initial problems were behind AT5, the station was able to develop a sizeable group of viewers. By the end of the first year of operation, 20 per cent of the Amsterdam

22. Much of the information in this section on MTV, including the audience data, comes from the brochure 'Migrantentelevisie Amsterdam', February 1993.

population, on the average, attended to AT5 programming.[23] The news programme was by far the most popular: each week about half of the population viewed one or more of these programmes. About a quarter of the population reported not watching AT5 programming at all. And according to audience research conducted as recently as October 1993, 14.6 per cent of the Amsterdam residents were watching the six o'clock local news on AT5 – a higher percentage than any of the national channels attained at that time in the Amsterdam region[24].

Presently, AT5 programming begins just before 6 p.m. with an overview of local news highlights. Then the national news programme is carried, followed by about a half-hour local news show. Various additional items related to sport, local politics, culture and weather are inserted until the next national news journal is broadcast at 8 pm. AT5 programming is repeated until around midnight. The AT5 programming format has served as a model for other regional television stations. Both TV Oost and Omrop Fryslân programme producers have consulted with AT5 personnel regarding a suitable formula for their own operations. There is, as a consequence, much similarity between the programming of TV Oost and AT5.

Present and future issues

A central issue on SALTO's agenda during the coming years is possible co-operation between the professional television division, AT5, and the regional radio station in the province, Radio Noord Holland. As elsewhere in the country, this provincial radio station is considering providing a television service. Unlike TV Oost and Omrop Fryslân which initiated regional television divisions from within their own organizations, Radio Noord Holland has no experience with this medium.[25] This kind of co-operative venture between a local and regional station is what, incidentally, the Ministry of Culture would like to see happen on a larger scale around the country (see discussion elsewhere in chapter on 1993 Ministerial memorandum).

Another serious concern is the decline in sufficient programming slots for open channel television offerings. Time on the current Open Kanaal is essentially fully booked with programming; new initiatives can hardly be allotted broadcasting time because of current demand. This situation led SALTO's Board of Directors to request a second channel on the cable system from the city for public access programming. The request was denied in late 1993, but in all likelihood will be honoured when allocation of channel space on the cable system is again reviewed in late 1994. An additional television channel would allow SALTO to not only increase the volume of access programming, but also to begin organizing programming into thematically related slots.

Finally, SALTO is very concerned about developing new television-based interactive services. It already commissioned development of a local teletext service since 1990 on the

23. Figures reported in SALTO Annual Report 1992.

24. Reported by Van Horn (1993: 6).

25. Interestingly, Radio Noord Holland is the organizational metamorphosis Radio STAD underwent some years ago when the station changed its programming focus from the city to the province. Radio STAD, as noted above, helped create SALTO in the early 1980s and now is considering 'marriage' with one of its own offspring.

open television channel and has stimulated experimentation with two-way cable communication related to televized public debates (see Jankowski and Mendel, 1990). The broadcasting organization considers development of telematics of major importance and a policy document has recently been distributed internally to promote consideration of possible applications. Furthermore, one of the programming groups which makes regular use of SALTO's Open Kanaal facilities is involved in the initiative 'Digital City', taking place in Amsterdam during the first four months of 1994. This project is intended to utilize a variety of computer communication possibilities and relate them to Amsterdam political and cultural issues. SALTO is lending its facilities to a series of public debates on the potential applications of computer mediated communication.[26]

Conclusions and outlook for the future

Looking at the media scene in the Netherlands, it is difficult not to be struck by the flurry of activity around regional television initiatives and pioneering stations. There are, particularly for the size of the country, a surprisingly large number – three – already in operation and another three in the 'starting blocks'. The economic and organizational realities of regional television, however, will certainly impede, if not prohibit, the number of permanent successes in this new media adventure. No one anticipates regional television to develop alongside all 13 regional radio stations. The most positive estimate is that six to seven stations will emerge and survive.

These stations are anticipated in major metropolitan areas – such as around Rotterdam, Amsterdam, and The Hague – where existing local television stations can relatively easily expand operations to neighbouring municipalities. This development is, in a sense, a logical result of the already existing tendency to connect neighbouring cable television systems – such as described in the case of Amsterdam and the local station SALTO. These regional stations will probably only cablecast their programming inasmuch as cable penetration is close to complete.

Regional television is not only destined for urban areas, however. A number of initiatives in primarily rural regions are also well underway. Regional television in areas like the province of Friesland, where a strong cultural basis already exists, will do well. Friesland has the added advantage of its own language which intertwines closely with cultural life in the province. Dialects of Dutch are particularly strong in other provinces and also linked with regional culture (e.g. Limburg, Drenthe), and these regions or provinces may also provide sufficient 'nutrient' for the development of regional television.

Wherever regional television develops, however, ties with broadcasting organizations at both the local and national level will be explored. This development is, in part, an outcome of

26. Involvement in this project is, in fact, an extension of SALTO policy to remain on the 'cutting edge' of television activities. In early 1993 SALTO was co-host and sponsor to an international festival, Tactical Television, where a wide variety of innovations with television were demonstrated: the emergence of local stations in Eastern Europe, utilization of satellite television facilities for action and citizen groups, and demonstrations of video technology for both artistic and political objectives. See Van Bergeijk *et al.* (1993) for further information.

concern by the national government to reduce the complexity (and expense) of three levels of electronic media. It is also part of station policy to combine resources where possible. Such alliances, however, will not develop easily; the differences in philosophy, intention, and practice among stations at the three levels are substantial.

Finally, the matter of money. At a recent 'meeting of experts' on media concentration, a major publisher in the Netherlands advised the director of the ROOS, co-ordinating body of the regional stations, to disband plans for developing regional television and, instead, concentrate on what regional stations are already good at: radio programming. His advice was based on a purely economic rationale: estimates suggest that between Dfl. 4–5 million per year is needed to produce an hour of regional television programming on a daily basis. That kind of capital, he asserted, will be difficult to raise, year in, year out.

It is no exaggeration, then, to assert that the central concern in the development of regional television is where the money is going to come from necessary to properly finance the enterprise. As stations become increasing dependent on advertising, this concern merges with another issue: whether and, if so, to what degree stations may be able to remain public service institutions. The director of the regional broadcasting organization ROOS maintains that a purely commercial financial basis, from advertising and sponsoring, will not generate adequate resources for regional stations in the long run. Support from cable companies, under consideration with some stations such as TV Oost, is also inadequate, according to the ROOS director. The only option which can be seriously considered is that at least an important portion of the financing comes from public funds, in particular from an increase in the licence fee collected from households with television sets. It is anticipated that the national government will allow provincial governments to increase this fee in the future. Should the fee be raised by another Dfl. 10 per household, regional television stations will then have a stable financial basis; commercial funding can then serve as a supplement to this amount. At this point in time, however, there is no assurance whether the national government will permit such an increase and, even if allowed, whether the provinces will be willing to levy such an additional burden. In the province of Overijssel where TV Oost operates, for example, there has already been protest against such a move.

The rationale for regional television is, of course, independent of financial concerns. The ROOS (1993) released a memorandum on this new medium at the end of 1993, and one of the central questions addressed was 'why regional television'. The authors first stated, for the record, that regional radio has achieved a substantial share of the market and that, together with the regional newspaper, it has become one of the most important sources of journalistic information about city and region. At the same time, television has become, on a national scale, the most dominant source of information for people. It is reasonable to assume, according to the memorandum authors, that this public preference for television is not only applicable to the national and international levels. Regional television, it is reasoned, could fulfil the same function at the level of city and geographic region.

In the same memorandum, three alternatives for distribution of regional television programming are compared. There is, first of all, cable-delivered programming. This is the alternative, currently available on an experimental basis, which most of the regional stations considering television programming are employing. Second, there is over-the-air or ether distribution of programming. Omrop Fryslân has purchased a transmitter for this mode of programme distribution and other stations are considering such an investment, particularly those in provinces with relatively low penetrations of cable or where the cable systems are not interconnected. Finally, there is the so-called 'window' alternative: where regional stations are allotted a portion of the transmission time of one of the national channels and the programming is distributed over-the-air via a transmitter covering most of a particular province. Although this is an alternative practised in some other European countries, such as England, it is expected to take several years before solutions will be found for the logistic and organizational problems accompanying its implementation in the Netherlands.

Areas for research

It seems fitting, inasmuch as this book is part of a larger research-oriented project, to end this chapter with suggestions for research questions related to regional television. Since the mid-1970s, in fact, the Dutch government has commissioned substantial amounts of social science research to aid designers of media policy. In 1976, for example, an exploratory study identified several areas of concern for media policy (Kempers, 1977). This was followed by a series of in-depth investigations which led to a major report intended to promote an integrated media policy (WRR, 1982). Regional broadcasting occupied an explicit – albeit modest – place in these studies. More recent investigations (Hollander *et al.*, 1992; Van der Linden and Hollander, 1993) have specifically focused on small scale electronic and print media.

In a certain sense, the questions relevant for researching regional television are no different than those for any other medium at any other level in an electronic media system. One commonly employed framework for categorizing areas of media research suggests four foci of attention: the overall media and policy environment, the specific media organization, aspects of the message system, and – last but not least – the audience. Different theoretical perspectives often guide the research questions for each of these categories.

Media Environment

Regarding the environment in which regional television is developing, the role this medium (along with other media) may play in a democratic state is perhaps the most dominant theoretical perspective behind questions formulated. Media pluralism, media access and citizen participation are frequently noted terms derived from this perspective (Jankowski, 1988). Several questions flow directly form these concepts which are relevant to the development of regional television: To what degree does regional television contribute to pluralism of the media at the regional level? To what extent does regional television increase access to the media at the regional level? To what degree does regional television contribute to increased participation in the political and social life of citizens at the regional level? Yet another question relates to the current trend to merge or encourage co-operation between the three levels of electronic media: What is the impact of the proposed forms of co-operation between electronic media at different levels on the pluriformity of the media system, on access to the different media, and finally on the participation of citizen in community and regional life?

Media organization

Much research has focused on the internal workings of media organizations (Altheide, 1974; Gans, 1979; Tuchman, 1978), but little of this work has been related to either local or regional level media. One particular concern for the development of regional television in the Netherlands is how the distinctly different organizational cultures of local and regional broadcasting interact where forms of co-operation develop. Central to present-day concerns is what form of financing develops for regional television. The potential influence commercial sources may have on the public service nature of regional television programming deserves systematic attention by investigators.

Media content

Students of local broadcasting in the Netherlands have noted that there has been essentially no investigation of the content of these media (Hollander *et al.*, 1992). The observation also applies to regional radio and television programming. This is a particularly unfortunate omission because without analysis of programming content it is not possible to determine the degree and manner regionally and locally related topics are present. Such information is essential to determining whether the addition of yet another medium such as regional television contributes to any greater diversity of opinion and expression – the primary reason, it should be remembered, for advocating a policy of media pluralism.

Media audience

A major research programme is presently underway in the Netherlands to examine changes in media use as a consequence of the increasing diversity of media offerings. Data collected in this project have been examined at the local and regional levels (see e.g. Hollander, Vergeer and Verschuren, 1993; Verschuren and Memelink, 1989). Moreover, the audience research division of the Netherlands Broadcasting Corporation periodically conducts surveys of listener and viewer attention to regional broadcasting. Data from studies such as these may help determine whether regional television becomes an important source of news and information. Although proponents of regional television say the medium will eventually become the primary news and information source at the regional level as it already is at the national level, this assertion has not yet been documented. Given the degree of media diversity and competition, it is not entirely certain this promise for regional television will be fulfilled.

To conclude, the issue whether the Netherlands is large enough for three levels of broadcasting – national, regional and local – can only be adequately addressed once information has been collected on all four of the above foci of research. Regional television is only possible on the condition sufficient structural funding is found. It acquires legitimacy once the programming is shown to be distinct from that offered at either the national or local level. Perhaps most important, both financially and principally, is that an adequately large audience must develop which regularly attends to and values regional television programming. It is much too early, of course, to expect a documented response to the questions posed in this section. It is not too early, however, to begin with the systematic collection of data for formulating a response in the future.

References

Altheide, D.L. (1974): *Creating Reality*. London: Sage.

Beenen, A., Binder, P., Capel, L., Herpt, M., Naber, J., Meijs, J., Spinhof, H., Bekkers, W. & Middel, R. (1982): *Kanaal 42; twee weken Utrechtse radio en televisie; geschiedenis en public access*. Hilversum: NOS.

Bergeijk, van J., Van Dijk, G., Koch, K. & Raijmakers, B. (1993): *The Next Five Minutes: A Conference, Exhibition and TV Program on Tactical Television*. Amsterdam: Paradiso.

Gans, H.J. (1979): *Deciding What's News*. New York: Vintage Books.

Gooskins, I. (1992): 'Experimenting with Minority Television in Amsterdam', in N. Jankowski, O. Prehn & J.G. Stappers (eds.): *The People's Voice: Local Radio and Television in Europe*. London: Libbey.

Hammersma, M. (1992): *Omrop Fryslân op televisie*, Hilversum: NOS, Afdeling Kijk- en Luisteronderzoek.

Hollander, E. & Renckstorf, K. (1993): 'Gefährdung des Prinzips der Bürgerbeteiligung Partizipationskonzepte im niederländischen', in *Media Perspektiven*, 7, 342–349.

Hollander, E., Van der Linden, C., Vergeer, M. & Verschuren, P. (1992): *Het belang van kleinschalige informatievoorziening en de wenselijkheid van een beleid inzake kleinschalige informatievoorziening: Een advies aan de mediaraad*. Nijmegen: Het Persinstituut/Vakgroep Communicatiewetenschap Katholieke Universiteit Nijmegen.

Hollander, E., Vergeer M. & Verschuren, P. (1993): 'Het publiek van lokale en regionale media'. *Massacommunicatie*, 21.

Horn, B. van (1993): 'Fons van Westerloo: Graag nog meer tegendraadsheid', in *VPRO Gids,* 49.

Jankowski, N.W. (1988): *Community Television in Amsterdam: Access to, Participation in and Use of the Lokale Omroep Bijlmermeer* (dissertation). Amsterdam: Universiteit van Amsterdam.

Jankowski, N.W. & Mendel, R. (1990): *The Public Sphere and Interactive Media: A Conceptual and Methodological Framework*. Paper presented at International Association of Mass Communication Research, Bled, Yugoslavia.

Kempers, F. (1987): *Mediabeleid en mediaonderzoek*. Amsterdam: Institute of the Press, University of Amsterdam.

Meijs, J. (1993): *TV Oost. Regionale televisie verzorgd door Radio Oost*. Hilversum: NOS, Afdeling Kijk- en Luisteronderzoek.

Rapport Adviesgroep (n.d.): *Rapport adviesgroep regional televisie Omrop Fryslân* (Report of independent Advisory Commission installed to review possibility of regional television in Friesland).

ROOS (1993): *Regionale televisie, een uitdaging aan Hilversum* (Final report of ROOS working group television). Hilversum: ROOS.

SALTO (1992): *Jaarverslag 1992.* Amsterdam: SALTO.

SALTO (1992): *Salto beleidsplan,* report. Amsterdam: SALTO.

SALTO (1993, august): *Toelichting op de aanvraag voor een extra televisie kanaal voor de programma's van SALTO Omroep Amsterdam,* stencil. Amsterdam: SALTO.

Televisiecommissie (1993): *Aanpak en opzet an de Friese televisie in de lucht en op de kabel* (report of the television commission of Omrop Fryslân).

Tuchman, G. (1978): *Making News: A Study in the Construction of Reality.* New York: Free Press.

Verschuren, P.J. & Memelink, R.J. (1989): *Media atlas van Nederland.* The Hague: SDU.

WRR (1982): *Samenhangend mediabeleid.* The Hague: State Publishing House.

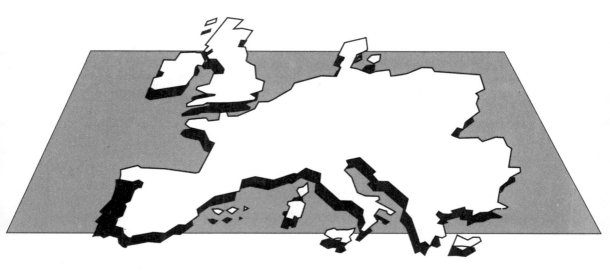

11 Portugal: Insularity, the basis of regional television

Francisco Rui Cádima[1]

The general political framework, the nation and the regions

The nation of Portugal covers an area of 91,985 km² and is made up of the mainland area (18 districts in the Iberian peninsula) and the two autonomous regions of Madeira and the Azores, islands lying to the west of the mainland territory in the Atlantic Ocean.

Portugal is a democratic state with a parliamentary regime. Its government is responsible to the President of the Republic and the Assembly. The autonomous regions of the Azores and Madeira have administrative and financial autonomy and regional governments.

Constitutionalism came to Portugal in 1820 as a result of the Liberal Revolution. The Republic was established in 1910. The revolutionary process to install it began in 1891 and can be traced back to the liberal reformist ideas of Antero de Quental and Oliveira Martins, among others. The Republic, of a democratic and liberal nature, was finally installed on 5 October, 1910. The new regime issued laws which revolutionized key sectors of Portuguese socio-political life such as the religious sector, which energetically reacted to these changes. Thus, the following 16 years of government were characterized by constant instability caused by the series of military *coups d'etats*, by the crises caused by the radical positions of political and party groups and by the social unrest of the people most affected by the resolutions adopted on economic and financial matters of national importance.

1. With the cooperation of Marta Civil and Rosabel Argote.

28 May 1926 marked the beginning of a right-wing military movement which, while attempting to restore political order to the country through a stable government, ended up establishing a dictatorship headed first by Salazar and later, after 1968, by Marcello Caetano. The dictatorial regime came to an end with the *Revoluçao dos Cravos* (Carnation Revolution) on 25 April 1974. Two years later, on 25 April 1976, the new Constitution of the Democratic State of Portugal was approved. This document recognized the statute of autonomy of Madeira and the Azores.

Specific characteristics of the regions in Portugal

The State of Portugal is divided into two primary geographic regions: mainland Portugal on the one hand and the two Atlantic archipelagos – the Azores and Madeira – on the other. Insularity, climate, and distance from the Iberian peninsula of the latter, together with their source of funding, clearly differentiate the islands from mainland Portugal and are the basis of the autonomous policy from which they have benefited since the Constitution was adopted in 1976. The Constitution includes the principle of the political and administrative decentralization of Portugal, although in practice this principle has only been developed in the case of the autonomous regions of Madeira and the Azores.

The archipelago of Madeira consists mainly of the islands of Madeira and Porto Santo with a territorial area of 795 km^2 and 253,000 inhabitants. The capital city is Funchal, in the island of Madeira. Its main revenues come from tourism, vineyards, sugar cane and fruit.

The archipelago of the Azores is made up of the islands of Santa María, S. Miguel, Terceira, Pico, Faial, S. Jorge, Flores, Corvo and Graciosa. The population is 237,600 and the territorial area totals 2,333 km^2. The tobacco and dairy industries together with beet sugar, fish canneries and tourism are the basis of the economy. The capital city is Ponta Delgada.

It should be pointed out that both archipelagos share a common language and culture with the rest of Portugal, so that with the exception of some cultural features peculiar to the islands, we cannot talk in terms of their having a distinctive identity different from that of mainland Portugal.

As for the latter, regional differences are not negligible. In fact, the 89,000 km^2 of which the mainland consists encompass ''two Portugal' – the atlantic north and the mediterranean south, as well as a very mosaic of landscapes and populations' (Navarro, 1992: 602). The northern zone (above the river Tagus), on the one hand, is divided into a prosperous, industrial coastal area (80 per cent of industries and rich wine-producing areas are concentrated there), along the Lisbon-Porto axis, and the mountainous, under-developed inland area. The whole region is traditionally Catholic and conservative. The region stretching south of the Tagus to São Vicente Cape may also be divided into two areas: on the one hand, the Alentejo region, with its cereal farming and large estates, one of the cradles of the Carnation Revolution, and on the other, the arid south of the Algarve, which lives almost entirely on the tourist industry.

On a linguistic level, mainland Portugal constitutes a homogeneous territory, with no distinctive linguistic or cultural identities apart from the obvious differences of dialect from region to region. In this context, according to a study by the European Community, 'There are clear differences between the Portuguese spoken in the north and the south of the country ..., which do not, however, pose a threat to the unity of the language'. The only noteworthy exception to this uniformity is the existence of 'Mirandès, a language variant related to the Asturian-Leonese dialect of Spanish', spoken in the area of Miranda do Douro (north-east of the country) by a few thousand individuals. Its use is confined exclusively to spoken language and it is not supported by any measures of protection or promotion (Siguan, 1990: 51–52).

Table 1. The Regions in Portugal

	Area (km^2)	Population
North	21,290	3,452,263
Central	23,672	1,720,787
Lisbon & the Tagus Valley	11,926	3,500,000
Alentejo	26,766	572,506
Algarve	4,991	340,000
The Azores	2,333	237,583
Madeira	795	253,045

Source: ICEP, 1994.

Political, socio-economic and administrative dimensions

As already pointed out, the Portuguese Constitution contemplates the possibility of a general decentralization of the State, even if political and administrative regionalization has only been carried out in the two Atlantic archipelagos. Since 1992, there has been constant debate on the extension of the autonomous model to the mainland regions. There would appear to be a certain consensus regarding the opportuneness of this extension, but differences of opinion arise regarding the demarcation of the regional boundaries: 'seven regions are to be created, according to economic units, or even nine, according to administrative criteria?' (Navarro, 1992: 602). Meanwhile, mainland Portugal continues to use the old purely administrative division into districts and provinces.

The islands of Madeira and the Azores base their autonomy on a formal statute and have their own Parliament elected by universal suffrage, which enjoys wide legislative powers (except in matters of defence, foreign policy and education). This assembly gives rise to an executive body called the *Junta*. Autonomous institutions are controlled by a representative of central government (the Minister of the Republic), appointed by the President of the Republic. From a political and administrative point of view, the autonomous regions enjoy a stable situation in respect to the central government. The only source of conflict that occasionally arises is due to the presence and activities of the representative of the central government. Nevertheless, radical and independent movements are not expected on the islands' political horizons.

The Portuguese autonomous regions, Azores and Madeira, often point out the weaknesses of not being on the mainland: the so called costs of being an island. However, despite the fact that these regions are geographically small and remote from the large markets and centres which are found on the Portuguese mainland and in the rest of Europe, they have proven their capacity for growth and development in the last decade.

The population of Madeira grew by 0.08 per cent in the 80s, totalling 253.000 in 1991, following a drop during the 1960s and a stabilizing period during the 1970s. The active population at the end of the last decade reached 140,000. The unemployment rate is 4.4 per cent of the active population (1993). According to the indicators for 1989, 56.3 per cent of the GDP came from the tertiary sector, 28.8 per cent from the secondary, and 15 per cent from the primary sector, with a clear growth of the tertiary sector during the 80s. The public sector is the major investment area, accounting for 85 per cent of the total investments in Madeira between 1981 and 1986. It should be noted that investments from the public sector through EC help for outlying regions (ERDF, RPD, etc.) and remittances from immigrants have greatly affected the GDP.

The demographic evolution of the autonomous region of the Azores during the period 1981–91 underwent a moderate decline, with a decrease of approximately 2.4 per cent, a small figure when compared with that of preceding periods (–11.7 per cent during the 1960s; –15.8 per cent during the 1970s). In 1993 the population stood at 237,583 inhabitants. During the period 1986–90, the average growth rate of GDP in the Azores was 3.65 per cent, which is relatively high, but lower than in mainland Portugal. In the economy as a whole, the secondary sector (27.5 per cent of GDP in 1990) and the tertiary sector (51.1 per cent) gained importance throughout the 1980s, to the detriment of the primary sector (21.4 per cent). The unemployment has remained relatively stable; in 1991 it was 3.7 per cent, and in 1993 it was 4.3 per cent. Our observations concerning the leading role of the public sector in investments made in Madeira, together with those regarding the importance of funding from Community subsidies and revenue from emigrants, can equally well be applied to the Azores.[2]

The legal framework and structure of television in Portugal

In mid-1993, Nelson Traquina stated that 'The basic feature of the current situation in Portugal, little more than six months after the commencement of broadcasts by private television operators, is the frantic competition in television activity' (Traquina, 1994). According to this portuguese researcher, the commercialization of the television system resulting from regulatory measures in Portugal has led to a great increase in the volume of television available, together with a general decline in the quality of programming, which in all cases is dominated by the entertainment genre: series, films, quiz programmes, variety shows and television dramas. Another characteristic underlined by Traquina and identified by other commentators, including the President of the Republic, Mr. Mario Soares, is the excessive influence of government on public television in Portugal, due to the various governments adopting 'an instrumentalist stance ... regarding television as an information/propaganda vehicle indispensable to maintaining power' (Traquina, 1994).

Television has existed in Portugal since 1958, when the first channel of Portuguese Television

2. Data from Secretaria de Estado do Planeamento e do Desenvolvimento Regional, 1993 and ICEP, 1994.

(RTP) began broadcasting. Its second channel (RTP2) began operating in 1969. The 1976 Constitution, resulting from the 'Carnation Revolution', establishes that television cannot be privately owned. Thus, for decades Portuguese television has developed under a regime of public monopoly. However, in the late 1980s Portugal experienced the wave of deregulation which has swept through and transformed the television scene in the majority of European Community States. The legal framework on which the current television system in Portugal is based, designed by socialist and social-democratic governments and dating from the beginning of the 1990s, has introduced a clearly commercial character into a system which until that time was distinguished by its strict State monopoly.

Act no. 15/90, dated 30 June, created the *Alta Autoridade para a Comunicação Social* (High Authority for Social Communication), the public body responsible for supervising the entire system of the communication media in Portugal, including public television and the proposed private television. This acquired legal status with the Television Act (22 August, 1990), which opened the Portuguese television scene. According to this Act, television is a public service, but 'may be carried out by public and private operators' by means of concessions (Art. 3.2). In February, 1991, the Government announced that after consultation with the Higher Authority it had granted two 15-year licences for use by private television services to the private companies SIC (Sociedade Independente de Comunicação, controlled by the multi-media group SOICOM of the former Prime Minister and the former leader of the Portuguese social-democrats, Francisco Pinto Balsemão, and with a 15 per cent participation by the Brazilian TV-Globo) and TV-Independente or TVI, controlled by various institutions connected with the Catholic Church. The first began broadcasting in October, 1992, and the second in February, 1993.

With regard to public television, in 1990 the Government abolished the television licence fee, and as a result RTP lost a major source of income (approximately 5 billion escudos in 1988, which complemented the 11 billion obtained through advertising and the 1.5 billion received in the form of government subsidies) and came to depend exclusively on government subsidies and revenue from advertising. RTP was given new statutes by Act 21/92 of 14 August, which transformed RTP into a limited company with entirely public capital. The Board of RTP is elected exclusively by the shareholders of the company, all of which belong to the State. Thus, the Government has control over its composition. This Act also institutes a consultative council (the *Conselho de Opinião*) for RTP, which is made up by a wide variety of collectives representing civil society, and with authority in matters of planning, review of budgets, financial balances and programming. However, the decisions of this consultative council are not binding. The structure of RTP is completed with the autonomous centres in Madeira and the Azores, which enjoy full independence in terms of organization, budgeting and programming by virtue of a legal statute dating from 1980 (see below, 'Public television in the Autonomous Regions').

The contract of concession was signed by the State and RTP in 1993; according to this document, RTP's Channel 1 (Canal 1) consolidated its general interest approach, while Channel 2 adopted a complementary role providing public service television for potential minority groups.

Table 2. Prime-time television programming according to genres on the four
Portuguese channels (week from 5 to 12 April, 1993) (%)

	RTP1	RTP2	Total RTP	SIC	TVI
News	13	10	12	23	14
Sport	0	42	19	6	5
Films	11	0	5	20	23
Series	47	37	41	44	27
Children's/young people's programmes	0	0	0	0	9
Entertainment	28	0	14	7	15
Cultural	0	10	4	0	9
Other	1	0	4	0	0

Source: Traquina, 1993.

Regional audio-visual map of Portugal

Regional television activity in Portugal is very scarce. In fact, it can be said to be limited to the existence of RTP's autonomous centres in the Azores and Madeira archipelagos. The only 'regional TV centre' of RTP besides the autonomous regional stations is the Oporto Production Centre, which broadcasts nation-wide and produces the morning programme space of Channel 1. This RTP centre in Oporto was officially opened on 20 October 1989 as a Production Centre, to complete the activities of the Lisbon Production Centre. From that moment, various phases of development and improvement converted it into an important Production Centre, which achieved considerable success from 1991. However, in spite of the fact that it is located in a privileged region in terms of social, economic and cultural development, RTP Oporto's production, activities and broadcasting scope are only national. It has three studios, employs a staff of thirty journalists and its national broadcasting share on Channel 1 amounted to over 1,444 hours in 1992 (approximately 20 per cent of the total broadcasting time in RTP). In fact, it is neither an autonomous nor a regional channel.

The private channels do not engage in any specific production or broadcasting activity on the regional level.

Public TV in the autonomous regions

Administrative and financial autonomy of regional Portuguese stations came about with the legal setting-up of the regional autonomous centres of the Azores and Madeira, thus going beyond the old statute of the RTP regional delegations (Madeira's delegation was founded in 1972, and Azores' in 1975). This autonomy was achieved mainly with the promulgation of the Decree-Law no. 156/80 of 24 May 1980. This text clearly defines the operating principles of regional television stations. Two years later, the new Decree 283/82 of 22 August explicitly granted them financial and administrative autonomy and the powers needed to establish their own programming and news. Thus, in the second article, it was said to be the 'legislators' aim' to 'endow the regional centres with financial and management autonomy, considering these centres to be 'decentralized representations' with decision-making structures, and complete powers to define their programming, news and broadcasting criteria concerning the interests of their regional area'.

RTP Madeira

Regular broadcasting on RTP Madeira began on 6 August 1972 during the dictatorship. 55 per cent of the Island of Madeira, centred on the city of Funchal and the south-west, was covered at this time.

In the initial period, daily broadcasting amounted to almost four hours a day from Monday to Friday and eight on Saturdays and Sundays. During this phase, the stations did not produce their own programmes. Programming consisted solely of packaged programmes sent from Lisbon on one inch magnetic supports. The only local contributions were the studio live shots of the anchor or journalist who showed news items with pictures from the news broadcast on the mainland the previous day. The first equipment, such as VTP's to make reports in the field, was obtained in 1976. Thus, the first locally produced programmes were made.

In 1980, RTP's Madeira branch acquired the legal status of an autonomous centre. New retransmitters were set up on the island in the early 1980s and 96 per cent of the archipelago was covered in 1984; the first broadcasts via satellite between the islands and the mainland were carried out in 1981, allowing Madeira first broadcast for the mainland on the occasion of and for special events. On 24 September 1982, RTP Madeira began broadcasting in colour.

The audio-visual field was strengthened by the first training course offered in 1985 and a year later, RTP-Madeira received its first mobile field unit. The late 1980s were marked by a considerable increase in regionally produced programmes once the technical and creative requirements had been met. This is also when the project for the new production centre was launched.

RTP Madeira currently employs a professional staff of more than a hundred, and broadcasts 14 hours a day from Monday to Friday (from 10:00 to 24:00) and 15 hours a day on Saturdays and Sundays (from 9:00 to 24:00). In 1991, the station was able to add 71 hours of daily news while maintaining the level of programming production reached in 1990 in spite of the severe lack of space and staff, especially in the production, news, and technical divisions. In 1992, nearly 527 of the 6,100 hours broadcast by RTP-Madeira were local productions and of these 371 were news.

That same year RTP-Madeira took part in several programming shows such as 'CIRCOM' (Holland), 'Prix Europa' (Berlin), 'Man and the Sea' (Riga), 'Mat' (the Azores) and 'Euromusic' (Nuremberg). It should also be noted that some of the programmes produced by the station were chosen and sent to the Exchange of the Portuguese Language Television Organization.[3]

Through the terrestrial broadcasting network which is managed by the state-owned *Teledifusora de Portugal* RTP Madeira covers 99.9 per cent of the inhabited area of the archipelago.

More than 70 hours of news are the overall result of the material produced by the news service in 1991. 154 programmes were also produced that year which amounted to over 181 hours.

3. Data from *Relatório e Contas de RTP 1991.*

Worthy of special mention among the regional programmes are the game shows *Cá Entre Nos* (Here Among Us) and *Os Nossos Jogos* (Our Games).[4]

Table 3. Distribution of Broadcasting Time in RTP Madeira, 1991 (by programme groups)

Areas	Time	Percentage
Daily news	499 h 04 min	8.2
Non daily news	154 h 04 min	2.5
Sports news	622 h 21 min	10.2
Documentaries and cultural programmes	416 h 53 min	6.9
Fiction (Films & serials)	2,360 h 59 min	38.7
Children and youth programmes	661 h 47 min	10.9
Recreational and music programmes	870 h 31 min	14.2
Institutional programmes[1]	124 h 34 min	2.0
Advertising	63 h 08 min	1.0
Other	326 h 32 min	5.4
TOTAL	6,099 h 56 min	100.0

[1] Including religious (70.5 per cent), political (11.6 per cent) and other official information (17.9 per cent) programmes.
Source: *RTP 1992 Yearbook*

RTP Açores

In 1975 the regional television of the Azores began regular broadcasting for three hours daily from Monday to Friday and six hours a day on Saturdays and Sundays. During its initial period, RTP Açores covered 60 per cent of the archipelago in spite of the severe lack of technical and production means. In any case, greater coverage of the archipelago was to be slow due to the widespread geographic location of the islands and their difficult terrain. It should also be noted that the Regional Government did not grant final approval for the station to allow complete coverage of the territory until 1985.

A production centre was launched in the island of S. Miguel in December of 1977. As of that moment the means were made available to guarantee broadcasting continuity and the use of the studio for news programmes. Satellite connections between Lisbon and the Azores were inaugurated that same month. The considerable increase in regional production was thus understandable, although it was almost totally made up of studio produced material.

In 1980, as pointed out above, the Azores centre became officially autonomous. Colour television became available on a regular basis in 1982. The first ENG equipment was acquired in 1983 and the Azores station began sending reports to Lisbon. In 1991 the correspondent network was completed: each of the nine Azorean islands had at least one RTP Açores camera.

It should be pointed out that from the first moments, programming was only partially based on broadcasts from the mainland in an effort to respond to the culture and outlook frame of the regional population. Within the regionally produced material from the beginning of the

4. Data from *Relatório e Contas de RTP 1991.*

168

80s, programmes such as *Crónicas de minha terra* (Chronicles of My Land) or *Os Açores e o património* (The Azores and its Heritage) by Jorge Forjaz are worthy of comment. In 1982, the Azorean station retransmitted the first Portuguese soap opera, *Vila Faia*; and in 1984 *TV Rural* by Forjaz Sampaio appeared. Azorean television gained a prestigious reputation in 1985 thanks to some fiction and documentaries on current events. This is also the case of *Xailes Negros*, by José de Medeiros, which is considered to be one of the most outstanding works of fiction on Portuguese television (Teleconfronto Award, Siena 1987).

From 1987, with financial support from the regional government, news about the region are provided weekly to the immigrant communities in the United States and Canada: broadcasts of the bulletin *Notícias dos Açores* (The Azores News) began to be passed through two Portuguese language channels in North America with viewers estimated at 500,000.

At present, RTP Açores broadcasts from 10:00 to 24:00 Monday to Friday and from 9:00 to 24:00 on Saturdays and Sundays. In relation to regional programming, it can be seen that RTP Açores produced 344 hours of regional information in 1991. 273 hours were made up of daily news and 71 of non daily news. The total gives an average of one hour a day of news on the Azores.

In any case, the percentage of locally produced material (adding TV films and serials to the news) is not especially significant when compared to the total number of hours broadcast (6,230 in 1992), as most of these hours are made up of broadcasts taken from RTP1 and RTP2 on the Portuguese mainland.

It should be taken into account that national public channels (RTP1 and RTP2), which transmit on the Peninsula, do not all reach the autonomous regions. Only certain RTP1 and RTP2 programmes are rebroadcast on regional RTP channels as part of their daily schedule. This is mainly due to political reasons: the clear autonomous demarcation in the field of the

Table 4. Distribution of Broadcasting Time in RTP Açores, 1991 (by programme groups)

Areas	Time	Percentage
Daily news	539 h 11 min	9.6
Non daily news	185 h 13 min	3.0
Sports news	501 h 48 min	8.0
Documentaries and cultural programmes	183 h 26 min	2.9
Fiction (Films & serials)	2,272 h 49 min	36.5
Children and youth programmes	2 h 26 min	–
Recreational and music programmes	709 h 50 min	11.4
Institutional programmes[1]	937 h 05 min	15.0
Advertising	167 h 41 min	2.7
Other	68 h 03 min	1.1
	608 h 24 min	9.8
TOTAL	6,229 h 58 min	100.0

[1] Including religious (67.6 per cent), political (9.5 per cent) and other programmes such as Farm Bulletins (22.9 per cent).
Source: *RTP 1992 Yearbook*.

specific television system in the autonomous regions. In any case, RTP is currently preparing for the diffusion of all its mainland programmes by cable in the Madeira and Azores regions, which will be in addition to the two regional channels of RTP (RTP Madeira and RTP Azores), which broadcast over the air.

On the other hand, both the Regional Government of Madeira and that of the Azores are continuing to put pressure on the central government in an effort to obtain a second regional channel. This struggle has been going on for years. The reason is simple. According to Mota Amaral, head of the Azorean government, there is a lack of public television service in the Azores in the sense that, in spite of the fact that the Law on Television establishes that there should be two public channels to complete 'the public television service', the Azorean Archipelago has only one regional channel. Mota Amaral is opposed to having the system completed with the addition of one of the channels from the mainland, and says 'yes to a second channel, but pro-autonomous administration, with management approved by the head of the Regional Government, the same as in the present RTP Açores'.

Regional broadcasting on private national television

The Law on Television allows for the possibility of regional private television networks coming into existence. According to this law, private channels may cover a district or group of districts on the mainland, or an island or group of islands in the autonomous regions. Although five candidates came forward during the period 1986–90 to set up private regional channels, these initiatives have come to nothing (Peyregne, 1990: 4). The two existing private channels (SIC and TVI) do not broadcast specifically regional programmes in Portugal, while Madeiran Cable TV and Cable TV Azores (the two regional companies of the public Cable TV Portugal), which have been in operation since 1992, cablecast only private national television programmes in their respective regions. TVI has recently signed an agreement with these companies to retransmit its broadcasts in both regions. SIC, however, limits its scope of activity to be distributed through the cable network of the capital city in Madeira (Funchal).

This is occurring within the context of RTP's Board of Directors having lodged an appeal against Madeiran Cable TV at the end of August in 1993. This company is the first cable television network in Portugal to offer regular cablecasting. Note that this is a cable operating company and by law, cannot possess its own television station which therefore limits its function to that of distributing the signal. Madeiran Cable Television had been transmitting football matches played in Funchal without the previous authorization of RTP. This was in violation of the conditions specified in the contract signed between RTP and the football clubs. Thus, this matter and other breaches of contract forced the company to discontinue the transmission of RTP International programmes in Madeira because the contract that gave it sole distribution rights had not been fulfilled. SIC immediately came on the scene to substitute RTP International, under the condition that it 'would not have to assume obligations such as sending the signal to Madeira', according to the technical director Trigo de Sousa, as this would imply expenses amounting to several million escudos a month.

In relation to the case of Madeira, it should be noted that TVI is the favourite channel of the

Cabo TV Madeirense subscribers, with 75.7 per cent preferring it, followed by RTP/Madeira, with 65.7 per cent, Eurosport, with 60 per cent, and RTP International, with 55.7 per cent.[5]

References

Alves, M.J. & Gomes, I. (1989): *A RTP Açores: o seu aparecimento, desenvolvimento e respectiva influencia na vida açoreana*, Lisbon: DCS/UNL (cadeira de História dos Media, typed, 30 pp.).

Hasse Ferreira, J. (1992): 'Portugal', in The Euromedia Handbook: *The Media in Western Europe*. London: Sage.

ICEP (1994): *Portugal, The Infrastructure*. Lisbon: Investimentos, Comércio e Turismo de Portugal.

INE: *Estatísticas da Cultura, Desporto e Recreio 1990*.

Navarro Pedro, A. (1992): 'Portugal', in Féron, D. and A. Thoraval (eds.): *L'état de l'Europe*. Paris: La Découverte.

'Olhar atento à TV e à Rádio', in *Comunicações* 43 (July-August 1992).

Peyregne, V. (1990): 'La télévision au Portugal, une réforme indécise', in *Dossiers de l'Audiovisuel*, 33.

Quaresma, M. do R. (1987): *12 Anos de Televisão nos Açores*. Lisbon: DCS/UNL (cadeira de História dos Media, typed, 30 pp.).

RTP (1991): *Relatório e Contas da RTP 1991*. Lisboa.

RTP (1992): *Anuario da RTP 1992*. Lisboa.

Secretaria de Estado do Planeamento e do Desenvolvimento Regional (1993): *Preparar Portugal para o Século XXI – Análise Económica e Social*. Lisboa: Ministério do Planeamento e da Administração do Território.

Siguan, M. (1990): *Les minorités linguistiques dans la Communauté Economique Européenne: Espagne, Portugal, Grèce*. Luxembourg: Office des Publications Officielles des Communautés Européennes.

Traquina, N. (1994): 'As indústrias Culturais em Portugal: A Alta Indefinição no Triângulo do audio-visual', in Parés, M. (ed.): *Cultura y comunicación social: América latina y Europa ibérica – Cultura e comunicação social: América latina e Europa Ibérica – Cultura i comunicació social: Amèrica llatina i Europa ibèrica*. Barcelona: Centre d'Investigació de la Comunicació/Universitat Autònoma de Barcelona.

---

5. Data from *TV Mais*, 9.10.93.

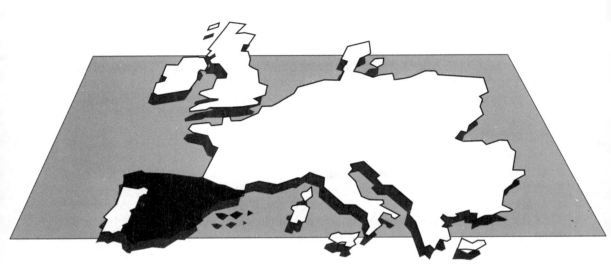

12 Spain: The contradictions of the autonomous model

Bernat López and Maria Corominas[1]

The general political framework, the nation and the regions

The Spanish State is a parliamentary monarchy which was organized into 17 Autonomous Communities in 1978. According to their official names, these communities are Andalusia, Aragon, Asturias, Balearic Islands, Basque Country, Canary Isles, Cantabria, Castile and Leon, Castile-La Mancha, Catalonia, Extremadura, Galicia, Madrid, Murcia, Navarre, La Rioja and Valencian Community. The 1978 Constitution explicitly recognizes and guarantees the right of autonomy to the nationalities and regions that make up the state.

While all of these regions have certain administrative and political powers, some differences do exist, especially in relation to the degree of their authority. The maximum autonomous level is that of communities which are defined as 'historical nationalities' (Catalonia, Galicia, the Basque Country) and Andalusia.

Spain is a culturally diverse State in which four large linguistic communities coexist: speakers of Castilian (Spanish), Catalan, Galician and Basque. It should be noted that some of these communities extend over state boundaries. Thus the Basque and Catalan speaking com-

1. The authors would like to acknowledge the information and opinions provided by José Vicente Idoyaga (University of the Basque Country); Elena Goixens (CCRTV); Ana Cristina Navarro and Enric Giralt (TVE); Josep Maria Vidal Bertran (RTVV).

munities include territories under French rule (south of Aquitaine and Roussillon, respectively). In the case of the Catalan speaking community, the micro state of Andorra should be taken into account. It is the only UN member state whose official language is Catalan.

Historical origins

The regional issue in Spain has historically been an unresolved matter caused by a long process of centralization that began under the reign of the House of Austria (XVIth and XVIIth Centuries) and which became more pronounced with the Bourbons (since 1714). Regionalist vindication were first evident in the Carlist Wars in the XIX century during which the Basque provinces, Navarre and a large part of Catalonia and Valencia fought for their old liberties. In XXth Century, a first recognition of regional differences was made by the passing of the so called *Ley de Mancomunidades* (1913), which allowed a very elementary degree of decentralization; nevertheless, it was applied only in Catalonia (1914). This first attempt at regional politics was put to an end by the establishment of Primo de Rivera's dictatorship (1923).

The II Republic with its new Constitution (1931) was the framework within which the fist statute of regional autonomy was set up: Catalonia (1932). The Basque Country and Galicia urgently vindicated their statutes of autonomy, but only the former succeeded in October 1st 1936, after the start of the Civil War (1936–39).

From 1939, the end of the war with General Franco's triumph marked the beginning of a dictatorship which lasted until 1975–76. One of the most pronounced characteristics of this regime was the repression of any manifestation of the differences between the various nationalities or regional communities. Thus, the life of these statutes was extremely short, as they were abolished by the Franco dictatorship.

The decentralization of the Spanish State would not again be dealt with until the Constitution of 1978 was established after the dictatorship had ended and the parliamentary monarchy reinstated.

Political-administrative dimension

The seventeen communities resulting from the application of the 1978 Constitution have their own parliaments and executive branches which coexist and share powers and scope of authority with the central institutions of the Spanish state.

In terms of division of powers in the field of communications, article 149 of the Spanish Constitution grants the state sole authority for drawing up the basic norms for a system of press, radio and television and in general, for all social means of communication. However, it foresees that the Autonomous Communities, through their Statutes of Autonomy, should take over the legislative development and implementation of this system.

In addition to these generally designated powers, the Statutes of Autonomy allow that the communities should regulate, create and maintain their own television, radio and press, and in general, all the means of social communication to satisfy their ends. Nevertheless, in terms

Table 1. Ranking of the Autonomous Communities according to GDP at market price (1992)

	Million pesetas
Catalonia	12,183,924
Madrid	10,049,256
Andalusia	7,511,040
Valencian Community	6,261,246
Basque Country	3,525,809
Castile and Leon	3,471,527
Galicia	3,453,278
Canary Isles	2,226,107
Castile-La Mancha	2,017,921
Aragon	1,988,385
Balearic Islands	1,517,976
Asturias	1,472,950
Murcia	1,326,150
Extremadura	1,057.437
Navarre	939,116
Cantabria	752,866
La Rioja	445,760

Source: *Anuario El País* 1994.

of television, this authority is limited to the possibility of obtaining a licence for a 'third channel' of regional scope, whose title of ownership would remain in state hands.

Cultural–linguistic dimension

The coexistence of four large linguistic communities creates a complex situation if we consider that, for the most part, the linguistic and administrative borders of the territories do not coincide and that a high immigrant population exists in some areas while in others it is negligible.

Recognition of the linguistic diversity of the Spanish state is clearly reflected in the Constitution as it considers Castilian the official language of the state and at the same time its envisages that 'the other Spanish languages will also be official in the respective Autonomous Communities in accordance with their Statutes'.

Six Autonomous Communities established linguistic policy criteria in their respective statutes of autonomy.[2] An analysis of these criteria reveals two general tendencies. On the one hand, a group of Autonomous Communities has considered their own language as the official one, together with Castilian, in the whole community. Catalonia (Catalan), Balearic Islands (Catalan), Galicia (Galician) and the Basque Country (Basque) fall into this category. On the other hand, the Autonomous Community of Navarre and the Valencian Community have divided the community into two linguistic zones: one with Castilian as the sole official language and another with two 'official' languages, Castilian and their own (Basque[3] and Catalan,[4] respectively).

2. Aragon and Asturias should be added to this list of communities, as they established, respectively, that the different linguistic models of Aragonés and Bable (the Asturian language) would be protected.

175

Table 2. Ranking of the Autonomous Communities according to GDP per inhabitant (1992)

	Pesetas
Balearic Islands	2,135,255
Madrid	2,023,265
Catalonia	2,005,302
Navarre	1,806,340
La Rioja	1,690,932
Aragon	1,673,914
Basque Country	1,673,557
Valencian Community	1,619,684
Canary Isles	1,481,800
Cantabria	1,426,991
Castile and Leon	1,361,496
Asturias	1,349,165
Galicia	1,264,544
Murcia	1,261,502
Castile-La Mancha	1,213,720
Andalusia	1,077,246
Extremadura	993,656

Source: *Anuario El País* 1994.

In the same manner, the Autonomous Communities have developed specific legislative measures in order to regulate the use and/or normalization of the native language. In general, the role of the media is considered vital in these endeavours.

Socio-economic framework

The Spanish economy underwent considerable growth in the 80s. This tendency was even more noticeable in the second half of the decade and Spain was included in the group of the main industrial world powers. In 1991, Spain ranked eighth world-wide according to its GNP. Nevertheless, the world recession which began after 1991 made the main weaknesses of this growth evident.

A review of the figures on regional distribution of economic activity shows the profiles of the internal socio-economic map of the country. On one side, the indicators on wealth created by each Autonomous Community (Table 1) reflect that, together with Madrid -which is located in the centre and has benefited historically as the national capital- the external areas dominate over the interior on the regional development map. Of a total of 17, four of the five leading positions in the autonomies' ranking according to their gross added value are occupied by external regions: Catalonia, Andalusia, Valencian Community and the Basque Country. Even Galicia is close to the top positions. Insofar as these (Andalusia, Basque Country, Catalonia, Galicia, Madrid and Valencian Community) are the Autonomous Communities that currently possess their own television channel, this could suggest a causality link between the economic factor and the development of regional television.

3. Also known as *Euskera*.

4. The official name of the Catalan language in the Valencian Community is 'Valencian'. See 'Autonomous television's development' below for an explanation of this fact.

176

Nevertheless, when considering other indicators such as GDP per inhabitant (Table 2), the pre-eminence of this economic factor appears as only relative, as we see that some Communities which have not developed a regional TV channel appear at the top of the table (Balearic Islands, Navarre) while Andalusia or Galicia are at the bottom.

This implies that the economic factor cannot be considered the sole determinant when explaining the geographic location of autonomous television, and that other factors – such as the cultural–linguistic or the geopolitical; i.e. distance and relations with the political centre – are more decisive, specially in Catalonia, the Basque Country and Galicia.

Legal framework of television in Spain[5]

The organization of television in Spain is similar to the system used in many other European states: a mixed model whose characteristics include coexistence and competition between public broadcasters and private stations.

The basic rule on state regulation in the field of television, the 1980 *Estatuto de la Radio y la Televisión*, has a broader scope than the general approach written into the Constitution. The first article of this Statute sets down that 'radio and television are essential public services whose ownership corresponds to the state' (art. 1.2.).

Under this law the old RTVE (*Radiotelevisión Española*) became a public enterprise, independent from the government and assumed all the 'powers that correspond to the state as owner of the radio and television public services' (art. 5).

Nevertheless, the 1980 Statute also foresees that the central Government 'can, on previous authorization by law from the General Courts, grant the Autonomous Communities direct management of a state-owned television channel created specifically for the territorial area of each Autonomous Community' (art. 2.2). For this purpose, the *Ley reguladora del Tercer Canal de Televisión* (Third Channel Law, 1983) was passed[6] and to date six autonomous communities have begun operating their own television: Andalusia, Catalonia, Galicia, Madrid, the Valencian Community and the Basque Country.

One of the features of the Third Channel Law is the large number of 'powers retained by RTVE in view of potential competition' (Garitaonandía and Idoyaga, 1986: 62). In terms of programming, the law foresees that, in cases of competition between RTVE and a third channel for the purchase of programmes, the latter will be entitled to acquire a programme on condition that it is to be broadcast 'exclusively in the native language of the community' (art. 15.3). Along the same lines, while retaining RTVE's priority in live rebroadcasting of international events, the third channel can rebroadcast 'but only in the native language' (art. 16) when these events are of specific interest to a community and it is a community with a

5. For a more detailed description of legal aspects of television in Spain, see Corominas and López, 1995.

6. In spite of this provision, Basque autonomous television and Catalan autonomous television began broadcasting before the law was passed. This was a source of conflict between the Catalonian and Basque television and TVE and between the autonomous and central governments.

native language. It is worth pointing that these restrictive rules have not much to do with real practices, as explained below (see 'Autonomous televisions' programming' in Chapter 4).[7]

In the initial phase the Basque Country, Catalonia, and Galicia, in this order, passed laws for the creation of their own television channel. In the three cases these are communities with a native language, whose promotion and greater use are defined in the law as one of the guiding programming principles of the new channels.

The legal framework of television was later completed with the Regulatory Law on Telecommunications (1987), the Law on Private Television (1988) and the Law on Satellite Television (1992). In general, these laws reinforce the presence and main role of central government to the detriment of the Autonomous Communities in two ways: through the establishment of exclusive state authority on regulated broadcasting matters and through the consideration of the state as the obligatory area of coverage.

Thus, the Law on Telecommunications states that Telecommunications are an exclusive competence of the Central State (art. 1.1.). The Law on Private Television, which made possible the entry of this type of broadcasters in Spain, defines a model in which the state grants three licences to private companies to carry out television broadcasts with state-wide coverage.[8] This eradicated the possibility of private regional television existing in Spain. The companies awarded these licences (Antena 3, Canal Plus and Tele 5) have made practically no use of the disconnection mode. Antena 3 was the only one of the three to develop a decentralization plan which covered its first phases in 1990–93. It set up several different regional delegations, disconnected news broadcasts and regional advertising in some Autonomous Communities.[9] Likewise, the Law on Satellite Television does not envisage autonomous television's access to the Hispasat direct broadcasting channels.

The legal framework of cable and local television had not yet been drawn up by the end of 1994. Both are presently operating in Spain, having been created and implanted outside legal provisions (at present, some 300 local over the air television stations and 750 cable television networks). The draft bill on cable television grants very limited powers to the Autonomous Communities, while the draft bill on local over the air television stations envisages that the Autonomous Communities should have the authority to adjudicate the broadcasting licences.

Regional television broadcasting in Spain

While the model of Spanish state-wide television is characterized by the dual condition of public/private, Spanish regional television's design is almost exclusively public in nature (as said above, the private broadcaster Antena 3 also provides some regional broadcasts).

This Spanish regional TV structure is based on two main points: a public State television with decentralized broadcasting and a series of independent stations which specifically offer regional coverage: the so called autonomous televisions.

7. For further discussion on these issues, see Carreras, 1987, and Chinchilla, 1988.

8. Even if including the possibility of regional disconnected broadcasts. See below, 'Regional programming of statewide private channels'.

9. See below, 'Regional programming of statewide private channels'.

178

In the first case, Televisión Española (TVE) currently covers the whole country with two channels: TVE 1 and La 2. Its regional structure is formed by two 'programme production centres', in the Canary Isles and Catalonia, as well as 15 'territorial centres' in Andalusia, Aragon, Asturias, Balearic Islands, Basque Country, Cantabria, Castile and Leon, Castile-La Mancha, Extremadura, Galicia, Madrid, Murcia, Navarre, La Rioja and Valencian Community. These function mainly as daily regional news broadcasting 'windows' for the respective communities and as news providers of the two state-wide channels.

In the second case, a group of six autonomous television stations covers the six respective communities of Andalusia, Catalonia, the Valencian Community, Galicia, Madrid and the Basque Country. Each station offers its community coverage through an autonomous channel except in the communities that make up the Basque Country and Catalonia, which have two autonomous channels each.

The total figure of all the autonomous channels' yearly hours of programming time exceeds 42,000 hours (see Table 5) and reaches 87 per cent of the Spanish population. The overall annual budget is around 100,000 million pesetas and the channels give employment to some 4,800 people (see Table 7).

The autonomous televisions, whose coverage is limited to their respective Autonomous Community territory, gear programming to compete with other television stations. In 1989, in view of the start up of new private stations, the six autonomous television bodies and Radiotelevisión de Murcia (which is still in an organizational phase) formed a federation known as FORTA ('Federación de Organismos Televisivos Autonómicos') to strengthen their position.

In agreement with articles 1 and 2 of its statutes, FORTA is conceived as a body to enable co-operation between autonomous televisions -which, nevertheless, conserve their distinguishing characteristics, legal status, structure and independence- especially 'for future agreements on property rights, sports and cultural rebroadcasting, broadcast connections, reception of news services and broadcasts, and participation in national and international professional radio and television organizations'.

Acquiring rights to films, serials, programmes and sports rebroadcasts, organizing a daily exchange of current news items among the six member stations and the coproduction of different entertainment, documentary and serial programmes have been the federation's most fruitful activities. However, its yet to be achieved goal is to participate in professional radio and television organizations and specifically the European Broadcasting Union (EBU). The autonomous televisions' entry into the EBU has been blocked by pressure from RTVE based on conditions established in article 3 of the organization's statutes which requires that candidate stations wishing to form part of the union must broadcast state-wide.

TVE regional broadcasts

The TVE Centre in Barcelona was inaugurated in 1959, only three years after Spanish Television TVE began broadcasting in Madrid. This first 'decentralizing' experience came under direct authority of Central Government through the Ministry of Information and Tourism. Within the framework of the dictatorship, this venture should in no way be considered as a sign of democracy or decentralization. Barcelona is Spain's second largest city and the new centre's role was auxiliary in programme production during the first difficult years of television in Spain (Baget, 1994).

This situation was modified in 1964 when new studios in Madrid began operating, which considerably increased resources in the capital of the state and noticeably reinforced centralized production. Parallel to this reinforced control of television, two new ventures which can be considered decentralizing in nature were begun in 1964. On the one hand, the TVE Canary Isles Production Centre was created with the aim of making television available in the islands. This was the only Spanish territory which was not covered by terrestrial broadcasting from the peninsula. Programming was first offered five hours a day and was broadcast separately from that of the peninsula until 1971, when link by satellite was established.

On the other hand, a TVE 'Catalan Circuit' which covered Catalonia and the Balearic Islands from its headquarters in Barcelona was created in 1964. It offered a monthly broadcast of one hour disconnected from the national channel, in Catalan language, increasing to two hours in 1967. Thus, during the 1960s the Canary Isles and Barcelona centres were able to produce and broadcast the only 'regional' programmes in Spain.

It was not until 1971 that a base for TVE's regional structure was conceived. That same year, the Valencia (Valencian Community), Seville (Andalusia), Bilbao (Basque Country), Oviedo (Asturias) and Santiago de Compostela (Galicia) delegations were inaugurated and initially operated as news agencies for TVE. Some delegations began disconnected broadcasting of brief daily news bulletins in 1974. This process was consolidated throughout the late 1970s and even more so when the democratic constitution of 1978 went into effect, establishing political administrative decentralization of the state on a territorial level.

The 1980 Statute for Radio and Television adapted, although not without ambiguity, the structure of Radiotelevisión Española to the new territorial situation arisen from the Constitution. The outlines of the two tendencies towards decentralization of television were already present in this law: the third channels or autonomous televisions (under state ownership and Autonomous Community's management) and the 'territorial organs of RTVE'. In relation to the latter tendency, the statute stipulated that in 'each nationality or region that corresponds' RTVE will broadcast 'specific radio and television programming' subordinated to national programming. It was expected that regional television programming would be done by the pre-existing Regional Centres, although these are not explicitly cited in the law.

Although the law had come out, it was necessary to wait until 1987 for RTVE to embark on a plan of activities to remodel the old centres (building or improving the TVE Territorial Centres in Cantabria, Galicia, Asturias, the Basque Country, the Valencian Community, Murcia, Balearic Islands and Andalusia; furnishing material and staff) and to create offices in those communities lacking them (Castile-La Mancha and Extremadura). In 1990, the staff in the Territorial Centres was made up of some 1,000 employees (some 50 to 60 per Centre) and the whole operating budget was approximately 1,000 million pesetas.[10]

Present situation of TVE's regional broadcasts

As of 1988, when the Spanish Television Territorial Centres in the communities of Castile-La Mancha and Extremadura began operating, the seventeen Autonomous Communities that make up the Spanish state possessed the basic structure necessary for producing regional programmes and for broadcasting them as regional 'windows' in the two TVE channels programming: one permanent central office with the corresponding assignation of studios, production teams and staff, broadcasting and retransmitting structures able to cover the regional territory by disconnected broadcasting.

Within this framework it seems paradoxical that the territorial structure of TVE should have been consolidated with the beginning of TVE's decline on the Spanish television scene. The state television's drop in advertising revenue (due to growing competition from the new autonomous and private stations), in addition to a drop in viewer rates, have caused large yearly deficits and dramatic budget adjustments in the state-owned radio-television company. RTVE's bid for the Regional Centres at the end of the 1980s can be understood, therefore, as a strategy to face up to the competition and fight the autonomous stations on their own ground.

Nevertheless, this strategy of competition between public state and autonomous TV channels became weakened during the 1990s, which signal a new phase with less confrontation and even, exceptionally, some co-operation. On the one hand, the regional broadcasting of TVE Centres has been questioned due to allegedly unjustifiable and not altogether legal duplication of public service activities in the Communities possessing their own autonomous television. On the other, we have to take into account the emergence of a new political map where, for the first time since 1982, the ruling party (Socialist) at the national level has lost its absolute majority in Parliament, and now it needs the backing of the nationalist (Catalan and Basque) parties.

Although regionalizing should appear to be an important future strategy for securing resources (advertising, audience, etc.), RTVE does not seem to have a solid plan for regional television. As said below, TVE's present regional programming and production activities do not allow a more optimistic forecast.

Production, programming and advertising

In terms of production and programming, the TVE territorial centres produce and broadcast a similar programme structure for their territorial areas daily from Monday to Friday (there is no regional broadcasting at weekends on the two TVE's channels, except for Catalonia and the Canary Isles):

10. These figures do not include the Production Centres of Canary Isles and Catalonia. Source: *Amario RTVE 1989.*

- Daily news from Monday to Friday, lasting some 30 minutes, which included news from the Autonomous Community.

- A daily magazine from Monday to Friday, lasting some 30 minutes. It offers subjects of interest to the Autonomous Community. In some cases, the programme deals with only one subject and each day is devoted to a different theme (sports, parliamentary activity, agriculture, cultural life...). Both the news and the magazine are broadcast in the time band from 13:00 to 15:00, just preceding the national news broadcast.

- A short daily news flash, lasting approximately 10–15 minutes, between 18:00 and 20:00.

Table 3. TVE's regional programming in 1992

Andalusia	228 h 46 min
Aragon	247 h 22 min
Asturias	227 h 14 min
Balearic Islands	238 h 33 min
Basque Country	312 h 22 min
Canary Isles	not available
Cantabria	215 h 01 min
Castile and Leon	202 h 43 min
Castile-La Mancha/Extremadura	200 h 49 min
Catalonia	1,148 h 30 min
Galicia	232 h 26 min
Madrid	274 h 24 min
Murcia	253 h 49 min
Navarre	240 h 50 min
Rioja	225 h 38 min
Valencian Community	250 h 51 min

Latest data available with regional detail.
Source: *Memoria de RTVE 1992.*

These centres rebroadcast certain cultural events of great interest such as sports and electoral specials in their territories in addition to the regular programmes. In 1992, the regional circuits broadcast an average of 225 hours on disconnection. This figure is quite low if we consider the considerable potential the centres have (staff, equipment) and the number of available broadcasting hours per year on the two TVE channels.

The Regional Centres also participate in national programming, although to a short degree: mainly through news items created for news broadcast or through live broadcasting of events of national interest. It is very unusual that centres regularly produced programmes destined to national audiences, excepting the Catalan centre.

The Catalan Centre alongside with the Canary Isles deserve special mention as they have greater programming autonomy since the mid 1970s and because of their seniority and independence are officially called *Centros de Producción de Programas* instead of *Centros Territoriales*. In 1993 TVE Canarias broadcast 1,309 hours of regional programming, while its 1994/95 regional schedule consists of approx. 16 weekly hours of disconnected programmes, including two daily news bulletins (midday and early evening), magazines, talk-shows, current affairs, sports and sports rebroadcasts. The Catalan Centre (TVE Catalunya) supplies the two national channels with a wide range of programmes (sports, game shows, TV serials, musical, children's programmes, current events magazines, debates, talk-shows etc.), being the second TVE's most important production centre besides Madrid. It produces and broadcasts also special programming for Catalonia in Catalan language, disconnected on the two national channels. In 1992, TVE Catalunya contributed 965 h 30 min of programming to the two TVE's state-wide channels, and broadcast 1,148 h of regional programming, including 615 hours of news and current affairs programmes. The 1994–95 TVE's regional schedule for Catalonia consists of 17 to 20 weekly hours of Catalan language programming, including two daily news bulletins (midday and early evening), the popular children programme *Sesame Street* in Catalan language (Monday–Friday, early evening), two weekly current affairs programmes and several weekly talk shows. Much of the sports live rebroadcasts of statewide scope in the two TVE's channels are broadcast in Catalan specifically for Catalonia. These figures and activities make TVE Canarias and TVE Catalunya an exceptional case within the regional structure of TVE.

Besides the degree to which the rest of the regional centres participate in national programming, or the different amounts of disconnected programming broadcast by each one, one fact is evident: regional programming is subordinated to national programming. On the one hand, the slight amount of daily regional programming is inserted in lower viewership time bands generally before the midday or nightly prime times. On the other hand, the regularity and punctuality of regional broadcasting is affected by TVE's programming policy which is dictated from Madrid.

The regional centres' task in relation to securing regional advertising for disconnected broadcasting responds to increased demand from regional and local advertisers to offer methods able to reach smaller market segments. Spanish Television collected some 17,000 million pesetas for regional advertising broadcast by regional circuits in 1991. 92,000 million must be added to this amount for advertising of statewide reach on the two TVE's channels. Thus, 15 per cent of TVE's advertising revenues came from the regional circuits in 1991.

While regional advertising is normally inserted in schedule bands on disconnected programme broadcasting, TVE has not overlooked the technical possibilities offered by the network and has organized disconnections solely devoted to advertising during nightly prime time on the first channel. This method allows TVE to multiply profits made for the same fraction of advertising time.

In the context of growing competition for stakes in advertising revenues, the state television's disconnections represent a considerable source of income which gives it an edge over private television and sets it in direct competition with autonomous television for regional advertising markets. The six existing autonomous televisions raised a total of 28,700 million pesetas on advertising in 1991, while TVE collected 17,000 million pesetas on the same year for regional advertising. This heated competition has damaged the autonomous channels' revenues as well as Spanish Television itself which had collected a total of 23,000 million pesetas for regional advertising in 1989.

The future of TVE's regional centres

In the last two years, the development of TVE's territorial structure has been affected by the controversy over its future. In those Autonomous Communities that have their own TV channel, the TVE regional centres have been qualified as subsidiary television, subjected to central TVE decisions. Their main function is pointed out to be a back up to general programming and they are said to lack sufficient time space for their own programming. Differing opinions come from the regional centres themselves which point out that the autonomous televisions 'carry out programming as an alternative to that of TVE, rather than as an alternative to that of their regional centres. Their news programmes are copies of the TVE's *Telediario* and they devote little time to news from their Autonomous Community' (Agudo, 1991: 81).

On the other hand, the Autonomous Communities which do not have their own channel and for budget reasons cannot set one up consider the possibility of carrying out 'autonomous programming' by increasing the number of disconnected programming hours on TVE's second channel ('La 2') based on the infrastructure and experience of the respective TVE regional centres. This new programming would be financed by the corresponding Autonomous government. The Presidents of the communities of Asturias, Extremadura, Castile and Leon, Castile-La Mancha, La Rioja, Navarre, Canary Isles, Murcia and Aragon met with RTVE management during 1992 and 1993 to discuss this possibility.[11] In any case, we are witnessing the potential opening up of a new phase in the regionalization of TVE in which the state television would make political pacts with different autonomous governments, thus enabling it to make their regional installations more profitable. This would be achieved in exchange for offering the Autonomous Communities the possibility of miniprogramming at a reasonable price.

Regional broadcasting of statewide private channels

No section of the Law on Private Television (law 10/1988, 3 May) mentions the Autonomous Communities which are thus legally excluded from its application. It sets down that the objective of government licences will be 'broadcasting programmes with statewide coverage' (art 4.1.), obligation which was clarified by the possibility of broadcasting programmes 'for each of the territorial zones outlined in the National Technical Plan on Private Television'

11. The last two Autonomous Communities mentioned, in particular, have engaged in intense activity to set up their own television stations, and these initiatives have taken them far beyond negotiations with TVE: Murcia has created and brought into operation its own radio and television corporation, TVMur, although so far only the the regional radio station is broadcasting. Aragon also has set up the 'Corporación Aragonesa de Radio y Televisión' (Aragonese Radio and Television Corporation), and has built and equipped a television centre, although successive political changes at the top level of the Aragonese administration have frustrated all attempts to set up 'autonomous' programming: the establishment of their own channel, negotiations with a private channel (Antena 3 Televisión) regarding the transfer of a programming band and negotiations with TVE regarding the cession of the Aragonese Regional Centre. The Canary Isles have also progressed quite a long way in their negotiations to establish an 'autonomous channel', although no particular model has yet been chosen (own independent channel, or transfer of TVE's Centre in the Canary Isles).

(art. 4.2.), 'provided that the daily duration of the limited coverage programme does not exceed the daily duration of programmes with state-wide coverage'.

This restrictive design was completed by the creation of territorial zones put into force by the mentioned technical plan: of the ten zones established, only five coincided with the territories of individual Autonomous Communities. In the other cases, the outlined zones included two or more Autonomous Communities. This organization totally disqualifies the Autonomous Communities grouped together in the aspect of organizing private broadcasting as the Constitution forbids the Autonomous Communities adopting norms of extra community scope.

Of the three private televisions that operate statewide, Antena 3 is the only one that has implemented activities to regionalize its broadcasts and has done so through the use of schemes that go beyond the conditions stipulated by the legal framework. In 1994, Tele 5 began broadcasting some statewide programmes dubbed in Catalan through the dual sound system. It has gone no further in this aspect than establishing news agencies in different Spanish cities.

The regional structure of Antena 3 TV consists, at the end of 1993, of a network of eight centres or delegations (Andalusia, Aragon, Balearic Islands, the Basque Country, Canary Isles with two centres, Catalonia and the Valencian Community) and three news agencies (Andalusia, Asturias and Galicia).

This centres have varying degrees of autonomy, but they primarily function as news agencies for the national channel, although the Catalan delegation also produces programmes for state-wide broadcasting. Moreover, centres located in Aragon, Balearic Islands and Canary Isles offer regular programmes to the respective Autonomous Community: daily 30' news bulletins from Monday to Friday after 14:00. On the other hand, Antena 3 also broadcasts between four and five daily advertising blocks on disconnection through the eight delegations.

The company status vary as well: Centres in Andalusia, Aragon, the Basque Country, Catalonia and the Valencian Community are companies fully owned by Antena 3 TV, while Centre in Balearic Islands is handled by an Associate Centre whose capital is equally divided between Antena 3 and a Balearic press group. The three news agencies are the result of a collaboration agreement with the Spanish News Agency EFE.

The experience of Antena 3 TV offers a clear picture of the regional strategy of this private broadcaster: news agencies for the network's news services are created in the first phase; advertising disconnections to increase the financial takings on each advertising block are organized in the second phase; and in the final phase an attempt to fill up the regional television spaces with programming in those Autonomous Communities that lack their own channel and which, due to the existing social demand or the potential of their advertising market, are attractive as a television venture. Thus, the Antena 3 news bulletins in Aragon, Balearic Islands and Canary Isles only compete with the TVE Regional Centres' programmes and act as a bridgehead toward amplifying Antena 3 regional programming in those and other Autonomous Communities.

Autonomous television

The introduction of autonomous television in Spain from 1982 onwards involved a great transformation on the Spanish television scene. This meant the final breakdown of the monopoly enjoyed by TVE, the public broadcasting corporation, which until that time had been the sole television broadcaster in Spain. In addition, however, it also involved the clear introduction of the regional dimension into the television model, which until that time had been characterized by state coverage via two channels of TVE. Nevertheless, this model would continue to remain exclusively public until 1989.

The 1980 Statute for Radio and Television and the 1983 Third Channel Law foresee the creation of a public body for management of radio and television services in the Autonomous Communities. Thus, the way the Autonomous Communities structured their respective radio and television public corporations showed slight variations: The *Ente Público Euskal Irrati Telebista* (Basque Country), the *Corporació Catalana de Ràdio i Televisió* (Catalonia), the *Compañía de Radio y Televisión de Galicia*, the *Ente Público Radiotelevisión de Madrid*, the *Ente Público Radiotelevisión de Andalucía*, the *Ente Público Radiotelevisión Valenciana* and the *Ente Público Radiotelevisión Murciana*.

All of these corporations have followed the *Radiotelevisión Española* (RTVE) model in that each entity has created 100 per cent public limited companies specialized in management of radio and television services whose direct management organs are appointed by the General Director of the entity. These companies have management autonomy but are under the control of the General Director and the Board of Directors (*Consejo de Administración*).

Moreover, in terms of financing also, the autonomous television companies have followed RTVE's model: public subsidies, advertising and sale of programmes and other products.

Autonomous television's development

As table 8 shows, the setting up of the autonomous television is carried out in two phases. In the initial phase (1982–85), the Basque Country, Catalonia and Galicia approve in this order, laws for the creation of their own television channel. In the three cases these are communities with a native language, whose promotion and greater use are defined in the law as one of the guiding programming principles of the new channel. Similarly, at the time at which the autonomous television stations came into operation, the three Communities were governed by political parties which at the State level (that is to say, in the Madrid Parliament) were in opposition to the ruling Socialist party. Thus, although never openly stated, the autonomous television was also begun as a political counterweight to the presumed influence of the ruling party in RTVE.

During the second phase (1986–89), there was a consolidation of autonomous television in two senses. On the one hand, through the creation of stations in three more Communities: Andalusia, Madrid and the Community of Valencia, all of which were governed by the same Socialist party which, at the State level, enjoyed an absolute majority. On the other hand, by the creation in the Basque Country and in Catalonia of a second channel of the existing autonomous television stations.

Autonomous televisions evolution has been marked by different issues, mainly *socio-linguistic*, even if they imply a political dimension (Basque Country, Catalonia, Galicia and Valencian Community), and *socio-political* (Andalusia and Madrid), backed by the *economic issues*.

Socio-linguistic issue. Euskal Telebista, Basque television was the pioneer of autonomous broadcasting in Spain. The Basque Parliament – where the Christian Democrat Basque Nationalist Party held the majority – passed a law creating the Basque Radio and Television Body on 20 May 1982. Four weeks later, the public company *Televisión Vasca-Euskal Telebista* was constituted. The first broadcast was on 1 January 1983, and this was normalized on and experimental basis, completely in Basque, on 2 February of the same year. Euskal Telebista was basically created to promote normalization of Basque culture and language. But it has run into considerable difficulties, especially in relation to the language, due to the low level of knowledge of the Basque language among the Basque population itself. Since then, the linguistic issue has been fundamental in determining the development of the Basque television and led to the creation of ETB 2 in 1986 (Garitaonandía *et al.*, 1989: 252). This was after lengthy public controversy on ETB as a 'closed linguistic reserve' or as an effective instrument to normalize Basque language. ETB 2 mainly broadcasts in Castilian (except for children's programmes) specifically in order to reach the whole of the population of the Basque Country.

Despite this attempt, ETB (two channels) have continued to register minority viewer rates registering 16.2 per cent of the total share in the Autonomous Community in 1993. This has led to a gradual reduction in the self-financing of ETB, which has decreased from 30 per cent in 1991 to 21 per cent in 1993. Thus, ETB has become an autonomous television with a high cost per inhabitant.

The Catalan Parliament, with a majority formed by a coalition between nationalist and christian democrat parties, passed a law creating the *Corporació Catalana de Ràdio i Televisió* in May 1983. The company responsible for television broadcasts is Televisió de Catalunya. In November of the same year, the TV3 channel began experimental broadcasting only in Catalan. The creation of Catalonia's own television had been preceded by widespread popular demand to normalize in public use and ennoble the native culture and language. In contrast to the Basque language, Catalan is more widely diffused (95 per cent of the population declared itself able to understand it), and Catalan political situation has been characterized by greater consensus and stability. The cultural–linguistic issue has always been the central axis of Catalan television's existence; however, its development has also been affected by political controversies. A second channel in Catalan, Canal 33, began broadcasting in 1989. It was created by Televisió de Catalunya for a triple objective: attain a leading position in the face of an imminent increase in competition caused by the start up or private television, assure greater use of Catalan in the overall television offer in Catalonia and centre a certain type or programmes on the new channel (especially sports, cultural, informative and educational shows). It would then appeal to a 'minority' audience and offer specialized programmes.

1992 was another important date for Televisió de Catalunya due to its participation in the televised coverage of the Barcelona Olympic Games. The Catalan television reached an agreement with TVE, which was the sole owner of the broadcasting rights for the games in Spain to take part in the make-up of RTO (Olympic Radio and Television, company in charge of the production of the official televized signal for the Games) and for the start up of *Canal Olímpic* (Olympic Channel), a television channel that broadcast the Olympic Games for Catalonia in Catalan. It made use of the *Canal 33* frequency and the resources and staff furnished by TVE and Televisió de Catalunya to carry out this task (Moragas Spà, 1992). Notwithstanding the exceptionality of this co- operation between TVE and Televisió de Catalunya, it is a sign of its possibilities.

Televisió de Catalunya is the autonomous television with the highest budget: 23.051 million pesetas in 1993 for its two channels, but with the lowest cost per inhabitant. This is because it has the highest self-financing quota, although in recent years its self-financing has tended to decrease as a result of the growing competition from other television companies. Thus, in 1991 Televisió de Catalunya was 83 per cent self-financing, whereas in 1993 this figure had dropped to 74 per cent.

In Galicia, Autonomous television appeared somewhat later than in the Catalan and the Basque cases. The law creating the *Compañía de Radio y Televisión de Galicia* (Galician Radio and Television Company) was passed in June of 1984 and broadcasting began in July of 1985. This autonomous television appeared in a context which differed greatly from its predecessors. It can be stated that the only point Catalonia, the Basque Country and Galicia have in common is the possession of a native linguistic and cultural heritage different from Castilian and their status as 'historical communities'. Politically, the Galician Community has been governed by the *Partido Popular* (People's Party, formerly *Alianza Popular*), a conservative statewide party, since the beginning of autonomy. Socio-economically, Galicia ranked next to last among the Autonomous Communities in terms of development and purchasing power per inhabitant.

Galician Television originally began as an instrument to normalize in public use Galician culture and language in addition to serving as a sociocultural backbone for the community. The cultural aims soon gave way to two harsh facts: the stiff competition first from TVE and later to the private channels and the lack of resources from the Autonomous Community. Thus, the Galician Radio and Television Company has continued in recent years to be the autonomous television with the lowest budget – 7,900 million pesetas in 1991 and 8,100 million pesetas in 1993. It also has a low self-financing capacity – 32 per cent in 1991 and 31 per cent in 1993.

Canal 9, the Valencian autonomous television, was the last to begin broadcasting (October 1989). The bilingualism of the Valencian Community presents considerable socio-linguistic problems which have also been reflected in programming, part of which is broadcast in Castilian and part in Catalan. Catalan language is spoken in the Valencian Community, but it is called 'Valencian'. This indicates the existence of a conflictual linguistic identity in this community. The linguistic controversy has plagued this model from its beginnings and reached its most heated point when the *Canal 9* Director imposed an internal list of words and expressions which had been vetoed for being too 'Catalan' and therefore, not 'genuinely'

Valencian. However, Canal 9 has achieved a considerable degree of consolidation. In terms of its budget, it now occupies third place among the autonomous television companies, registering 9,200 million pesetas in 1991 and 10,400 in 1993. Its self-financing stands at just over 40 per cent.

Socio-Political Issue. The Andalusian government began the first study to establish its own autonomous channel in 1982. In 1984, the autonomous parliament passed a law creating the public company *Radiotelevisión de Andalucía* (Andalusian radio and television). Canal Sur Televisión began broadcasting in October 1989. This was first created as a rather simply structured televisions that would buy or contract a large part of its programmes. It later opted to increase its means to embark on greater production of its own material (in 1992 this represented some 65 per cent of total programming, the highest percentage in any of the Autonomous Communities).

In the Community of Madrid, the law creating the *Ente Público Radiotelevisión Madrid* (Public Body Radio and television Madrid) was passed in 1984, but it was not until the beginning of 1989 that the project for Madrid television actually materialized. It first broadcast in May 1989. Telemadrid began and became consolidated in a framework characterized by stiff competition to attract viewers (the country's capital is where the central offices of five state-wide channels -two public, three private- are located and is therefore, a priority target for them) and by lack of stability and political struggles in the government of the Autonomous Community itself. This political situation is the reason why *Radiotelevisión de Madrid* has received negligible public subsidies. Thus, the deficit resulting from the difference between operating expenses and advertising incomes has had to be covered by loans. *Telemadrid*'s level of indebtedness reached 26,400 million pesetas in 1993 (31,000 million in 1994); the figure corresponding to interest on the loans amounted to 2,150 million pesetas in 1992. This precarious financial situation is further aggravated by the fact that *Telemadrid* does not own a central office. From its founding, it has been housed in different buildings in Madrid where it pays high rent (2,400 million pesetas in 1993) which must also be added to the operating expenses and the debt services. The Autonomous Community of Madrid's budget for 1994 foresees an allotment for the future central office of *Telemadrid* although the starting date for the construction has not been set.

Autonomous televisions' programming

Deregulation of television in Spain has resulted in a greater number of stations and the establishment of a mixed public-private system. This has been reflected in the programming which has undergone increased commercialization on both private and public stations. The need to compete has imposed the bid for massive audiences.

Thus, a noticeable change took place in the Spanish television offer between 1989 and 1992. This can be summarized as a predominance of spectacular genres. According to Fundesco data, the overall percentage of broadcasting hours devoted to fiction reached 45.7 per cent in 1992 (*Comunicación social 1993/Tendencias*: 106). In 1993, the private channels headed the ranking according to volume of 'popular' programmes, but TVE and the autonomous channels were not far behind.

News has also appeared as an important genre in programming strategies, especially on public stations. However, this key role is not so much reflected in the amount of programme hours it occupies (news accounted for 12,4 per cent of the total broadcasts on public channels in 1993) as in its position on the grid (it mainly occupies prime time). In any case, news has also reflected this general tendency to spectacularize in content and presentation.

In general, the autonomous televisions' programmes reflect the tension that is created by the 'public service' characteristics of these channels and the need to attract acceptable audience rates in a highly competitive framework. All of them have programme make-ups considered as 'general television' and therefore, competitive, refusing to conform to the 'folklorist-an-thropological' or complementary model pointed out as being 'ideal' for the future Spanish regional television during the initial phases.

At present, autonomous television is facing up to the challenge of competing with a high percentage of entertainment programmes on its grid. These vary from 35 per cent to 58 per cent of total programming. These programmes (films, serials, variety and game shows) are generally homologous with those of public and private state-wide television in terms of presentation and content.

Table 4. Percentages by programme genre on Spanish channels, 1993

	TVE1	La 2	Tele5	Ant.3	C+	CST	TV3	C33	ETB1	ETB2	TVG	TVM	C9
Films	19.9	20.6	29.3	27.2	59.9	23.8	17.5	2.2	4.4	28.4	16.1	30.6	33.6
Series	18.2	7.0	20.2	24.9	4.2	9.9	23.7	7.2	11.5	19.6	24.3	15.9	10.7
Game shows	6.8	2.8	8.3	2.0	0.0	7.8	5.0	0.0	2.9	3.7	4.1	2.5	6.9
Bullfight	1.0	0.4	0.4	1.3	1.2	1.8	0.0	0.0	0.0	0.0	0.0	1.9	0.9
Sport	3.4	17.1	3.5	5.0	7.9	5.4	3.0	36.3	23.5	2.9	11.0	94	6.4
Music	1.2	5.0	0.8	0.9	9.1	4.3	0.4	10.6	4.6	1.4	4.3	0.0	1.6
Religious	0.9	1.5	0.0	0.0	0.0	1.2	0.0	2.0	1.7	0.3	1.7	0.0	0.1
Divulgative	5.6	17.9	1.9	4.6	6.2	14.2	7.7	30.8	12.2	20.3	8.0	5.1	6.4
Magazines	13.6	2.2	12.6	11.2	0.0	7.2	6.7	0.2	5.8	6.6	8.9	6.7	4.3
News	9.0	19.5	6.2	7.6	6.0	11.0	18.4	2.2	9.6	15.5	12.8	15.7	10.9
Children	17.7	4.9	16.6	14.6	4.1	12.8	16.7	6.6	21.5	0.0	8.4	11.5	17.6
Theatre	0.0	0.2	0.0	0.0	0.0	0.1	0.0	0.6	0.0	0.0	0.1	0.0	0.0
Other	2.6	0.9	0.0	0.7	1.3	0.5	1.0	1.3	2.2	1.4	0.4	0.6	0.6

This does not include programme previews, the channel's self-advertising, test cards and advertising between programmes.
Ant.3: Antena 3 televisión; C+: Canal Plus; CST: Canal Sur Televisión; C33: Canal 33; C9: Canal 9.
Source: Sofres, 1994.

Aware of having assigned a central role to this type of programme and the high costs it entails, the autonomous televisions have begun a group purchasing, production and broadcasting strategy in the FORTA headquarters, which is the federation they are members of. Different agreements of this type have been put into effect since 1990. In the field of joint purchase of rights, FORTA has obtained important film packages and successful television serials from large distributors such as Orion, Metro Goldwyn Mayer and Columbia. However, the most important and controversial intervention of this type was the joint acquisition with the private channel Canal+ of the Spanish Professional Football League rights for 1989–1997. This operation cost 54,500 million pesetas. The ranking of the most widely viewed programmes in Spain is usually headed by football rebroadcasts, which clearly shows the strategic role of football in the fight for viewers. Through cession of match summaries and broadcasting rights to TVE in those Autonomous Communities that lack their own television channel, FORTA has avoided the legal problems that could stem from the prohibitions stipulated in the Third Channel Law on the subject of autonomous televisions' acquiring exclusive rights. Concerning production and broadcast of programmes in common, different projects have been made possible, some of which have enjoyed considerable artistic and commercial success, like the coproduction *El joven Picasso*, that was filmed in 1990. This four chapter serial received an award in the New York Festival in 1994.

The public service characteristic, which is in theory an integral part of the autonomous televisions, seems to be reflected in greater attention to news. According to the Fundesco 1993 report, 'in general, autonomous televisions devote more time to news and current events commentaries'. According to available data, the Catalan TV3 devoted 19.4 per cent of its programming to news in 1992; Telemadrid, 17.1 per cent; ETB 1, 19.2 per cent; ETB 2, 28.3 per cent, etc. (*Comunicación social 1993/Tendencias*: 106).

One of the first differences to take into account when referring to autonomous programming is that one must distinguish between those Autonomous Communities that have two channels and those that have only one. Televisió de Catalunya and Euskal Telebista fall into the first category. In both cases, linguistic considerations have been important when starting up the second channels: Euskal Telebista took this step in 1986 due to the market penetration problems the first channel in Basque was experiencing. In 1989, Televisió de Catalunya inaugurated its second channel, Canal 33, in order to be able to compete in better conditions in the eminently competitive television scene and in order to assure greater presence of the Catalan language in the overall audio-visual offer in Catalonia.

ETB initially appeared as a television project based on few, high quality broadcasting hours in Basque. The situation has changed gradually and now the two channels are in operation. ETB–1 broadcasts nine hours daily on work days and fourteen on Sundays and holidays. ETB–2 broadcasts seven hours a day, with reruns of ETB–1 programmes in the remaining time. The percentage of own material produced by the Basque channels is around 50 per cent. In any case, the considerable rise in broadcasting time (increased by the appearance of the channel in Castilian) has caused a greater than desirable dependence on outside programming.

The programming offered by ETB is rounded off with miniprogramming specifically directed to the French Basque Country, where ETB broadcasts are regularly watched. Since 1992, the second ETB channel has broadcast a five minute daily news bulletin in Basque whose content is related to this territory. This bulletin has been complemented by broadcast of a 45 minute debate programme called *ETB Dimanche* since October 1993.

Televisió de Catalunya has opted to structure Canal 33 as a complementary channel specializing in sports, documentaries, news and cultural programmes. This is reflected in the minority audience it attracts: 5.6 per cent in 1993. That same year, 36.3 of Canal 33's programmes were sports or sports related (Sofres, 1994). The TV3 and Canal 33 channels

Table 5. Television broadcast time (1992)

Ranking by broadcast time (hours)		Ranking by % of home programmes production	
TVE1/La 2	14,977	Canal Sur	65.00
TV3/C33	10,545	TV/3/C33	56.59
ETB 1/ETB 2	9,583	ETB1/ETB 2	55.00
Tele 5	7,544	Antena 3	51.00
Canal +	7,481	TVE 1/La 2	49.99
TVM	7,256	TVM	49.63
Antena 3	7,244	Tele 5	41.74
Canal 9	6,745	Canal 9	41.00
Canal Sur	6,690	TVG	31.94
TVG	5,829	Canal +	data unavailable

Source: *Comunicación Social 1993/Tendencias*; *Comunicación Social 1994/Tendencias* and own study.

programming began and has continued to compete with TVE and the private stations, which is made evident by the broadcast of popular television serials, variety programmes and news programmes. *Televisió de Catalunya*, being itself an end product of the television decentralization process in Spain during the 80s, has, in turn, established a decentralized territorial structure with the start up of provincial news delegations and the broadcast of daily news programmes on disconnection for each of the four Catalan provinces. This odd regionalization process within regional television has been rounded off with the broadcast of news on disconnection for the small Pyrenees region of Vall d'Aran, in the Aranese language (a strain of Occitane) since 1990.

In the group of autonomous televisions that carry out the task of spreading and normalizing the use of a language other than Castilian one must also include *Televisión de Galicia* and *Canal 9-Televisió Valenciana*. The first of these channels broadcasts a general type of programme only in Galician and has attempted to find a balance between popular and quality programmes. However, the figures for own material produced (TVG was the station with the lowest amount in Spain for 1992) reveal the Galician television's problems in meeting the costs producing their own material implies (in 1993, its overall budget was the lowest of the six autonomous televisions).

Canal 9 broadcasts in Catalan ('Valencian'), although not exclusively as it also included broadcasts in Castilian. Its programming policy has been characterized by the key role played by entertainment programmes. In 1993, 57 per cent of the grid was taken up by entertainment while cultural shows only made up 8 per cent of the total. This strategy has achieved considerable audience rates. In fact, Canal 9 was the autonomous channel that reached the highest audience share in its own Autonomous Community in 1992 and 1993.

TeleMadrid programming has also given the leading role to entertainment since its beginnings. This was the result of a direct bid for massive audiences in the Autonomous Community where the competition was stiffest between the different channels. In 1994, disagreement on this model of TV programming has lead the director of TeleMadrid to resignation.

Canal Sur also began with popular programmes where fiction and entertainment items were predominant. In 1990, the Andalusian television's broadcasts were 55 per cent entertainment in comparison to 4.75 per cent cultural and informative programmes. In 1993, these figures where 48.7 per cent and 19.7 per cent respectively. As was the case with *Televisió de Catalunya* concerning the Olympics, *Canal Sur* actively took part in coverage of the 1992 events related to the Seville Universal Expo. It was co founder and participant in TeleExpo S.A., the company responsible for the Expo television services in collaboration with TVE and Sociedad Expo 92. TeleExpo produced 1,000 programme hours.[12]

Canal Sur has a decentralized structure of provincial news delegations which enables it to offer a daily news bulletin in which each of these delegations broadcasts local news live for the whole Autonomous Community. In 1992, Canal Sur was the autonomous television that registered the highest percentage of own programmes produced in its broadcasting grid (some 65 per cent).

Autonomous television audiences

Overall, the autonomous televisions have registered an increase in audience share in the last years, rising from 15.8 per cent statewide in 1990 to 17 per cent in 1993.[13] This is a meaningful increase as it took place during the period of greatest upheaval on the Spanish audio-visual scene coinciding with the appearance and consolidation of the private channels. The private channels had an audience share of 42.2 per cent in January of 1993 in comparison to TVE's 40.8 per cent.

In any case, the data which refer to the Spanish state as a whole should be considered relative as a precise analysis of the autonomous broadcasting penetration level should be done taking into account the exclusive area where each one of the autonomous stations broadcasts. Thus, Canal 9 and TV 3 were the second leading channels in their respective Autonomous Communities in 1992. Canal Sur, TVG and TVM were the third leading channels in their respective communities although the latter was practically at a draw with the private channel Antena 3. The two Basque channels, ETB1 and 2, occupied marginal positions on the audience charts with relatively low penetration rates. It is meaningful that ETB 2 had a much larger audience than ETB 1. The linguistic issue has been noted here as ETB 2 mainly broadcasts in Castilian and ETB 1 exclusively in Basque. Even if data of 1993 show a general decrease of Autonomous channels' audience rates, in front of the increase of private channels' audience, both data from 1992 and 1993 reveal, on the one hand, a more consolidated market position of those televisions that broadcast in languages that are completely or considerably normalized in their respective territories (Castilian in the case of Canal Sur and Telemadrid, Catalan in the case of TV3, Catalan and Castilian in the case of Canal 9) in comparison to the lower penetration levels of those televisions that broadcast in non-normalized languages (Televisión de Galicia: Galician; ETB: Basque). On the other hand, it is also evident that autonomous televisions which have followed a commercial policy presenting a more aggressive image have obtained better viewer rates (TV3, Canal 9). Thus, it is necessary to

12. *Noticias de la Comunicación* 47, 4–10 May 1992.

13. According to data from Sofres (Ecotel) for the months of January from the 1990–1993 period, quoted in *Comunicación Social 1993/Tendencias*, p. 101

Table 6. Television audiences by Autonomous Communities (1993)

	Andalusia	Catalonia	Galicia	Madrid	Valencian Comm.	Basque Country	Remaining	Total Pen. & Baleares
TVE	33.4	32.7	45.3	34.1	35.7	39.9	49.8	39.4
TVE1	25.7	24.1	35.8	24.8	27.3	29.1	38.1	29.8
La 2	7.7	8.6	9.5	9.3	8.4	10.8	11.7	9.6
Autonomous	29.1	25.4	15.5	18.8	21.2	16.2	4.0	15.6
2Canal Sur	19.1	–	–	–	–	–	–	–
TV3	–	19.2	–	–	1.3	–	–	–
Canal 33	–	5.6	–	–	–	–	–	–
TVG	–	–	15.5	–	–	–	–	–
Telemadrid	–	–	–	18.8	–	–	–	–
Canal 9	–	–	–	–	19.9	–	–	–
ETB–1	–	–	–	–	–	5.5	–	–
ETB–2	–	–	–	–	–	10.7	–	–
Commercial	46.0	41.7	39.0	47.0	42.7	43.4	45.7	44.4
Antena 3	20.5	21.0	16.7	23.0	21.5	23.3	21.2	21.1
Tele 5	23.5	19.5	20.6	21.3	19.8	18.5	22.6	21.4
Canal +	2.0	1.2	1.7	2.7	1.4	1.6	1.9	1.9
Other	1.5	0.2	0.2	0.1	0.4	0.5	0.5	0.6
Total	100.0	100.0	100.0	100.0	100.0	100.0	100.0	100.0
Daily viewing time (min.)	212	207	171	219	210	174	203	204

Source: Sofres, 1994: 28.

Table 7. The autonomous televisions

Autonomous televisions	Inhabitants	Public corporation channels	Date of law approval	Beginning of broadcasts	Language of broadcasts	Broadcasting hours 1992	% home made progs. 1992	Annual budget 1993	Income TV advertising 1993	Public subsidy for TV 1993	Personnel
Basque Country	2,093,415	Euskal Irrati-Telebista – ETB1 – ETB2	5/1982	12/1982 5/1986	Euskera (Basque) Castilian	8200 (2 channels)	55 (2 channels)	14,326 (11,938 for TV)	1,700	8,787	652
Catalonia	5,959,929	Corporació Catalana de Ràdio i Televisió – TV3 – Canal 33	5/1983	9/1983 4/1989	Catalan Catalan	9,894 (2 channels)	56.59 (2 channels)	36,384 (26418 for TV)	13,340	6,060	1,338
Galicia	2,709,723	Compañía de Radio y Televisión de Galicia – TVG	6/1984	7/1985	Galician	5,275	31.94	10,315 (8,205 for TV)	1,620	5,566	722
Madrid	4,845,851	Radiotelevisión de Madrid – Telemadrid	6/1984	5/1989	Castilian	7,331	49.63	16,537 (10,638 for TV)	5,860	No subsidy	570
Andalusia	6,859,958	Radiotelevisión Andalucía – Canal Sur	7/1984	10/1989	Castilian	4,957	65	21,808	6,568	10,362	795
Valencian Community	3,831,197	Radiotelevisión Valenciana – Canal 9	12/1987	2/1989	Catalan/Castilian	6,591	41	13,505 (10,673 for TV)	4,150	5,447	580
(Murcia)	1,032,275	Radiotelevisión Murciana	11/1988	No broadcasts	–	–	–	396	–	–	–

Source: *Comunicación Social 1993/Tendencias* and FORTA. Budget figures in million pesetas.

point out that audience data from March and April 1994 put the two Televisió de Catalunya channels (TV3 and Canal 33) in the leading audience share position in the Autonomous Community of Catalonia for the first time of autonomous televisions' history.

Conclusions and outlook for the future

The last two years of the 1980s would seem to mark the culmination of the first phase in adapting television structures to the political, territorial and cultural conditions of the Spanish State. Between 1988 and 1990, in fact, the regionalization of TVE which had begun in the early 1970's was completed, and three new autonomous television companies were added to the three already in existence. Since then, the regional structure of television in Spain has remained stable, the only movement being due to abortive attempts to create a number of autonomous television companies (Aragon, Murcia and the Canary Isles), and to contacts established between RTVE and a broad group of Autonomous Communities in order to study the possibility of setting up 'autonomous programming' schedules, based on TVE's regional structure (Regional Centres).

The period 1990–1994 has been characterized by the rapid growth of tough competition among television stations. From the time that the Spanish State began to operate two nation-wide public channels, three commercial channels, also nation-wide, eight public regional channels and some 400 local television stations have been competing to capture audiences and financial resources, and that is not taking into account the ever-increasing number of satellite channels broadcasting in Spanish. All this has taken place within a context now extending beyond Spain to Europe and the whole world, and dominated by the increasing commercialization of communication.

In this new competitive scenario, the predominantly political direction taken by the development of television in Spain between 1980 and 1988 gave way to commercial and economic criteria. Regional television companies, which were born out of that earlier political, ideological and cultural will, struggled to adapt to the new, competitive situation in financial circumstances characterized by their limited source of income (given their territorial location). Liberal opinions came under attack on grounds of their economic 'inefficiency', and there was no lack of support for privatization. There were also criticisms voiced by those defending the principles of public television as a service, in this case due to the excessively commercial nature and poor overall quality of some programming schedules which were forced to capture audience ratings in order to attract advertisers and thereby win political and social approval.

As for TVE, the significant decline in audience ratings and in income from advertising due to the loss of a monopoly, has forced its executive into adopting a competitive, commercial strategy based on its two nation-wide channels on the one hand, and on an internationalization of broadcasting[14] on the other, while at the same time tending to cut back on expenditure

14. By means of the establishment of two Europe-wide satellite channels (Canal Clásico and Teledeporte), and two channels directed at Latin America, thanks to the frequencies reserved for TVE in the Hispasat satellite.

deriving from what were formerly 'free' services: the Official Radio and Television Institute, publications and research, training... Thus, the expansion of regional programming has remained frozen, as a result of its unfavourable cost-benefit ratio in economic terms. Nevertheless, TVE has endeavoured to capitalize on the technical possibilities arising from the regionalization of the hertzian network, by means of disconnection for regional advertising. There is, however, a lack of planning or of a strategy capable of balancing the political and cultural objective of decentralization (both necessary and desirable within a democratic public television framework) and the economic means available.

However, the current stable situation of regional television in Spain does not mean that it has exhausted its potential. On the contrary, we can see that the capacity for growth and the numerous experiments in regional television are still very considerable, especially if we bear in mind the following factors:

(a) Current legal and politico-territorial ruling in Spain envisages the possibility of each of the 17 Autonomous Communities constituting the Spanish State developing some kind of television service of its own. Considering that only 6 Autonomous Communities have actually set up such a service, there are still 11 regional bodies who might choose to do so in the future. However, it is unlikely that structures as exhaustive and complex as those seen in the present autonomous television stations will be developed, given the current high costs involved and the degree of saturation in conventional television in Spain. It is probable that the hypothetical autonomous television stations of the future will take advantage of the technical possibilities made available by the new production and broadcasting systems, or that they will use pre-existing structures, such as the local television networks.[15] The most likely scenario, however, is that future strategies will be developed along the lines of those described in sections (c) and (e).

(b) In those Autonomous Communities which have their own television service, the choice of a conventional television formula does not exhaust all the technical and organizational possibilities of the audio-visual field. This is the tenor of an initiative undertaken by the Catalan government (Generalitat de Catalunya), which involves its forming part of a consortium, together with the Barcelona's Town Hall and the North American Time Warner and US West to develop cable television services in Barcelona.

(c) The present stability of the regional structure of TVE could give rise to a situation charged with major political, economic and cultural potential if the talks between the chairman of RTVE and some autonomous communities prosper. Among other things, they have studied possible co-operation between the latter and the public television authority in order to exploit the regional structure of TVE for autonomous broadcasting off the network under the supervision and control of the autonomous community authorities.

(d) RTVE could itself decide to implement a strategic plan for the development of the

15. A project based on exactly this option exists in the Community of Castile and Leon.

regional structure of TVE, consisting of an extension of the off-the-network programming, including advertising, in conjunction with regional institutions and companies of various kinds. Conversations with a top executive of RTVE, however, have confirmed the absence of any such plan, 'basically because of economic reasons': as long as RTVE receives no regular subsidies from the government, it will have to review some of its public service activities, including regional programming.

(e) Private television companies, keen to capture mass audiences given their nature as nation-wide commercial television channels, are unlikely to develop complex regionalization strategies, particularly bearing in mind the existing autonomous television stations and the regional structure of TVE. A possible trend in this field is the regional experiment of Antena 3 Televisión, with its tendency to occupy with off-the-network mini-programming the television spaces left vacant by those Autonomous Communities without their own television stations, taking economic advantage of the situation by off-the-network advertising. The experience of Antena 3 in Aragon also points to another possible path towards regionalization for private television, a broader but at the same time much more controversial path in legal and political terms: agreements between regional governments in order to develop autonomous programming within the framework of private television.

References

Agudo, J.L. (1991): 'Producción y programación en los centros territoriales de TVE' in Reig Cruañes, José (ed.): *Jornadas sobre le papel de la TV estatal en las comunidades autónomas.* Valencia: Consell Assesor de RTVE Comunitat Valenciana.

Alvira, F. (1991): 'Estudio sobre audiencia y publicidad en Aragón', in Guillén Pardos, E.: *Aragón en la televisión sin fronteras* Zaragoza: Oroel.

Baget, J.M. (1993): *Historia de la televisión en España (1956–1975).* Barcelona: Feed-Back.

Baget, J.M. (1994): *Història de la televisió a Catalunya.* Barcelona: Centre d'Investigació de la Comunicació.

BOE (1992): *Legislación sobre radio y televisión.* Madrid: Boletín Oficial del Estado.

Carreras Serra, L. (1987): *La ràdio i la televisió a Catalunya avui.* Barcelona: Edicions 62.

Corominas, M. & López, B. (1995): 'Espanya: les contradiccions del model autonòmic', in *Anàlisi. Quaderns de Comunicació i Cultura* 17. Bellaterra: Universitat Autònoma de Barcelona.

Corominas, M. & Llinés, M. (1988): *La televisió a Catalunya.* Barcelona: Libros de la frontera.

Chinchilla, C. (1987): 'Les competències de les Comunitats Autònomes en matèria de televisió', in *Autonomies. Revista Catalana de Dret Públic* 8.

Chinchilla, C. (1988): *La radiotelevisión como servicio público esencial.* Madrid: Tecnos.

Diputación General de Aragón (1991): *Segundas jornadas sobre Televisión Autonómica.* Minutes of the convention held in Zaragoza on 25, 26 April 1991. Zaragoza: Diputación General de Aragón.

El País: *Anuario El País*, 1992, 1993 and 1994. Madrid: El País.

Even, M. (1989) *L'Espagne et sa télévision*. Paris: INA.

Fundesco: *Comunicación social/Tendencias,* 1990, 1991, 1992, 1993. Madrid: Fundesco.

Garitaonandía, C. (1993): 'Regional Television in Europe', in *European Journal of Communication* 8, 3.

Garitaonandía, C. & Idoyaga, J.V. (1986): 'Televisión y lenguas minorizadas en el Estado Español', in ISPROM: *Lingue meno diffuse e mezzi d'informazione nella Comunità Europea: Problemi della Radio-televisione*. Nuoro: Isprom, vol. 1.

Garitaonandía, C. *et al.* (1989): 'Estructura y Política de Comunicación en Euskadi', in *Various La Comunicación en las Naciones sin Estado*. Bilbao: UPV-EHU.

Gifreu, J. (dir.) (1991): *Construir l'espai català de comunicació*. Barcelona: Centre d'Investigació de la Comunicació.

Martínez, G. (1991): 'Criterios presupuestarios y autofinanciación de Radiotelevisión valenciana', in RTVV: *Financiación y Publicidad de las radiotelevisiones públicas y privadas*. Valencia: RTVV.

Mateo, R. de (dir.) (1993): *Els mitjans de comunicació social als 'Quatre Motors per a Europa': Baden-Württemberg, Catalunya, Lombardia, Roine-Alps*. Barcelona: Centre d'Investigació de la Comunicació.

Moragas Spà, M. de (1988): *Espais de Comunicació*. Barcelona: Edicions 62.

Moragas Spà, M. de (1992): *Los juegos de la comunicación*. Madrid: Fundesco.

Reig Cruañes, José (ed.) (1991): *Jornadas sobre el papel de la televisión estatal en las Comunidades Autónomas*. Valencia: Consell Assesor de RTVE Comunitat Valenciana.

RTVE: *Memoria de RTVE,* 1988, 1989, 1990, 1991, 1992. Madrid: Ente Público Radiotelevisión Española.

RTVV (1990): *Las radiotelevisiones en el espacio europeo*. Valencia: RTVV.

RTVV (1991): *Financiación y publicidad de las Radiotelevisiones públicas y privadas*. Valencia: RTVV.

Sofres (1994): *Anuario de audiencias de televisión 1993*. Madrid: Sofres.

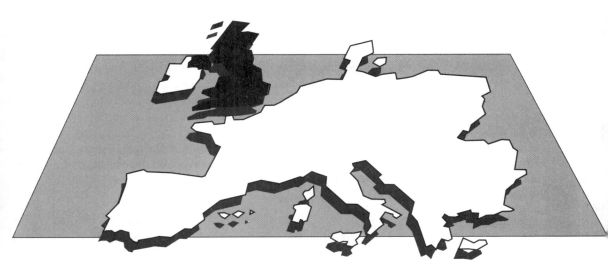

13 United Kingdom: More centralization than meets the eye

Mike Cormack

The general political framework, the nation and the regions

The United Kingdom is a plurinational state consisting of England, Scotland, Wales and Northern Ireland. In addition to these the Isle of Man and the Channel Islands have their own parliaments, and have the status of being dependencies of the British Crown. In the cases of both Scotland and Wales there is general recognition of their status as nations within the British state, distinct from England. Northern Ireland is a more complex case, with its nationality in dispute between those (described as 'nationalists' within Northern Ireland and largely consisting of the Catholic community) who see it as a region of the Irish nation and those (described as 'loyalists' and largely consisting of the Protestant community) who see it as a region of the United Kingdom. In terms of population, England is by far the largest. According to the 1991 Census, the population of England is 49,890,000, the population of Scotland is 4,999,000 and the population of Wales is 2,512,000.

Within these national areas there are important regional divisions. In England there is a well-known and long existing division between the north (roughly north of Nottingham and Derby) and the south. Smaller areas such as the south-west (Cornwall, Devon and Somerset), East Anglia (Norfolk and Suffolk), Yorkshire, the north-east (including Newcastle and Sunderland), and Lancashire (including Liverpool and Manchester) all have strong regional identities, frequently tied to a particular regional dialect. Economically the most important of these areas is the south-east (London and the 'home counties' surrounding it). In Scotland the major regional division is the geographical division between the highlands and islands in the north and west, and the lowlands elsewhere. This is a major cultural division which was also formerly linguistic. But here again there are other notable regional identities, such as in the north-east (around Aberdeen), the Borders (the area to the immediate north-west of the Scotland-England border), the south-west (Galloway), and the various island areas. As in England, one area dominates — in Scotland the central belt including the two largest cities of Edinburgh and Glasgow. In Wales the major division is between, on the one hand, the rural north and west and, on the other hand, the industrial areas of South Wales (including the cities of Cardiff and Swansea).

These various divisions are reflected in linguistic variations. The pronunciation of English varies significantly between the south and north of England, and in many rural areas strong regional dialects can still be heard. In lowland Scotland language ranges from an identifiably Scottish version of English ('Scots English') through to the Scots language itself (which was once as distinct from English as Catalan is from Castilian), still heard in rural areas such as Aberdeenshire and the Borders. In addition to these, there are the Celtic languages. Welsh is spoken in Wales, with different dialects in the north and the south. Scottish Gaelic now survives mainly in the western isles (with each major island having its own dialect) and the more westerly parts of the highlands.

In Northern Ireland Irish Gaelic exists largely as a symbol of the nationalist community, rather than as an everyday language, the nearest Gaelic speaking community being in Donegal in the north-west of the Irish Republic. Manx Gaelic on the Isle of Man has virtually died out (although efforts are being made to revive it).

Historic origins

England, Wales, Scotland and Ireland each evolved as separate countries during the Middle Ages, often in conflict with each other, and political and administrative union occurred only gradually over several centuries. After much conflict, especially in the 15th century, Wales was incorporated into a union with England by the Act of Union of 1536. Scotland became linked to England in 1603 when King James VI of Scotland inherited the English crown on the death of Queen Elizabeth I, and moved his court from Edinburgh to London. A century later in 1707 the Scottish Parliament in Edinburgh voted to merge with the English Parliament in London. By this Act of Union, however, Scotland (unlike Wales in 1536) kept its own distinctive legal system, its own educational system, and its own established church (Calvinist in origin, as opposed to the Episcopal Church of England). The situation in Ireland was more complex. Invasion of Ireland by Normans from England began in the later 12th century and was followed by centuries of conflict, with large parts of Ireland frequently under direct English control. An Act of Union finally took place in 1800 but was eventually repealed by the Anglo-Irish Treaty of 1922 which split the island, creating the Irish Free State in the larger part of the country, predominantly Roman Catholic in religion, and leaving Northern Ireland, predominantly Protestant in religion and descended over several centuries from Scottish and English settlers, as a part of the United Kingdom. However the presence of a large minority (40 per cent) of Catholics in Northern Ireland, many of whom wished for union with the rest of Ireland, gave rise to the conflicts which have marked Northern Ireland's history, particularly since 1969.

During the twentieth century, separatist movements have periodically emerged in Wales and Scotland. As the British Empire was gradually transformed into the Commonwealth of Nations, and as the United Kingdom moved closer economically and politically to the rest of Western Europe, the economic advantages of union with England became less obvious. From the 1960s onwards the nationalist parties Plaid Cymru (in Wales) and the Scottish National Party (SNP) recorded significant numbers of votes although neither has ever managed to achieve the electoral majority necessary to convince the British government of the necessity of change.

Politics and administration

The nations of the United Kingdom have varying relationships with the central government. Scotland's administration is headed by the Scottish Office, created in 1885. It is a department of the British government but since 1939 has been situated in Edinburgh. Its head is the Secretary of State for Scotland who is a member of the government and appointed by the Prime Minister. The Welsh Office (modelled on the Scottish Office) is a much more recent development, dating from 1964, and, as in the Scottish case, the Secretary of State for Wales is a member of the government. The situation of Northern Ireland has changed over the years. Currently there is a Secretary of State for Northern Ireland, appointed by the Prime Minister, but until 1972 Northern Ireland had its own parliament, meeting in Belfast. This was suspended as 'the Troubles' developed and direct rule from London imposed. Like the people of Scotland and Wales, the Northern Irish elect members of the United Kingdom parliament in London.

Despite these very minor measures of devolution, most power is retained in London. The Secretary of State for Scotland, for example, only has power over a limited range —local government, housing, education, health, road construction, social work, law, agriculture and fisheries, economic development. The budget for the Scottish Office has to be argued for by the Secretary of State against the bids of other government ministers. All control of the mass media is retained by government departments in London, with the Department of National Heritage, created in 1992, responsible for the media (along with the arts and sport).

Local government in Britain is based on relatively small areas, with only the Scottish, Welsh and Northern Ireland Offices coming between these smaller regions and the central government. Since the reform of local government in the mid 1970s (1974 for England and Wales, 1975 for Scotland), the picture is as follows (with further reforms currently being discussed in Parliament). England is divided into 45 Counties and 32 London Boroughs. Wales consists of 8 Counties. The English and Welsh Counties are all subdivided into Districts. Scotland is divided into 9 Regions (all of which are subdivided into Districts) and 3 Island Authorities (Western Isles, Orkney and Shetland) which are not further subdivided. All of these regions, districts and counties are run by elected officials. The only elected local government organizations in Northern Ireland are 26 Districts with very restricted powers. Other services are provided by non-elected Area Boards and by central government.

The boundaries of parliamentary constituencies frequently do not coincide with local authority boundaries. The 650 Members of Parliament are made up of 72 from Scotland, 35 from Wales, 17 from Northern Ireland and the rest from England. In recent years, political movements for Welsh and Scottish independence have developed with varying fortunes. After the general election of October 1974, the SNP had 11 MPs and Plaid Cymru had 3, and a Bill for political devolution in Scotland was introduced. It was passed by Parliament and became the Scotland Act of 1979 but was required to receive a majority of at least 40 per cent of those voting in a Scottish referendum. A majority was achieved but it did not reach the required figure and so the Act was abandoned.

Since the 1980s the policies of the Conservative governments of Margaret Thatcher and John Major have exacerbated political differences between the various parts of the United Kingdom. Scotland and the north of England regularly voted for the Labour Party, whereas the more densely populated south of England voted for the Conservatives. In the 1992 general election overall voting figures were Conservatives 43 per cent, Labour 35 per cent, Liberal Democrats 18 per cent, whereas in Scotland the figures were Conservatives 25.7 per cent, Labour 39 per cent, Liberal Democrats 13.1 per cent and SNP 21.5 per cent.

Support for devolution of power increased in Scotland during the 80s to the extent that, as well as the SNP's policy on complete political separation from England but retaining membership of the EC (the 'Scotland in Europe' campaign), both the Labour and the Liberal Democrat Parties supported the creation of an elected Scottish Assembly. In 1989 an unofficial and unelected Scottish Constitutional Convention was set up in Edinburgh with membership drawn from political parties, local government organizations and other groups to discuss constitutional questions.

Culture and language

As noted earlier, there are major differences amongst the regional variations of English, and speakers of other languages are small minorities within this dominant, but varied, English-speaking culture. Of the Celtic languages in Britain, the best surviving is Welsh, spoken today by 18.7 per cent of the Welsh population, that is, about 200,000 people. This figure (from the 1991 Census) was a decrease of 0.3 per cent since the 1981 census, but the percentage of speakers in the age range 3–15 was significantly up (from 17.6 per cent to 24.3 per cent), suggesting that the future of the language is secure. Gaelic is spoken by about 65,000 people in Scotland, mainly living in the Western Isles and adjacent coastal areas, although there are significant numbers of speakers scattered throughout Scotland, particularly in Glasgow. This number is 1.4 per cent of the Scottish population, a decrease from 1.6 per cent in 1951. However it has been argued that the low point for the language was in the mid 1980s and, with the development of Gaelic schools and pre-school groups, the figure should increase in the future. Gaelic speakers and Welsh speakers are all bilingual with English.

Since the Welsh Language Act of 1967, Welsh has had equal status with English within Wales. However Gaelic has no official status and native Gaelic speakers who can speak English as well are not allowed such basic rights as speaking in their own language in law courts or getting official forms in Gaelic. Even within the Gaelic speaking areas in the

Western Isles, it is only in recent years that bilingual road signs have been erected. In 1974 the Western Isles local authority (calling itself *Comhairle nan Eilean*, Council of the Isles) began its own bilingual policy, concentrating particularly on education.

In addition to the remaining Celtic languages, there are now significant communities of speakers of Asian languages in Britain, particularly the languages of the Indian subcontinent, such as Hindi, Urdu, Punjabi, Gujerati and Bengali. According to the 1991 Census there were 1,479,645 people claiming South Asian ethnic origin in Britain, 44 per cent of whom were British born. Clearly many of these will not be speakers of Asian languages, but equally clearly many will. Although they are spread throughout the United Kingdom, they are found particularly in the larger industrial cities. Punjabi is commonly spoken in Bradford and in the London Borough of Southall; Gujerati is common in Leicester, Coventry and in the London Boroughs of Brent and Harrow; and Bengali is common in the London Borough of Tower Hamlets. There are also significant numbers of Chinese-speakers, particularly in central London.

The socio-economic framework

The central socio-economic fact of life in the United Kingdom is the contrast between the relatively prosperous south and south- east, centred around London, and the rest of the country. In Scotland, Wales, the northern half of England and, to some extent, the English West Midlands (around Birmingham) economic life has been centred on heavy industries (such as ship-building, car-building, coal-mining and iron-smelting) which have been in decline. These areas (with the exception of the West Midlands) also include the more remote rural areas in which agriculture has also been in decline.

Under the Thatcher government in the 1980s, this north-south socio-economic divide was exacerbated. Because of the civil conflict, Northern Ireland has always been in an even worse economic state than the other areas. The sets of statistics of table 1 will indicate the broad pattern. The first figure is the unemployment rate and the second is the Gross Domestic Product as a percentage of the European Community average (both sets of figures are for 1990). The statistics are given for Northern Ireland, Scotland and Wales, along with the English economic regions. For comparison, the corresponding figures for Germany and Ireland are also given.

Hidden within such figures are starker contrasts. Many of the larger industrial cities contain classic examples of inner city deprivation, and the remoter rural areas, particularly the highlands and islands of Scotland, are also relatively deprived. Social indicators such as high unemployment, poor housing, alcohol and drug-related problems, are found in both sectors. Although economic indicators show that the general standard of life in Britain is higher than in poorer European countries, such as Greece and Portugal, it is clearly well behind countries such as Germany and France, and when the more prosperous south-east of England is discounted, the contrast becomes more evident.

Table 1

Area	Unemployment rate (%)	GDP (%) EU average = 100
Northern Ireland	17.1	74.3
Scotland	10.1	92.6
Wales	7.6	83.7
North of England	10.1	86.9
North-west England	9.1	90.7
Yorkshire & Humberside	8.0	91.6
West Midlands	6.9	92.1
East Midlands	5.9	96.7
East Anglia	4.2	102.4
South-west England	4.9	96.1
South-east England	4.7	121.3
Germany	4.9	117.0
Ireland	14.2	68.2

Source: *Regional Trends*, 28. London: HMSO, 1993

The legal framework for television

The legal framework for British television is given by the BBC's Charter and by the various Acts of Parliament which govern commercial television. The BBC was incorporated as a public body in 1927. It is governed by a Royal Charter and a 'Licence and Agreement' which together set out its powers and functions. Although strictly speaking coming from the crown, in fact the Charter is granted by the government and is regularly renewed. The current charter was issued in 1981 and is due for renewal in 1996. The Licence runs for the same period of time. The BBC is a public service broadcaster financed almost entirely by a licence fee payable by all television owners. It is required to submit its 'Annual Report and Accounts' each year to the Secretary of State for National Heritage. As well as the main BBC television channel (BBC 1), which began broadcasting in 1936 but was closed down between 1939 and 1946, there is also a second channel (BBC 2), which was started in 1964 and is aimed less at the large popular audience than the first channel.

Commercial television was introduced to Britain by the Television Act of 1954 which permitted privately-owned television companies, financed by advertising and regulated by the Independent Television Authority (ITA). From the beginning, commercial television (which, calling itself Independent Television, became universally known as ITV) was organized on a regional basis with companies being granted licences to broadcast in specific areas for specific periods of time. Later legislation has developed this sector, most notably the Sound Broadcasting Act of 1972 which legalized commercial radio and changed the ITA into the Independent Broadcasting Authority (IBA), the Broadcasting Act of 1980 which set up a second commercial channel (Channel 4) organized as a single national channel, and, most recently, the Broadcasting Act of 1990, which changed the IBA into the Independent Television Commission (ITC). A separate Radio Authority was created to oversee commercial radio. The 1990 Act also changed the basis for awarding the regional television licences. Whereas under previous Acts the ITA/IBA was free to select whichever application it preferred, under the 1990 Act the ITC is required to award the licence to the applicant who offers the highest annual 'cash bid' (creating what became known as the 'franchise auction'), with the only discretion available to the ITC being that all applicants must first pass a 'quality hurdle', that is, an assessment to ensure that the quality of their proposed programming passed a basic minimum level, and that in undefined 'exceptional circumstances' a lower bidder might be accepted. These new regulations came into play in 1991 when new licences were announced, to run for ten years from January 1993. Three of the regional licences changed hands. The 1990 Act also allows take-overs and mergers amongst the ITV regional companies and between them and other non-British EU companies (although this was not allowed to happen until after 1993).

The 1990 Act also allowed for the creation of a fifth channel, over and above the two national BBC channels, the ITV network (which the Act renamed Channel 3) and Channel 4. This was to be a national commercial channel, without regional variations, but which (because of technical limitations) would only reach about 74 per cent of the population. Because of doubts about the economic viability of setting up such a channel (partly due to the fact that the licensee would need to pay for the retuning of all video recorders in the areas of reception in order to avoid interference), when the franchise was advertised in 1992 only one application was received, and the ITC refused to grant the licence because of doubts as to the viability of that application. At the moment Channel 5 remains a possibility for the future.

The legal framework for cable and satellite television in Britain was created by the Cable and Broadcasting Act of 1984. This created a Cable Authority to award licences for cable television in specific areas, and the first cable stations began in 1985. However the 1990 Broadcasting Act did away with the Cable Authority, giving its powers to the ITC. By the spring of 1993 there were 58 cable stations in Britain, with several more franchises awarded but not yet operational. The total number of homes connected up was about half a million. Of the 58 franchises, six were in Scotland (in Aberdeen, Dundee, Edinburgh, Glasgow, Motherwell and Glenrothes in Fife) and one in Wales (in Swansea). The rest were all in England, with 19 in the Greater London area alone. In their applications for franchises, cable operators are required to make provision for local programming. However when financial problems have arisen, local programmes have usually been the first to suffer.

The 1984 Cable and Broadcasting Act also set the scene for the development of satellite broadcasting. In 1986 British Satellite Broadcasting (BSB) was awarded the IBA satellite contract and began broadcasting in April 1990. However in February 1989 Rupert Murdoch's Sky Television had begun broadcasting to Britain as a rival satellite service (based in Luxembourg but aimed at the British audience). The fourteen-month advantage proved to be crucial and in November 1990 Murdoch took over BSB, creating a single satellite service BSkyB. Initially satellite services were financed partly by advertising but since September 1993 BSkyB has been almost entirely subscription based. Although estimates vary, in August 1993 BARB (Britain's official broadcasting research organization) announced that 2,500,000 homes in Britain had satellite dishes and that another 700,000 received satellite channels via a cable operator.

For some linguistic minorities, cable and satellite have been very important. Channels such as Asia Vision and TV Asia have included much material in Asian languages, with TV Asia, for example, including daily news broadcasts in Punjabi, Gujerati, Bengali, Hindi and Urdu.

Regional broadcasting in the United Kingdom

The most important fact about regional television in Britain is that it scarcely exists at all. This is partly because of the British tradition of heavily centralized administration and partly because of geographical factors —the United Kingdom is a fairly compact state, with the only large remote and sparsely populated area being in the north-west of Scotland. Regional broadcasting has become the preserve of radio, rather than television. It should not be surprising then that, despite the many differences between the BBC and the commercial television companies, the basic pattern of regional programming is remarkably similar in both sectors. A central network schedule is worked out in London, allowing regional programmers some room to insert local programmes, most of which are news programmes. This pattern is strongest in the BBC but also exists in the ITV network, despite its seemingly federal structure. The larger ITV companies make most of the networked material, with the smallest companies doing little more than producing local news programmes, inserted into the national network. In earlier years, the ITV network was dominated by programmes made by the five biggest companies (all in England). More recently the other companies have gained more access to the network with their own programmes and since the 1990 reorganization under the ITC, a Network Centre has been created (inevitably sited in London). As an ITC publicity booklet puts it, 'executive decisions about commissioning, acquiring and scheduling network programmes are taken by staff at the Network Centre' (Independent Television Commission, 1993: 17).

It is also important to note that the various broadcasting divisions in the BBC and ITV networks do not coincide with local authority areas. For example Scotland, as noted earlier, is administratively divided into nine Regions and three Island Authorities, but has no overall Scottish elected authority other than the government-appointed Scottish Office. On the other hand, the broadcasters divide the country very differently. The BBC treats the whole area as one 'national region' for the purposes of television (although with various local opt-out areas for radio broadcasts). The three Scottish ITV companies divide up the Regions as follows. Grampian Television's north of Scotland region covers Grampian Region, Tayside Region, the northern half of Fife Region, and most of Highland Region, apart from its most southerly districts. It also covers the northern Island Authorities of Orkney and Shetland, and most of the Western Isles. Scottish Television's central Scotland region covers all of Strathclyde, Lothian, Central and Fife Regions, along with a part of Highland Region and the island of Barra in the Western Isles. Border Television's region covers Borders Region, Dumfries and Galloway Region, and the English areas of Cumbria and the Isle of Man (with the company being based in the English town of Carlisle).

The BBC and regional television

As part of its public service obligations, the BBC is required to provide a certain amount of regional broadcasting. It does this through six subdivisions: three 'regions' in England

(Midlands and East, based in Birmingham; South, based in Bristol; and North, based in Manchester) and three 'national regions' (Scotland, based in Glasgow; Wales, based in Cardiff; and Northern Ireland, based in Belfast). These regions make both radio and television programmes for their own areas as well as for the national network. Part of the BBC South region is London and the south-east, although this area is normally regarded as the centre, rather than as a region. In overall charge of these is a Director of Regional Broadcasting, based in London. The Charter instructs that the BBC shall appoint a National Governor for each of the national regions (which the Charter also refers to as individual countries) and that these individuals will be members of the BBC's Board of Governors, the topmost level in the organization.

The Charter also instructs that National Broadcasting Councils shall be set up in Scotland, Wales and Northern Ireland with the primary function of 'controlling the policy and content' of BBC programmes in their respective countries. Despite this seemingly powerful remit, the National Broadcasting Councils tend to be organizations for passing on advice to the central BBC organization. As far as the members of these councils are concerned, as one recent commentator has remarked, 'none of the individual members perhaps realizes quite how strong in constitutional terms they are; BBC senior staff in the regions are not particularly anxious to tell them' (Madge, 1989: 101). Their existence is not well-known within their respective countries and it would be very unusual to find anyone who could name their country's National Governor. In each of the English regions, the Charter sets up a Regional Advisory Council but here their role is quite explicitly limited to advice on programmes and policy. Like the National Councils, their existence is not particularly well-known. It is worth noting that the BBC's Board of Management, the principal committee in charge of the day-to-day running of the Corporation, includes the London-based Managing Director of Regional Broadcasting, but does not include any representatives of the BBC's Regions or National Regions.

In 1993 little more than one fifth of all BBC programmes were made in the regions, the rest being made in London. The more expensive of these regionally made programmes were ones made for the national network and containing little if any regional identity (for example, the BBC in Bristol is well-known for making wildlife programmes). The BBC has committed itself to increasing the amount of regional production but despite this the organization remains a heavily centralized one, with all important decisions being taken in London. Some indication of how the system works will be given by looking at BBC programming as it was at the time of writing (January 1994). The more popular BBC1 channel consisted entirely of nationally networked programmes apart from 15 minutes of Gaelic children's programmes each weekday morning (all the non-Scottish regions broadcast the same programme while this was on in Scotland), a half-hour of regional news in the early weekday evenings (each region having its own programme) following the national news, and a five minute weekday late evening regional news programme (again following the national news). In addition to these daily programmes, BBC Scotland had a number of weekly programmes —a half-hour sports programme on Fridays and one and a half hours of sports programmes on Saturdays, a half-hour quiz programme, a half-hour general current affairs programme and a half-hour programme of political comment. This was at a time when BBC1 was broadcasting between

18 and 20 hours each day. The more specialized second channel, BBC2, included a weekly two-hour slot of Gaelic programmes in Scotland (the other regions included a half-hour local programme as part of this slot, but shared the same film in the other one and a half hours). In addition to this there were two other weekly half-hour slots for regional current affairs programmes. At this time BBC2 was broadcasting for around 17 hours each day.

The ITV companies

There are currently fourteen ITV regions, one of which (London) has two companies, one for weekend television (Friday evening to Sunday evening) and one for weekday television (Monday morning to Friday afternoon) (See table 2).

Table 2. ITV's companies

ITV Region	Company
London and south-east (weekday)	Carlton Television (London)
London and south-east (weekend)	London Weekend Television (London)
Southern England	Meridian Broadcasting (Southampton)
Channel Islands	Channel Television (St. Helier)
South-west England	Westcountry Television (Plymouth)
English Midlands	Central Television (Birmingham)
East Anglia and East Midlands	Anglia Television (Norwich)
Wales and west of England	HTV (Cardiff and Bristol)
Yorkshire	Yorkshire Television (Leeds)
Lancashire	Granada Television (Manchester)
North-east England	Tyne Tees Television (Newcastle)
Cumbria and south of Scotland	Border Television (Carlisle)
Central Scotland	Scottish Television (Glasgow)
North and north-east of Scotland	Grampian Television (Aberdeen)
Northern Ireland	UTV (Belfast)

Since 1983 there has also been an early morning (6:00 am–9:25 am) television company which broadcasts to the whole ITV network from a London base. This licence changed hands under the 1991 reallocation and is currently held by GMTV.

As with the BBC, there is comparatively little regional programming in the ITV network. Most of the networked programmes are made by Carlton, Central, LWT, Granada and Yorkshire. In recent years other companies have been getting more on the network, often with programmes containing some local flavour. Thus Scottish Television's police series 'Taggart' (set in Glasgow) has been popular throughout the national network. The larger companies still dominate, however. Some idea of the weakness of local ITV programming will be given by considering the situation in January 1994. At this time most of the ITV companies were broadcasting for 24 hours each day. Weekday opt-outs, when regional companies provided their own programmes, consisted of 35 minutes in the middle of the day, one hour in the early evening (of which the first half would be a local news programme), and a ten-minute news programme in the later evening. Occasionally local programmes would also be broadcast in the middle of the night. As noted earlier, Channel 4 (broadcasting around 21 to 22 hours daily) has no regional opt-outs at all, although it does broadcast programmes for specific social groups, such as English language programmes for ethnic minorities. Independent producers outside of London have regularly complained about the lack of commissions which non-London producers have received from Channel 4.

Sianel Pedwar Cymru (S4C)

In Wales the Channel 4 frequencies are used by Sianel Pedwar Cymru (S4C), the Welsh Fourth Channel Authority, to broadcast programmes in Welsh. S4C has a rather anomalous position within British broadcasting. It was created under the 1980 Broadcasting Act (after a vigorous campaign which culminated with a Welsh Member of Parliament going on hunger strike) and began broadcasting in 1982. It transmits about 30 hours of Welsh evening programming each week, made by BBC Wales, HTV (the ITV company which covers Wales and the West of England) and independent producers. When not transmitting Welsh programmes, Channel 4 programmes in English are broadcast. It is financed by a payment of a percentage (fixed at 3,2 per cent in the 1990 Act) of the total television revenues paid by the commercial companies to the government. In effect, the ITV companies are subsidizing Welsh language television.

The most popular programme on S4C has usually been the soap opera *Pobol y Cwm* which has regularly reached audiences of 100,000. Other programmes, even more popular ones, have seldom passed the 20,000 mark. The programmes have not usually been seen elsewhere on British television, although in January 1994 the BBC started transmitting *Pobol y Cwm* nationally on BBC2, with English subtitles. The only other programmes to get wider audiences have been children's animation programmes which have dubbed into other languages.

Comataidh Telebhisein Ghàidhlig (CTG)

Gaelic language television in Scotland has recently been expanded with the creation of the CTG. Following a campaign by Gaelic language activists in 1989, provisions were added to the 1990 Broadcasting Act to set up a Gaelic Television Committee (*Comataidh Telebhisein Gàidhlig*). This committee is awarded a sum of money, the Gaelic Television Fund, from central government, with the precise amount being decided by the Secretary of State for Scotland. The CTG's role is to commission Gaelic television programmes. These programmes are made by independent producers, as well as by BBC Scotland, Scottish Television and Grampian Television, and are broadcast by BBC Scotland and by the two larger Scottish commercial companies (Border Television does not take any of the Gaelic programmes). Before the CTG was set up, about 100 hours of Gaelic programmes were broadcast annually by the three companies combined. The CTG was set up to triple that amount. It started with an annual fund of £9.5 million, with the new programmes beginning in January 1993. In December of that year the Secretary of State announced that in the following year, instead of increasing the fund to £9.7 million to account for inflation (as the CTG had expected), the fund was cut back to £8.7 million as part of a costcutting exercise.

The programmes made by CTG funded producers have included a short daily news broadcast and a weekly soap opera. Most of the programmes have been broadcast with English subtitles and although the audiences have been comparatively small by the standards of popular English language primetime programmes, they have been large when compared with the number of Gaelic speakers. Thus the soap opera has regularly reached audiences of between 300,000 and 400,000.

Conclusions and outlook for the future

The major events to affect the future of regional broadcasting in the United Kingdom are the relaxation of the rules concerning the ownership of commercial television companies and the renewal of the BBC's charter in 1996. Already in June 1992 the ITC had permitted the merger of two English regional companies - Yorkshire Television and Tyne-Tess Television. In November 1993 the Secretary of State for National Heritage, Peter Brooke, announced that television companies would be allowed to hold two regional licences. He also announced that there would be no special protection for Welsh and Scottish broadcasters, despite many people having argued that the cultural importance of these regional companies should be recognized by giving them special protection against take-over bids from the English companies. Within a few months from this announcement three mergers had taken place. Carlton merged with Central, Granada bought London Weekend Television, and Meridian bought Anglia. Thus of the ten purely English regional companies, there are now four large merged companies and two small companies (Westcountry and Channel). These merged companies are still subject to the same regulations as before so that they still have a requirement to provide some local programming, such as news programmes. It remains to be seen, however, whether these larger companies have the will or inclination to expand or even to protect local programmes in the increasingly competitive television environment of the future. The non-English regional broadcasters are still independent (although Mirror Group Newspapers bought a 20 per cent share in Scottish Television in September 1994). Behind these various moves is the worrying prospect of non-British companies (such as Fininvest or Bertelsmann) taking over some of the regional companies and having no interest in the continued provision of the little regional programming which still exists.

Debates about the renewal of the BBC's Charter in 1996 have been underway for some time now, with some people arguing for an enhanced regional role for the BBC in the future (see, for example, the essays collected in Harvey and Robins' *The Regions, the Nations and the BBC*, London: BFI, 1993). It has even been argued that the best way of preserving the public service role of the BBC is for it to become a regional broadcaster, rather than a network one. Thus Jonathan Davis has argued that 'The BBC, for its own sake, ought to be pursuing a policy which makes the regions its corner-stone, which is about the BBC representing the diversity of life in Britain, maintaining a United Kingdom-wide programme-making base, and providing viewers with a service which belongs to them as much as it does, say, to London's middle class' (Harvey and Robins, 1994: 80) In Scotland a campaign called 'Broadcasting for Scotland' was set up in the autumn of 1993 with the aim of getting more autonomy for BBC Scotland written into the new Charter.

The government's plans for the BBC were finally published in July 1994 (Department of

National Heritage, 1994). These plans included the renewal of the BBC's Charter for 10 years, the retention of the licence fee as the main source of finance for at least the next five years, and the expansion of the BBC's various commercial activities. There was very little in the plans about regional services, apart from a rather vague statement of continued support for them.

> The BBC's programmes should reflect the interests and cultural traditions of the United Kingdom as a whole. Programme-makers, presenters and performers in all parts of the United Kingdom should contribute fully to the BBC's national output, as well as to its regional and local services.
> (Department of National Heritage, 1994: 1).

It was, however, noted that BBC programmes are frequently criticized for reflecting too much the life of the South-East of England, and that such criticisms are made particularly strongly in Scotland and Wales. Thus the report recommends that 'it is important that the BBC should make and commission a reasonable proportion and range of its national output, as well as programmes for local audiences, in Scotland, Wales ands Northern Ireland and in the English regions' (Department of National Heritage, 1994: 16). Two points are worth noting here. The first is that the emphasis is not on truly regional broadcasting, but on regionally-made programmes which would be broadcast throughout the United Kingdom. The second point is that there was a lot more in the plans about the BBC developing international television services than there was about regional services, showing clearly where the government's interests lie.

With these points in mind, and remembering the cut in the Gaelic Television Fund, it is difficult to be optimistic about the future of even the very small amount of regional television which currently exists in Britain – at least until there is a major change of government policy.

References

Bevan, D. (1984): 'The Mobilization of Cultural Minorities: The Case of Sianel Pedwar Cymru', in *Media, Culture and Society*, 6.

Broadcasting Act 1990. London: HMSO.

Cathcart, R. (1984): *The Most Contrary Region: The BBC in Northern Ireland, 1924–84*. Belfast: Blackstaff Press.

Coe, J. (1983): 'Sianel Pedwar Cymru: Fighting for a Future', in Blanchard, S. & D. Morley (eds.): *What's This Channel Fo(u)r?* London: Comedia.

Cormack, M. (1993): 'Problems of Minority Language Broadcasting: Gaelic in Scotland', in *European Journal of Communication*, 8, 1.

Cormack, M. (1994): 'Programming for Cultural Defence: The Expansion of Gaelic Television', in *Scottish Affairs*, 6.

Department of National Heritage (1994): *The Future of the BBC: Serving the Nation, Competing World-wide*. London: HMSO.

Griffiths, A. (1993): 'Pobol y Cwm: The Construction of National and Cultural Identity in a

Welsh-Language Soap Opera', in Drummond, P., R. Paterson and J. Willis (eds.): *National Identity and Europe: The Television Revolution*. London: British Film Institute.

Harvey, S. & Robins, K. (1994): 'Voices and Places: The BBC and Regional Policy', in *The Political Quarterly*, 65, 1.

Harvey, S. & Robins, K. (eds.) (1993): *The Regions, the Nations and the BBC*. London: British Film Institute.

Hetherington, A. (1989): *News in the Regions*. London: Macmillan.

Hetherington, A. (1992): *Inside BBC Scotland, 1975–1980: A Personal View*. Whitewater Press.

Howell, W.J. (1982): 'Bilingual Broadcasting and the Survival of Authentic Culture in Wales and Ireland', in *Journal of Communication*, Autumn 1982.

Independent Television Commission (1993): *Factfile '93*. London: ITC.

MacInnes, J. (1992): 'Broadcasting in Scotland', in *Scottish Affairs*, 2.

Madge, T. (1989): *Beyond the BBC*. London: Macmillan.

McDowell, W.H. (1992): *The History of BBC Broadcasting in Scotland, 1923–1983*. Edinburgh: Edinburgh University Press.

McLoone, M. (ed.) (1991): *Culture, Identity and Broadcasting in Ireland: Local Issues, Global Perspectives*. Belfast: Institute of Irish Studies, Queen's University.

Meech, P. (1987): 'Television in Scotland: A Fair Day's Programming for a Fair Day's Pay?', in McCrone, D. (ed.): *Scottish Government Yearbook 1987*. Edinburgh: Unit for the Study of Government in Scotland.

Meech, P. & Kilborn, R. (1992): 'Media and Identity in a Stateless Nation: The Case of Scotland', in *Media, Culture and Society*, 14, 2.

Tomos, A. (1983): 'Realising a Dream', in Blanchard, S. and D. Morley (eds.): *What's This Channel Fo(u)r?* London: Comedia.

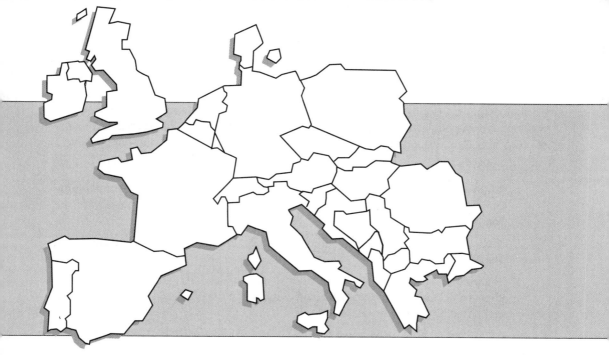

14 The regions: An unsolved problem in European audio-visual policy

Miquel de Moragas Spà and Bernat López

The aim of this chapter is to analyse the existing documentation on European audio-visual policy (Directives, Agreements, Reports, Programmes, Recommendations, Green Papers, etc.) in order to assess the relevance of this policy to regional television. Our primary conclusion is that the attention so far received by regional television from European institutions has been limited. However, it should also be said that, in the documentation analysed, mainly of the less legal type, we can discern the basic ideas for a new policy recognizing the importance of regional television on the European audio-visual scene at the turn of the century.

The measures taken by European institutions in relation to television and their regard to regional television

An analysis of European policy in relation to television must consider three main areas: intervention in the audio-visual field, intervention in the cultural field and intervention in telecommunications.

This chapter will make no detailed, explicit reference to cultural policy programmes unless they are directly concerned with the communication media; nor will it refer to measures in the field of telecommunications concerned with, for example, rulings on the standardization of techniques for direct television broadcasting via satellite (Mac/Packet) or those involved in high definition television. Similarly, no reference will be made to some aspects of communication policies which affect all the media, without distinction, such as the matter of copyright (Commission of the European Communities, 1991).

Within each of the areas selected for our analysis, we shall consider three types of measure:

1. Political directives, which define the general framework for European planning and action and, more specifically, have as their goal the standardization of the various legislations of the member states.

2. Action, consisting of specific aid programmes within the audio-visual field (e.g. the MEDIA programme).

3. Recommendations, resolutions, reports, etc., which, although they are not in themselves legally binding, are of an undoubted moral and political value, at least in prospective terms.

Regarding the case in question, we should underline the distinction between, on the one hand, those measures relating to the European audio-visual space without explicit reference to the regions, and on the other hand, those measures which make some explicit reference to regional television.

Political directives

In terms of European political directives concerning the audio-visual field, there is a great deal of literature by both the EU and the Council of Europe,[1] stressing the economic, political and cultural importance of television and of the audio-visual sector in general.

It is a fact that, since the 1980s, the problems of the audio-visual sector have become a top priority in Europe's cultural (and even industrial) policy.

With regard to the European Union, the major principles and measures adopted in relation to the subject in hand are laid out in a number of documents,[2] the most important of which are as follows:

> *Television Without Frontiers. Green Paper on the Establishment of the Common Market for Broadcasting, Especially by Satellite and Cable.* (COM (84) 300, 14 June, 1984).

> *Council Directive of 3 October 1989 on the Co-ordination of Certain Provisions Laid Down by Law, Regulation or Administrative Action in Member States Concerning the Pursuit of Television Broadcasting Activities,* known as the 'Directive on Television without Barriers' (Directive 89/552/CEE, 3 October, 1989).

> *Communication from the Commission to the Council and Parliament on Audio-visual Policy* (COM (90) 78 fin, 21 February, 1990).

1. See Council of Europe, 1991a and 1991b; Commission of the European Communities, 1990a

2. See Commission of the European Communities, 1992.

Pluralism and Media Concentration in the Internal Market. An Assessment of the Need for Community Action (COM (92), 480 fin, 23 December, 1992).

Communication from the Commission to the Council and the Parliament Concerning New Perspectives for Community Action in the Field of Culture (COM (92), 149 fin, 29 April, 1992).

Growth, Competitiveness, Employment. The Challenges and Ways forward into the 21st Century. White Paper (COM (93) 700 fin, 5 December, 1993).

Strategy Options to Strengthen the European Programme Industry in the Context of the audio-visual Policy of the European Union (COM (94) 96 fin, 6 April, 1994).

To these basic texts of the European Community, we should add one of the most important legislative bodies of the Council of Europe as regards the audio-visual sector, the *European Agreement on Trans-border Television* (STE no. 132, 1989).

The development of this body of legislation has given rise to a great deal of interest and extensive debate among professionals and researchers in the field of social communication, not only in Europe, but also in the United States, where the evolution of the European Community's audio-visual policy has been followed with close attention (and concern). Most analysts agree that a number of peculiar features can be detected in this policy, which hinge on a narrow, predominantly economy-based view of official intervention:

Liberalization of the Community's internal audio-visual space, together with a growing protectionism in relation to the external audio-visual space.

Obstacles placed in the path of those public television monopolies which still operated in various of the European Community states, preference being given to the interests of large transnational private communications enterprises.[3]

Industrial approach to the audio-visual question.[4]

Clear insufficiency of cultural means to compensate for the liberal, economy-based focus; inefficiency of the Directive's quota system;[5] insufficient resources and lack of cohesion in the MEDIA programme's activities...

_____The new framework for deregulation on a Community level, which favours the

3. With reference to the Directive on *Television without Frontiers*, Delwit & Gobin (1991) have pointed out that 'this regulation also reflects, on a more political level, a liberal social philosophy based on the "greater market" project: it clearly arises from the political will to encourage the "commercialization" of information and culture, to the detriment of the public management of television'.

4. According to the members of the 'think tank' entrusted by the European Commission with preparing a report on the Community's audio-visual policy, 'in the film industry, to a greater degree even than in other economic sectors, the rule is that strength in the market and, therefore, cultural hegemony, are functions of quantity and size'. (Vasconcelos, 1994: 29).

5. In this connection, one analyst has pointed out that 'The Directive's final version has been largely regarded as a victory for commercial forces and those favouring anti-protectionist policies' (Papathanassopoulos, 1990).

formation of large, dominant pan-European communications groups, is not offset by any European policy regulating anti-concentration (Papathanassopoulos, 1990)

Measures designed to compensate less widespread cultures and languages for the creation of a great audio-visual market are clearly inadequate, not to say of merely token value (Burgelman and Pauwels, 1990 and 1992).

Regarding this last issue, a close reading of the texts enumerated above reveals very few references to the topic of regional television which concerns us here.

As various authors[6] have already amply observed, the Directive should be seen as an instrument of liberalization, aimed at eliminating internal barriers to the free circulation of broadcasts and advertising. In order to achieve consensus among the member States on this strategic aim, the document lays down various means for the regulation of advertising and programme content, as well as other cultural promotion measures, designed to ensure a majority programming quota for European productions. However, the loose wording of these 'obligatory' measures, together with the absence of control and sanctioning mechanisms, effectively cancels out their binding power. It is understandable, therefore, given that the principal aim of the Directive is the configuration of a great European television market, that matters relating to the safeguarding of minority languages and cultures should have been ignored. As Burgelman and Pauwels have pointed out, 'the development and final wording of this Directive show to what extent the Community's audio-visual policy represents the audio-visual interests of the larger States, whilst taking very little account of those of the smaller States' (Burgelman and Pauwels, 1990). Clearly, this statement can also be applied to the regions. The Directive mentions local television (Article 9), but makes no specific reference to television in the regions, or 'regional television', even though the commitments undertaken by the member States should naturally have repercussions on all their television spaces, on every level, including therefore regional television.

Another major document on European audio-visual policy, the *European Agreement on Trans-border Television* edited by the Council of Europe, which in wording and content resembles the Directive, makes only one reference to the audio-visual sector in the 'smaller countries', and nowhere does it specifically refer to the regions. In Article 10, it requires European television companies to devote the greater part of their broadcasting time to European productions, particularly fiction programmes. To facilitate this objective, it recommends a policy of protectionism to favour home audio-visual productions, particularly in the case of 'countries with low audio-visual production capacity, or those corresponding to a limited linguistic area' (Article 10, 3).

Regarding the regulation of the defence of languages (Article 8), the Directive leaves at the discretion of the member States 'the power, when they consider it necessary to carry out objectives of linguistic policy and providing that they respect Community law, to establish stricter or more detailed regulations concerning some or all of the broadcasts by the television

6. See Delwit and Gobin, 1991; Papathanassopoulos, 1990; Venturelli, 1993; Burgelman and Pauwels, 1992.

broadcasting bodies under their jurisdiction, and in particular in those matters pertaining to linguistic criteria'.[7] This article has been interpreted as the Directive's only concession to minority cultural interests (Burgelman and Pauwels, 1990). However, it should be understood as favouring the main official languages, rather than the 'regional' minority languages of the respective Community countries. Even so, as Hordies and Jongen (1991) have pointed out, the various attempts of member States to promote or protect broadcasting in certain languages and cultures (whether on a State or regional level) by imposing linguistic quotas, for example, can easily be thwarted by 'delocalization' tactics (the targeting of broadcasts from neighbouring States, aimed at the territory in question, in order to circumvent national regulations).

The Maastricht Treaty, notwithstanding its importance for the political construction of Europe, and the ensuing consequences on a cultural level, makes few references to cultural and communications policies, and there is only one explicit reference to 'culture' (Chapter IX, Article 128, 1), which states that 'the Community will contribute to the flourishing of the cultures corresponding to the member States, respecting their national and regional diversity, whilst encouraging their common cultural heritage'. It is important to stress that this reference to culture relates specifically to the 'regions', and not merely to States or smaller countries, thereby representing an advance on former documents concerning cultural and audio-visual policy, as regards the regional question.

The White Paper Growth, competitiveness and employment *and the Green Paper on the European Union's audio-visual policy*

December 1993 saw the publication of the White Paper *Growth, competitiveness, employment*, a document accorded the utmost importance by its promoter, President Delors, and by the Commission as a whole, since it formulates the European Union's major lines of strategy concerning future action to emerge from the recession, accelerate the process of the political union of Europe, as well as laying the foundations for the sustained, harmonious growth of the Old Continent. With the publication of this strategic document, European cultural policy has taken a new and important turn: in the face of the problems caused by recession and unemployment, we see for the first time a solution rooted in information and culture. The main recipe for overcoming the crisis is now to 'prepare without delay and lay the foundations for a society based on information'. In the project to create a common information space, a major role is assigned to the audio-visual sector in generating wealth and employment: if Europe succeeds in winning back its home market, which is now largely in the hands of the United States, and in developing the full potential of the audio-visual sector (which has been multiplied as a result of technological advances), as many as two million jobs can be created between 1994 and 2000. Leaving aside whether this figure is realistic, it is worth noting that major socio-economic aspects not strictly related to culture are for the first time appearing at the centre of cultural and communication policies.

7. This decision has been confirmed in subsequent Community documents. More recently, the 'Communication from the European Commission to the Council and Parliament on Audio-visual Policy' (Brussels, 28 February 1990) reiterated this adjudication of authority.

Proof of the Commission's commitment to an 'information society' and the audio-visual sector came with the publication in April, 1994, of the Green Paper on the European Union's Audio-visual Policy, and the European Conference on the Audio-visual Sector, held at the end of June the same year. With regard to the topic under consideration, a close reading of both these documents (the White Paper and the Green Paper) reveals that they barely mention the complex problem of the cultural and linguistic diversity of Europe, or the deficiencies in the audio-visual sector of the smaller countries and regions facing the challenge of the European audio-visual space. However, it would be untrue to say that these documents did not carry important implications for the topic in question.

A rough idea of the tone and content of the Green Paper may be gained from the Prologue which alone uses the word 'technology' (and its variants) nine times, the word 'industry' 13 times, and the term 'information society' seven times. Thus, the Green Paper aims to answer the question: 'How can the European Union contribute to the development of a European cinema and television programming industry, capable of competing on the world market, forward-looking, and able to guarantee both the dissemination of European cultures and the creation of employment in Europe?' (Commission of the European Communities, 1994: 2). Such wording clearly reveals the secondary importance of cultural concerns, as opposed to the central importance of economic, industrial and even social considerations (competitiveness, industrialization, creation of jobs). When the Green Paper does address the (unavoidable) question of the cultural diversity of the continent, it does so from a commercial and industrial angle: 'the problem of maintaining cultural diversity on a national and regional level ... is now clearly linked to the development of a largely European programming industry which will be profitable in the medium and long term' (Commission of the European Communities, 1994:3). What the Green Paper merely hints at, referring to the necessary 'critical standard' of European audio-visual companies, is categorically stated by the members of the think-tank on Community audio-visual policy set up by the Commission: 'above all, production must be concentrated in powerful companies' (Vasconcelos, 1994: 28); 'Financial aid and other forms of encouragement by the Community ... must be directed at creating and strengthening powerful, integrated companies whose large number of products and breadth of penetration in the territorial and multimedia market will in the near future enable them to become one of the driving forces behind the audio-visual industry that Europe needs' (Vasconcelos, 1994: 36). Moreover, throughout the text of the Green Paper we find numerous critical references to 'the excessively local character' of audio-visual production in Europe, or the 'tightening up' of national markets, phenomena which are brought about by 'national and regional' policies based 'more often on cultural rather than economic criteria' (Commission of the European Communities, 1994: 37).

The only section of the Green Paper to deal at some length with the problem of the possible conflict between a European audio-visual policy, on the one hand, and the interests of the member States and the regions on the other, also adopts an economy-based approach. According to the Commission, 'it is essential to ensure that an industrial policy within the sector does not lead to development 'at different speeds', which would be detrimental to those member States (or some of their regions) with a lower capacity in the audio-visual sector, or those corresponding to a limited linguistic area. It is important that all regions of the European Union should be able to participate in the development of the audio-visual industry' (Commission of the European Communities, 1994: 53). The solution is invariably an industrial one: the creation of a unified internal market will naturally solve the problem of those risks, since producers will no longer be restricted by the size of their respective markets. Meanwhile, the European Community may consider the possibility of adopting 'positive discrimination measures', that is to say specific (temporary) measures to promote audio-visual production in those States (and regions) which have a lower production capacity.

It should be pointed out that the Commission has not shied away from the thorny question of the possible risks involved in a liberalizing, industrialist European policy in the audio-visual sector, risks deriving from possible trends towards oligopolies, which could represent a threat to the plurality of opinions and world-views in a sector considered to be of central importance in the shaping of public opinion. Thus, in 1992 the Commission published its Green Paper *Pluralism and Media Concentration in the Internal Market. An Assessment of Need for Community Action* (COM (92), 480 fin, 23 December, 1992), in which it studied the current trends of the European audio-visual industry towards concentration, and the possible steps which could be taken at a Community level to avoid the potentially adverse consequences of this process of concentration for the plurality of information. So far, however, no concrete action has been adopted to this end.

Aid to audio-visual production

In recent years, European institutions have been remarkably active in their policies designed to support the audio-visual sector. There are three major programmes in this area:

- The MEDIA Programme (Mesures pour Encourager le Développement de l'Industrie Audiovisuelle) of the European Union.
- The EUREKA audio-visual Programme, with the participation of 33 European States, in conjunction with the European Union and the Council of Europe.
- The EURIMAGES Programme of the Council of Europe.

The most important of these is the MEDIA Programme,[8] managed by DG X (Information, Communication and Culture), with a budget of 200 million ECU's for the period 1991–95.[9] According to its original text, the MEDIA Programme is justified by the need 'to reinforce Europe's audio-visual capacity, both as regards the free circulation of programmes and the promotion of the European system of high definition television, and in a policy of encouraging creativity, production and dissemination, with the aim of reflecting the richness and diversity of European cultures'. Similarly, the MEDIA Programme recognizes the need to take into account small and medium size companies, as well as those countries ... with a

8. Commission of the European Communities, 1990b; Commission of the European Communities, 1993.

9. In February 1995, the Commission has adopted the MEDIA II Programme, for the period 1996–2000. Following the recommendations of an audit commissioned to an independent consultant, and the claims of representatives of the audio-visual industry, the Commission has doubled MEDIA's budget to 400 million ECU for the new period, and concentrated its activities in three main areas: aid for professional training, development of European programmes and films, and international distribution of European productions.

smaller audio-visual production capacity and/or corresponding to limited linguistic zones within Europe' (Commission of the European Communities, 1990b).

The MEDIA programme also clearly expresses predominantly economic and industrial considerations in relation to cultural matters. The SCALE Programme, the only MEDIA initiative committed to maintaining the cultural diversity of the European Union (deriving from the seven 'smaller' States in the Community), originated not as a result of the express will of the Commission, but as a result of political pressure exerted by those 'smaller' States within the Council of Ministers. According to those responsible for SCALE, this line of action was created 'for political reasons, arising from the commitments of the Commission and the governments of the 'large' countries to 'compensate' eventual disadvantages experienced by the 'small' countries as a result of the Directive 'Television without Barriers'. Furthermore, the inclusion of this line of action for some 'small' countries was a sine qua non condition for the unanimous vote in the MEDIA 91–95 Decision' (Associação SCALE, 1993).

MEDIA consists of a total of 19 initiatives devoted to the training of professionals, the improvement of production conditions, distribution mechanisms, the boosting of the film industry and financial incentives. Those initiatives which deal more closely with regional television are the above-mentioned SCALE Programme (Small Countries improve their audio-visual Level in Europe), with a modest budget of 15 million ECU's, and BABEL, which deals with aids for the dubbing and subtitling of audio-visual productions, and (according to its guide-lines) pays special attention to the less widely spoken languages; this initiative has a budget of 10 million ECU's. In any case, neither of these two programmes is aimed specifically at the development of audio-visual production in the regions. In 1988, the pilot programme entitled 'Audio-visual Development in the Regions', presented by Channel Four Television and Amber Films Workshop (UK), was not retained by those responsible for the MEDIA Programme. Similar conclusions can be reached regarding the development of the Eureka audio-visual and the EURIMAGES Programmes.

The Council of Europe's EURIMAGES Programme (Council of Europe, 1993a) bears some similarity to the general outlines of the MEDIA Programme and, like the latter, advocates no specific line of support to the audio-visual sector in the regions. Moreover, EURIMAGES has a much more limited budget than the MEDIA Programme (FF150 million in 1993). These funds are devoted to the promotion of European productions, as well as the distribution and showing of European films in countries outside the European Community which have major deficiencies in the sector and which do not participate in the MEDIA Programme (Turkey, Cyprus, Hungary, etc.). The regions' opportunities to participate are therefore very limited.

EUREKA audio-visual, born in Paris in 1989, in which both the European Union and the Council of Europe participate together with 33 European States, is another programme aimed at promoting European audio-visual production, although its activities involve promotion and encouragement rather that direct financial aid. Among its chief objectives are the strengthening of competitiveness in the audio-visual industry and respect for the cultural identity and interests of programme creators, in recognition of the need to defend the various cultural identities within Europe.

EUREKA audio-visual's constitutive documents reveal a desire to 'give all due attention to those projects likely to encourage the dissemination of the languages and cultures which constitute the rich heritage of Europe' and to 'give special attention to those European countries with small geographical or linguistic areas and to preserve the plurality of European cultures'.[10] Due to the narrow scope of this initiative's activities, such intentions can only be verified by studying its programme. Among the activities of the EUREKA Programme, we might underline the creation of the European audio-visual Observatory, which was officially opened in 1993, and which might be expected to have a section, programme or specific concern for regional and local television.

Recommendations and resolutions

From the 1980s onward, there have been numerous resolutions and recommendations on audio-visual development in the Regions, especially those with their own languages.

Concerning the audio-visual sector in the regions

As early as 1987, the *Barzanti Report* stated in relation to regional television that 'it is necessary to ensure that the rationalization of the market does not entail the disappearance of regional and local radio and television stations, since they have the task of expressing the values of everyday life, traditions and opinions, as well as preventing the increasing norm of acritical conformity'.

These statements and recommendations were taken into consideration in what may be described as the principal official document on a European level to support the existence of regional television, which emerged from the Council of Europe: *Resolution 253 (1993) on the Regional Dimension of the European audio-visual Space* by the Standing Conference on Regional and Local Powers.[11]

The clauses of this document reflect the existence of a great variety of regional television services, the impossibility of a single exportable 'model', the need for inter-regional co-operation in the television sector, a consideration of the main functions of regional television (to reflect the region's self-image and to project that image to neighbouring regions). Also, it states that regional television is the fruit of the marriage between political will and a genuine corporate identity. It therefore requests the appropriate authorities of European governments (both State and regional) to adopt the following measures:

- To facilitate the access of the various players in regional life to the local and regional information media.
- To contribute to the professional training and exchange of regional and local personnel at a national and international level.

10. Joint Declaration by Eureka Audiovisual, 2 October 1989.

11. See the document *Rapport sur la dimension régionale de l'espace audiovisuel européen* CPLR [28] 12, 18 January 1992. Rapporteur, Halvdan Skard. This document, like the resolution itself, was inspired in the studies by Pierre Musso on television and the regions in Europe, which were commissioned by the Council of Europe (see Musso, 1991 and 1993).

- To support co-productions, cross-border 'magazine' programmes and the exchange of programmes on a European level, giving special importance to regional television.
- To support the less developed regions, with a view to compensating for inequalities in the area of television.

Among the recommendations, there are various specific proposals, such as: the creation of an 'observatory or network of regional television services', in conjunction with CIRCOM Regional and the European audio-visual Observatory; organizing an annual regional television festival; the creation of an image bank which would assist regional television services; the creation of a European inter-regional channel, broadcast via cable and satellite, which would transmit the best programmes from the regional and local television stations; the setting up. within the EURIMAGES fund, of concrete support for pilot projects or experiments in regional television.

Concerning the audio-visual sector in regions with their own languages

In the recommendations and reports arising from the European Union and the Council of Europe, we find various references to those regions with their own distinctive cultures and languages, and to importance of developing their communication media and audio-visual production. The European Parliament has, on various occasions, expressed support for the less widely spoken languages and their right to avail themselves of the modern communication media (Resolution Arfé 1, 16 October, 1981, and Resolution Arfé 2, 11 February, 1983).[12]

These positions were later ratified in the *Kuijpers Resolution*[13] (1987), which recommends that the member States 'authorize and facilitate access to local, regional, national, public and commercial television and radio, in such a way as to guarantee the continuity and efficiency of broadcasts in regional and minority languages, ..., that they develop dubbing and subtitling techniques to encourage audio-visual productions in the regional and minority languages'. Subsequently, the Council of Europe has taken up these and other recommendations in its *European Charter of Regional and Minority Languages*, which acquired the status of European Convention on 29 June, 1992.

This Charter, drawn up by the Standing Conference on the Regional and Local Powers of Europe, constitutes the most important legal instrument to date in the field of international law on autochthonous linguistic minorities. Regarding the audio-visual media, it directs that those States which adopt the Charter should 'ensure the creation of at least one radio station and one television channel in the regional or minority languages' and 'support and/or facilitate the production and distribution of audio-visual and audio items in the regional or minority languages', among other determinations (Art. 11).[14]

12. Arfé 1: DOC no. C287, 9 November 1981; Arfé 2: DOC no. C68, 14 February 1983.

13. Resolution on the Regional and Ethnic Minority Languages and Cultures in the European Community, doc. A2-0150/87, DOC no. C318/160, 30 November 1987.

14. The antecedents of this Charter within the Council of Europe are to be found in documents such as *Cirici Report* of 1980, which identifies as many as 58 linguistic minorities in European countries which

Recommendation no. R (93) 5 [15] of the Committee of Ministers of the Council of Europe refers to principles designed to promote the distribution and dissemination on the European television markets of audio-visual products from those *Countries or Regions* with a low audio-visual production capacity, or with a limited geographical or linguistic area. Accordingly, the recommendation refers to 'those regions of the larger European countries which, as a result of their having their own distinctive language, experience similar difficulties in promoting the distribution and dissemination of audio-visual products reflecting their linguistic difference, both within the countries of which they are a part and in other European countries.[16]

The chief aim of this Recommendation is to 'create equality of opportunity in the construction of a European audio-visual space reflecting its cultural diversity'. The regions are treated as areas whose cultural and linguistic differences are 'under threat', and whose audio-visual expression must be protected.

Conclusions: the difficult balancing of hegemony/diversity and culture/business in the European project of the 'information society'

Despite the variety and the good intentions inherent in the range of resolutions, recommendations and other European documents which deal with the subject of cultural and linguistic diversity of the continent and its implications (real or potential) for European communication and cultural policies, one thing is clear in the process so far: the core of these policies is concentrated in a very few documents and measures which must be regarded as central. These are the Directive on Television without Barriers, the Media Programme, the Green Paper on European audio-visual Policy and, in particular, the White Paper *Growth, Competitiveness, Employment*. This document has gradually consolidated bridges between cultural and communication policy and R&D, Telecommunications and Advanced Technology Policies, the latter not having been discussed in the present chapter. The sum of these policies must be integrated, according to the nascent European argument, with a view to hastening toward the advent of the 'information society'. This adaptation, it says, is not only desirable but also irreversible: 'the dawn of a multimedia world (sound-text-image) represents a change comparable to the first industrial revolution'. According to the Commission, 'the rapid expansion of information and communication technologies made possible by digitalization

are members of the Council of Europe, Recommendations 928 and 1067, 1981 and 1987 respectively, of the Parliamentary Assembly, and the *Report on Regional or Minority Languages in Europe* , 1988. Within the European Union, the *Kililea Report* of the European Parliament (A3-0000/92 PE 201.963, 13 October 1992) once more insisted on the importance of member States and the appropriate regional authorities 'adopting the following measures regarding the media: to guarantee the establishment and maintenance of at least one radio station and one television channel in each minority language; to support and sustain the production and distribution of sound and audio-visual productions (for example, videos) in the minority languages' [Art. 71].

15. Recommendation no. R(93)5 by the Committee to the Member States Containing Principles Designed to Promote on the European Television Markets the Distribution and Dissemination of Audiovisual Products from Countries or Regions with a Low Audiovisual Production Capacity or with a Limited Geographical or Linguistic Area.

16. Relation of the Tenets of Recommendation no. R(93)5.

is a powerful factor of economic and social improvement: a factor of growth, of economic and social cohesion, of efficiency in the other major infrastructures, of development of new services and, therefore, of the creation of employment' (Commission of the European Communities, 1994: 18). The Community's discourse reveals that the information society will require 'critical status', a great unified market, the elimination of technical and regulatory barriers, and the liberalization of infrastructures and services.

The argument in favour of unity is given as a necessary condition for competitiveness (technological, economic, scientific, military, etc.) and therefore of *hegemony*. This term constitutes a meeting point of the cultural, industrial and economic interests of the various players (private and public) in the European States: the idea that only unity will enable them to withstand the cultural influence or hegemony (entailing the growing uniformity of European culture) and the economic and technological influence (implying dependence and subordination) exerted by the great world powers in industry, technology and culture: the United States and Japan. Economic union as a condition of the survival of cultural diversity: herein lies the difficult balance between unity, diversity, culture and business which the pro-European discourse has devised under the auspices of the 'information society' project.

The major problem now facing analysts is to unravel the reason and realism contained in all these promises and arguments. The affirmation, for example, that the audio-visual sector can create as many as two million jobs in Europe between now and the year 2000, at a time when the programme production industry is plunged in a deep crisis, and also bearing in mind the severe cut-backs that many television companies have had to implement in view of the crisis in the advertising market and growing competition. It is true that the process of convergence between culture, communication, technology and the economy must be seen as irreversible, but it is also true to say that the logic behind its evolution does not appear to be the logic of cultural interests, but rather that of the large industrial interests related to communication infrastructures. In this context, the survival of the cultural and linguistic diversity of the continent within the framework of the information society would seem problematic, especially in the case of the less widespread languages and cultures.

However, it is not necessarily the case that the above-mentioned process of convergence need be to the detriment of the regions. This is firmly borne out by the fact that the widely recognized return to economic centrality and political sovereignty by the regions in recent years. As far as communication technologies are concerned, the European regions (like the States themselves) clearly cannot draw up policies in the telematics sector in isolation from one another. It is precisely this sector which most clearly demonstrates the centrality of the new European and world dimension. This does not mean, however, that the regions cannot and should not plan the use of telematics in their territorial, cultural, educational, social, health policies, etc. With the new cable technologies, (especially fibre optics) and satellites, we find ourselves in a situation characterized by the technical multiplication of channels. This multiplication will enable, indeed even make advisable a more direct management of telecommunications in the smallest areas of cities and regions.

In relation to the audio-visual sector, which is the subject of our analysis, the debate on the European 'commonwealth' has served to underline the multiple dimensions of its diversity, and has made it even clearer that all the communication spaces, from the smallest to the largest in terms of territory, which make up the European audio-visual space: city, region, State, Europe, must be taken into account.

We have seen how European audio-visual policy is currently dominated by an economy-based approach, which nevertheless attempts to compensate for its 'realism' by measures aimed at guaranteeing that the construction of the European audio-visual Space is not carried out to the detriment of the Continent's cultural diversity. The clearest translation into practical terms of this political will is the SCALE Initiative of the MEDIA Programme, which, with limited resources, aims to promote the audio-visual sector in the 'small States' in the Union. However, the regional dimension has so far been neglected in the principal European documents and lines of action. Regional television undeniably occupies an irreplaceable position in the European audio-visual space. Therefore, the integral development of a European audio-visual policy would seem impossible without balanced action in all the various audio-visual spaces, from the local to the European Community level, including all the intervening communication spaces, both State and regional. This observation may be extended to the whole future strategy of the European Commission: the major lines of policy pointing towards the 'information society' should not fail to take into account the impact of cultural and technological changes on the infra-State levels. It is vital to design policies tailor-made to the new European space, which also take into consideration the multiplicity of spaces, both State and regional, of which it is comprised. Thus, and particularly in relation to audio-visual policy, the Commission should consider the possibility of including in the MEDIA Programme a project devoted essentially to promoting the production, dissemination and exchange of audio-visual works produced by regional television companies and bodies, with special attention to productions from regions corresponding to the less widespread cultures and languages. Similarly, co-operation between regional television companies should be encouraged, as also their participation in European broadcasting bodies, in particular the EBU.

In the field of research and study of the audio-visual sector in the European regions, the Committee of the European Regions might consider the possibility of promoting, in conjunction with the European Commission, the establishment of a European Regional Communication Observatory, along the lines of Resolution 253 (1993), on the Regional Dimension of the European audio-visual Space, under the Standing Conference on Regional and Local Powers, which Would Be Responsible for Gathering and Spreading Information among the Various Players in Regional Communication, and for Carrying out Prospective Studies. The European Parliament is similarly invited, together with the European Commission, to prepare a White Paper on the current situation of regional television in the European Union. All the foregoing measures should be undertaken on the basis of a single underlying principle: the recognition and promotion of audio-visual spaces by cultural identity groups should not be restricted to the State-nation level. The current process of European unification has underlined a need which for many years had been vindicated by minority groups: the State does not constitute the only level of representation of cultural identity. One of the chief dangers potentially involved in the European Union's communications policy would be to allow the process of relinquishing sovereignty by consent in one direction: that of transnationalization, while attempting to maintain strong systems of centralized cultural representation in each State. Such a trend would necessarily lead to the reinforcement and dominance of a few national identities, with the consequent impoverishment of the diverse and common European heritage.

References

Associação SCALE (1993): *Media audit. Report on SCALE activities*. Lisbon.

Bassand, M. and Delgado, E. (1992): *Cultura y Regiones en Europa*. Barcelona: Oikos Thau.

Burgelmann, J.-C & Pauwels, C. (1990): 'La politique audiovisuelle et l'indentité culturelle des petits états européens', in *Mediaspouvoirs* 20.

Burgelmann, J.-C & Pauwels, C. (1992): 'Audio-visual Policy and Cultural Identity in Small European States: the Challenge of a Unified Market', in *Media, Culture and Society* 14.

Commission of the European Communities (1990a): *Decision of the European Council, 21 December 1990, Concerning the Application of a Programme to Encourage the European Audiovisual Industry, 1991–1995*. Ref. 90/685/CEE.

Commission of the European Communities (1990b): *La política de la Comunidad Europea para la industria audiovisual. Recopilación de textos legislativos y políticos*. Luxembourg: Office des publications officielles des Communautés Européennes.

Commission of the European Communities (1991): *El derecho de autor y los derechos afines en la comunidad Europea*. Documentos Europeos, nº 9. Luxembourg: Office des publications officielles des Communautés Européennes.

Commission of the European Communities (1992): *La política de la Comunidad Europea*. Documentos Europeos, June. Luxembourg: Office des publications officielles des Communautés Européennes.

Commission of the European Communities (1993): *MEDIA, Guide pour les Professionels*. Brussels: Media Programme.

Commission of the European Communities (1994): *Livre vert options strategiques pour le renforcement de l'industrie des programmes dans le contexte de la politique audiovisuelle européenne*. COM (94) 96 fin. Luxembourg: Office des publications officielles des Communautés Européennes.

Council of Europe (1987): *El rol de la comunicación en el desarrollo regional*. Ref. CC-GP 10 (87) 17. Strasbourg.

Council of Europe (1991a): *Recommandations adoptées par le Comité des Ministres du Conseil de l'Europe dans le domaine des Média*, DOC. DH-MM (91) 1. Strasbourg: Direction des Droits de l'Homme.

Council of Europe (1991b): *Recommandations et résolutions adoptées par l'assemblée parlementaire du Conseil de l'Europe dans le domaine des Média*, DOC. DH-MM (91) 2. Strasbourg: Direction des Droits de l'Homme.

Council of Europe (1993a): *EURIMAGES, Guide*. Strasbourg, January.

Council of Europe (1993b): 'Symposium Presse, Télévision et Régions d'Europe'. Cracow, October.

Davies, J. (ed.) (1993): *The Mercator Media Guide*. Aberystwyth: University of Wales Press.

Delwit, P & Gobin, C. (1991): 'Etude du cheminement de la directive 'télévision sans frontières': synthèse des prises de position des institutions communautaires', in Vandersanden, G. (ed.): *L'espace audiovisuel européen*. Brussels: Université de Bruxelles.

EBLUL (1991): *Policy Document on Lesser Used Languages in Radio and Television*. Dublin: The European Bureau for Lesser Used Languages.

Hordies, J.P. & Jongen, F. (1991): 'La directive 'télévision sans frontières', analyse juridique', in Vandersanden, G. (ed.): *L'espace audiovisuel européen*. Brussels: Université de Bruxelles.

Moragas Spà, M. & Garitaonandía, C. (eds.) (1994): *The Role of Regional Television Sations*. Document presented at the Public Hearing held with the Committee on Regional Policy, Regional Planning and Relations with Regional and Local Authorities and the Committee on Culture, Youth, Education and the Media of the European Parliament, March 1994. Brussels.

Musso, P. *et al.* (1991): *Régions d'Europe et télévision*. Paris: Editions Miroirs.

Musso, P. *et al.* (1993): *Presse écrite et télévision dans les régions d'Europe. Rapport provisoire*. Strasbourg: Conseil de l'Europe.

Papathanassopoulos, S. (1990): 'The EC: "Television without Frontiers" but with Media Monopolies?', in *Intermedia*, 18, 3.

Servaes, J. (1992): '"Europe 1992": The audio-visual Challenge', in *Gazette* 49.

Various (1985): 'L'Audiovisuel en Région', in *Dossiers de l'Audiovisuel*, 4.

Various (1990): 'La télévision régionale en Europe', in *Dossiers de l'Audiovisuel*, 33.

Vasconcelos, A.P. *et al.* (1994): *Rapport de la cellule de réflexion sur la politique audiovisuelle dans l'Union Européenne*. Luxembourg: Office des publications officielles des Communautés Européennes.

Venturelli, S.S. (1993): 'The Imagined Transnational Public Sphere in the European Community's Broadcast Philosophy: Implications for Democracy', in *European Journal of Communication*, 8, 4.

About the Authors

EURORETV
Network for the Study of Television in the Regions, Nationalities and Small Countries of Europe

Gaëlle Canova-Lamarque has a degree in Communication and Information Sciences. She is a research fellow at the Université Michel de Montaigne-Bordeaux 3 with a research on time perception (comparative analysis of Spanish and French television).

Mike Cormack is Lecturer in the Department of Film and Media Studies at Stirling University and researcher in the Stirling Media Research Institute. He is author of *Ideology* (London: Bastford, 1992) and *Ideology and Cinematography in Hollywood, 1930–1939* (London: Macmillan, 1994). His principal current research interest is in the use of Gaelic language in the Scottish media and he has published several articles on this topic. He contributed a paper comparing the Scottish and Catalan media to the 1st Conference on Contemporary Catalan Studies in Scotland in 1994 which is due to be published in the conference proceedings in Barcelona in 1995.

Maria Corominas is Professor of Communication Sciences at the Autonomous University of Barcelona, where she teaches mainly on the fields of structure, theory and history of communication. One of her main research interest is the relationship between media and language from a sociolinguistical point of view. She is also interested in the study of Catalan communication system, with special emphasis on the developments of Catalan language. She is the author of *La Televisió a Catalunya* (Barcelona, 1988); *Models de ràdio als països occidentals. Evolució i perspectives* (Barcelona, 1990); *Construir l'espai català de comunicació* (Barcelona, 1991, with J. Gifreu); «Spain, Catalonia: Media and democratic participation in local communication», in Jankowski, N.et. al. (eds.), *The people's voice: local radio and television in Europe* (London, 1992, with M. Moragas Spà).

Panayote Elias Dimitras is Director of the Communication and Political Research Society (ETEPE) in Athens. Between 1989–1992, he has been assistant professor of Political Science at the Athens University of Economics (formerly ASOEE). He has also been a lecturer at the University of Laverne Nea Makri Residence Center (1980–1989), at the University of Maryland Hellenikon Center (1984–1987), and at South-eastern College (1987–1989). He has participated in several international conferences and published many books and articles in scholarly publications. He is the author of the book *Political Background, Parties and Elections in Greece* (Lychnos, 1991). He has reviewed articles for the *International Journal of Public Opinion Research* and the *European Journal of Communication*.

Carmelo Garitaonandía Garnacho, Professor of Journalism at the University of the Basque Country, has a wide and multivalent experience in research and teaching in the field of mass communication. He has been a founder member of the Council of the Public Radio and Television of the Basque Autonomous Community. He has carried out researches for the UNESCO on the structure of TV programming in Europe and, in the last years, he has specialized on the subject of regional TV. In 1992–93 he was a visiting professor at the School of Communication & Theatre of Philadelphia, where he carried out a research on cable TV in the USA. Some of his recent publications are the following: *La radio en España*; *Las empresas informativas en la Europa sin Fronteras* (1992, with others) and *Imágenes recíprocas en los medios de comunicación social. Francia-España. Aquitania-País Vasco* (1993, with others).

Ellen Hazelkorn PhD, is Lecturer in Politics in the Department of Communications, Dublin Institute of Technology. She is co-author of *The Dynamics of Irish Politics* (London, 1989), co-editor of *Let in the Light. Censorship, Secrecy and Democracy* [in Ireland] (Dingle, 1993) and of *Irish Communications Review* (Dublin), and a contributing editor to *Science and Society* (New York). She is currently writing a textbook on Irish politics (Dublin, 1995), co-authoring a history and analysis of the politics of birth control and abortion in Ireland (forthcoming London 1995), and researching the feminization of the media industry. She has published widely on Irish politics and society, labour history and migration.

Nicholas W. Jankowski is Assistant Professor at the Department of Mass Communication at the University of Nijmegen in the Netherlands. He has published extensively in the areas of small scale electronic media, qualitative research methodology and new communication technologies. He co-edited the Libbey volume *The People's Voice: Local Radio and Television in Europe* (1992) and the Routledge publication *A Handbook of Qualitative Methodologies for Mass Communication Research* (1991). He is currently preparing a volume of empirical studies related to multimedia an another regarding access to electronic media.

Hans J. Kleinsteuber is Professor at the Institute of Political Science, University of Hamburg, for comparative government, specializing in comparative media studies, including Europe, North America and other countries. He also teaches in the university's journalism programme and heads the 'Arbeitsgruppe Medien und politik' at the University. This research group has recently finished a number of research projects on European media developments. He is member of he Euromedia Research Group. His recent publications on

Europe include: *EG-Medienpolitik* (EC-Media Policy, Berlin 1990, together with Wiesser, Wilke), *Europa als Kommunikationsraum* (Europe as Communication Space, Opladen 1994, together with Rossmann).

Bernat López is a research fellow at the Journalism Department of the Autonomous University of Barcelona. He is preparing his doctoral thesis on *The Regions, Nationalities and Small Countries facing the challenge of the European audio-visual Space*, and studying the EC Media Policy from the point of view of minority cultures and languages. He is the author of 'Televisión regional en la Europa de las indetidades', in *Chasqui*, 47, 1993 and 'Minority cultures and audio-visual policy of the EC', in *Mercator Media Forum* (Aberystwyth, 1995).

Miquel de Moragas Spà is Professor in Communication Sciences at the Autonomous University of Barcelona and Director of the Olympic Studies Centre in this University. He is the author of *Teorías de la comunicación* (Barcelona, 1981); *Sociología de la comunicación de masas* (Barcelona, 1985–86); *Espais de comunicació. Experiències i perspectives a Catalunya* (Barcelona, 1988); *Televisiones locales. Tipología y aportaciones de la experiencia catalana* (Barcelona, 1991, with others); *Los Juegos de la comunicación: las múltiples dimensiones comunicativas de los Juegos Olímpicos* (Madrid, 1992), and *Television in the Olympics* (1995).

José-Manuel Nobre-Correia is Professor of Information and Communication at the Université Libre de Bruxelles (ULB), and director of the «Observatoire des Médias en Europe» in this University. He was the chairman of the Communication, Information and Journalism Section at the ULB. He is former director of the monthly *Média Magazine* (Bruxelles), and former collaborator of several publications (*Pub, Trends Tendances* and *Le Vif-Express* in Belgium, and *Público* in Portugal). At present he writes weekly in the Portuguese magazine *Expresso*. He is co-ordinator of the european consultants of the magazine *Médiaspouvoirs* (Paris). He is co-author of several collective books, as *Guide de la Presse* (Paris: Ofup), *L'État de l'Europe* (Paris: La Découverte) and *O 25 de Abril nos media internacionais* (Porto: Afrontamento).

Michel Perrot is Professor of Information Sciences at the Université Michel de Montaigne – Bordeaux 3; director of the UFR des Sciences de l'Information, de la Communication et des Arts; Director of the Common Audio-visual Service of the University and Responsible for the Centre d'Analyse de la Communication Interculturelle (CACIC). He has studied the media in many countries from a sociological point of view. Some of his main publications are the following: *L'attraction de l'informatique* (Bordeaux, 1981, with others); *Les usagers potentiels du câble. Pratiques culturelles actuelles* (LASIC, Bordeaux); 'La radiodiffusion par satellite: facteur d'intégration?' in *Communication* 9, 1, 1983.

Jørgen Poulsen, born 1948, M. Phil., 1975 (film, Copenhagen University). Since 1987 Associate Professor of Communications at the Department of Communications, Roskilde University, Denmark. Previously worked as Associated Professor at Aalborg University and Institute of Inuit Studies, Copenhagen University, Head of Section at the National Council for the Social Sciences and same position at the Ministry of Telecommunications. Consultant for the Danish Trade Unions Council and the Danish Chief of Police. Author and editor of several books and readers on film, informatics and mass communications.

Giuseppe Richeri is Professor of Theory and Technics of Communications at the Politecnico of Milano, and has a wide international experience in research and consultancy acquired through his work in several institutions like the UNESCO, the Council of Europe, the European Community, the Nippon Hoso Kiokai, the International Institute of Communications, Fundesco and the Centre National d'Études de Télécommunications. He taught in 1983–84 at the Ecole Nationale d'Administration of Paris and in 1993–94 at the Universitat Autònoma de Barcelona. He is the author of several books, some of which are: *La tv che conta* (Bologna: Baskerville 1993), *Los satélites de televisión en Europa* (Madrid: Fundesco 1988), *L'altro mondo quotidiano* (Torino: Edizioni Eri 1986, together with C. Lasagni), *L'universo telematico* (Bari: DeDonato 1982), *La radio, origine, storia, modelli* (Milano: Mondadori, 1980, together with D. Dolgio).

Francisco Rui Cádima is Assistant Professor at the Department of Communication Sciences of the Human and Social Sciences' Faculty of the Universidade Nova de Lisboa, that currently co-ordinates. He is specialized in History of the Media and Theory and History of Television. He has been member of several international research projects, among others: *Cable television Market in the USA, Europe and Portugal* (Portugal Telecom/TV Cabo Portugal/ASEA); *Television in the Regions, Nationalities and Small Countries of Europe* (Universitat Autònoma de Barcelona/Universidad del País Vasco); *Public television: what future?* (Sorbonne University, Media Business School, Secretariado Nacional para o audio-visual). At present he is member of the Portuguese Association fot the Development of Communications and the Association for the Study of audio-visual. He has published broadly on Mass Communication issues, in Portugal and abroad.

Barbara Tomaß is research fellow at the 'Arbeitsgruppe Medien un Politik' at the University of Hamburg, specialized in European media policy, journalism and ethics. After her studies of Communication Science, Political Science and Political Economy she had an education in journalism and was an editor of science. Her recent publication is 'Arbeit im kommerziellen Fernsehen' (Commercial Broadcasters: Their Impact on the Labour Market and the Working Conditions).